Azure OpenAI Service for Cloud Native Applications

Designing, Planning, and Implementing Generative AI Solutions

Adrián González Sánchez

Beijing · Boston · Farnham · Sebastopol · Tokyo

Azure OpenAI Service for Cloud Native Applications

by Adrián González Sánchez

Published by O'Reilly Media, Inc., 1005 Gravenstein Highway North, Sebastopol, CA 95472.

O'Reilly books may be purchased for educational, business, or sales promotional use. Online editions are also available for most titles (*http://oreilly.com*). For more information, contact our corporate/institutional sales department: 800-998-9938 or *corporate@oreilly.com*.

Acquisitions Editor: Megan Laddusaw
Development Editor: Melissa Potter
Production Editor: Gregory Hyman
Copyeditor: Charles Roumeliotis
Proofreader: Stephanie English

Indexer: Potomac Indexing, LLC
Interior Designer: David Futato
Cover Designer: Karen Montgomery
Illustrator: Kate Dullea

July 2024:   First Edition

Revision History for the First Edition
2024-06-27:   First Release

See *http://oreilly.com/catalog/errata.csp?isbn=9781098154998* for release details.

The O'Reilly logo is a registered trademark of O'Reilly Media, Inc. *Azure OpenAI Service for Cloud Native Applications*, the cover image, and related trade dress are trademarks of O'Reilly Media, Inc.

978-1-098-15499-8

[LSI]

Table of Contents

Preface

I cannot hide my excitement. The 2022–2024 period has been one of the most amazing moments of the modern technology era. Some call it the "iPhone moment" of artificial intelligence, and a lot of people are now discovering the actual potential of AI. But I don't think that's all it is. I believe we are entering an exponential phase where all technological advancements move so fast that it is difficult to keep track of them. But that is wonderful. Several years of progress and industry competition in just a few months. What was often thought of as impossible (or even magic) is now a reality…and it's just getting started.

That sense of innovation and complete disruption is how I felt the first time I tried the Azure OpenAI Studio. I got early access as an AI Specialist at Microsoft. It was a very early version, and definitely not the Studio and related features and models we have today, but it was very promising. Little did we know that this cloud-enabled service was about to become the superstar of the generative AI era. And it was a reality, not a concept or a future product. It was something we could use to create our very own GPT-style implementations, with different models and cost/performance trade-offs, but also with relatively low implementation and deployment complexity.

After a few months of testing and tracking new functionalities, OpenAI released ChatGPT. Boom. I have never seen such a viral moment related to AI technologies. Even at Microsoft, the feeling of being witnesses to something extraordinary was there, every day and evening, during countless "nerd" discussions with my colleagues. The key moment was the announcement of the "chat" functionality in Azure OpenAI Service, which allowed any company to test and deploy a ChatGPT-ish kind of instance for their own purposes for the first time. Then came Bing Chat (which would evolve into what we today call Microsoft Copilot). Boom ×2. That was the first time we saw the combination of classic search engines with a GPT chat experience, on the same screen…and it worked! People could get a direct answer to their precise needs instead of searching for information using keywords and having to determine the right answer themselves, and they were doing it with plain language. Not keywords, not complex combinations of words. Just asking for information and waiting for an answer.

Months passed and we started to deploy the first proof-of-concepts with Azure OpenAI. I'm part of a field team, so I was very close to the reality of the adopters—their understanding of what generative AI is, their envisioned use cases, their concerns, etc. I was also part of the AI community at Microsoft, which had plenty of energy and creativity to explore new approaches, discover new architectures, and learn about the most recent techniques and accelerators. Trust me, I wasn't the only one feeling lucky in those moments. This was pure energy.

At one point, and I assume this was due to my academic background as a university professor, I felt like the vast amount of information—while very useful for any learner or adopter—was also a bit overwhelming for any company or individual trying to get started with generative AI and the Azure OpenAI Service. There was a lot of demand from companies around the world, and this technology deserved to be massively adopted, in a safe, responsible manner.

It was then that I started drafting the main concepts of a technical guide for application development with Azure OpenAI Service. Initially, it was just a way to keep track of all the URLs and pieces of information I was continuously collecting. Then, I continued adding my notes, based on my own implementation experiences. Finally, I kept changing or adding content based on the recurrent questions and discussions I was getting from clients, friends, and even family!

This was a great baseline, and I knew it could become an official technical guide, or even a full book. I decided to talk to my O'Reilly colleagues and present the topic. These conversations took only a matter of weeks. The potential was clear, but the challenge was huge: creating high-quality O'Reilly-level content, in a timely manner (as soon as possible) so all generative AI adopters could start reading and learning.

This has been one of my most challenging, but still rewarding, experiences. I feel really honored to write this book. So many Microsoft folks around the world could have done it, and for this reason, I took the opportunity very seriously. My main goal was to create something that would include all critical elements for Azure OpenAI learning, keeping in mind the (constantly) evolving context—showing the best features and implementation approaches, but knowing that there will be others soon and a continuously changing mix of generative availability and new features in preview. But that's part of the charm, and the reason why I like this book and the creative process behind it so much.

One of my favorite things (and I hope you like it too) is the combination of the typical static content of a book, with the interactivity of online repositories, references to evolving documentation…and the incredible power of the guest interviews. Having such an amazing amount of talent and knowledge from a roster of AI pros is an authentic luxury, for you as readers and avid learners, but also for me as an AI professional.

Now, I hope that if you have decided to start reading this book, you are ready to explore each piece, from the core technical aspects to the other relevant business and ethical aspects that will help you during your first generative AI projects with Azure OpenAI Service.

— Truly yours,
Adrián

How This Book Is Organized

The content of this book is organized in a way that follows the typical adoption work-streams for new technologies: initial understanding of their potential, exploration of technical implementations, considerations for operationalization, and business requirements. Depending on the company and its level of maturity, the sequence of things may change. For example, experienced AI teams will have a clearer under-standing of the business aspects and future operationalization, then consolidate the technical part. Regardless of you and your company's context, the seven book chap-ters (plus an appendix) should cover what you need to leverage Azure OpenAI Ser-vice for your generative AI implementations:

Chapter 1, "Introduction to Generative AI and Azure OpenAI Service"
A 101 overview of AI, generative AI, and the role of Azure OpenAI Service for enterprise-grade implementations. Ideal if you are starting your generative AI journey from scratch.

Chapter 2, "Designing Cloud Native Architectures for Generative AI"
A top-down approach for architecting generative AI applications based on cloud native principles, with the most relevant building blocks, including those from the Microsoft Azure cloud. The key preliminary step before you start exploring Azure OpenAI Service.

Chapter 3, "Implementing Cloud Native Generative AI with Azure OpenAI Service"
The core chapter for you to explore the different Azure OpenAI interfaces, including visual playgrounds and APIs, as well as the main implementation approaches and patterns.

Chapter 4, "Additional Cloud and AI Capabilities"
The perfect complement to the third chapter. The place to go if you want to learn about all related "pieces," such as vector databases, orchestration engines, and other Azure-related services.

Chapter 5, "Operationalizing Generative AI Implementations"
> The most important chapter, from my point of view, if you want to understand what a "real life" generative AI implementation means. You can design a wonderful architecture and make the most of Azure OpenAI and other services, but it is important to implement all required measures to secure, scale, protect, and optimize your deployments. A must if you are creating generative AI applications for a company.

Chapter 6, "Elaborating Generative AI Business Cases"
> Even if you master every single technical aspect related to your generative AI apps with Azure OpenAI, you still need to make it work from a business point of view. This means creating sustainable business cases, supported by realistic cost estimations and project roadmaps. By the end of the day, no AI system will be adopted if these topics are not discussed up front.

Chapter 7, "Exploring the Big Picture"
> An overview of the future state of generative AI systems with Microsoft technology, along with interviews with some of the industry's top talent to give you key insights from the people on the ground.

Appendix, "Other Learning Resources"
> A collection of resources for you to expand your learning experience.

My goal is for this collection of chapters to give you a 360-degree view of what generative AI implementations mean today, which will enable you to start your new projects with all the required knowledge.

Conventions Used in This Book

The following typographical conventions are used in this book:

Italic
> Indicates new terms, URLs, email addresses, filenames, and file extensions.

`Constant width`
> Used for program listings, as well as within paragraphs to refer to program elements such as variable or function names, databases, data types, environment variables, statements, and keywords.

`Constant width bold`
> Used to call attention to snippets of interest in code blocks.

This element signifies a general note.

 This element indicates a warning or caution.

Using Code Examples

Supplemental material (code examples, exercises, etc.) is available for download at *https://oreil.ly/azure-openai-service-code*.

If you have a technical question or a problem using the code examples, please send email to *support@oreilly.com*.

This book is here to help you get your job done. In general, if example code is offered with this book, you may use it in your programs and documentation. You do not need to contact us for permission unless you're reproducing a significant portion of the code. For example, writing a program that uses several chunks of code from this book does not require permission. Selling or distributing examples from O'Reilly books does require permission. Answering a question by citing this book and quoting example code does not require permission. Incorporating a significant amount of example code from this book into your product's documentation does require permission.

We appreciate, but generally do not require, attribution. An attribution usually includes the title, author, publisher, and ISBN. For example: "*Azure OpenAI Service for Cloud Native Applications* by Adrián González Sánchez (O'Reilly). Copyright 2024 Adrián González Sánchez, 978-1-098-15499-8."

If you feel your use of code examples falls outside fair use or the permission given above, feel free to contact us at *permissions@oreilly.com*.

O'Reilly Online Learning

 For more than 40 years, *O'Reilly Media* has provided technology and business training, knowledge, and insight to help companies succeed.

Our unique network of experts and innovators share their knowledge and expertise through books, articles, and our online learning platform. O'Reilly's online learning platform gives you on-demand access to live training courses, in-depth learning paths, interactive coding environments, and a vast collection of text and video from O'Reilly and 200+ other publishers. For more information, visit *https://oreilly.com*.

How to Contact Us

Please address comments and questions concerning this book to the publisher:

O'Reilly Media, Inc.
1005 Gravenstein Highway North
Sebastopol, CA 95472
800-889-8969 (in the United States or Canada)
707-827-7019 (international or local)
707-829-0104 (fax)
support@oreilly.com
https://www.oreilly.com/about/contact.html

We have a web page for this book, where we list errata, examples, and any additional information. You can access this page at *https://oreil.ly/azure-openai*.

For news and information about our books and courses, visit *https://oreilly.com*.

Find us on LinkedIn: *https://linkedin.com/company/oreilly-media*

Watch us on YouTube: *https://youtube.com/oreillymedia*

Acknowledgments

Thanks to all involved "stakeholders" for helping me to make this happen. My wife Malini, the amazing O'Reilly team for their methodology (and their unlimited doses of patience and support, especially Melissa), my Microsoft colleagues for being a continuous source of inspiration (including my boss, Agustin, and his unwavering support), all technical reviewers and interviewees for their wealth of knowledge (many thanks to Jonah Anderson, Sergio Gonzalez, and Jorge Garcia Ximenez), and so many learners around the world showing their interest in this amazing topic. This book is for all of you. Please enjoy it.

Introduction

Artificial intelligence is finally here. While it was certainly already among us, we can consider the 2020s as the beginning of a new era for modern, more accessible, and powerful artificial intelligence.

If you are reading this book, you probably already know that AI is not a new concept. It's been several decades since its first appearance (at least as a concept, during a very famous university conference in the United States (*https://oreil.ly/kk-Ey*)), and we can now say that people from almost all walks of life are beginning to understand the potential and considerations of artificial intelligence. After several AI summers and winters (*https://oreil.ly/au2B6*) and cycles of hype and deception, the promise of AI value for companies and individuals is finally here, and terms such as generative AI, generative pre-trained transformer (GPT), and large language model (LLM) (*https://oreil.ly/8KuvO*) are everywhere.

The arrival of AI-enabled tools such as OpenAI's ChatGPT (*https://oreil.ly/HUWak*), Midjourney (*https://oreil.ly/ercyb*), and the new Microsoft Copilot (*https://oreil.ly/NofXj*) engine is facilitating the interaction between people and the algorithms. Even more, the generative AI wave can be considered a democratizing element for mainstream AI adoption, due to its unique value for natural language–based communication.

And this is not only for the general public. Companies, politicians, governments, observatories, startups, etc. are all talking about generative AI, adopting the technologies to improve their services to clients and citizens, analyzing its potential, and thinking about future AI regulations.

That's the key difference between then and now: *awareness*. Before, AI-enabled capabilities were kept behind the scenes (e.g., face detection and classification engines for image repositories, natural language processing and generation [NLP/NLG], and speech technologies for personal home assistants). Nowadays, most people are aware that behind a GPT type of application, there is a "machine" with AI capabilities and power algorithms.

And what comes after awareness? Plenty of things depending on the involved actor, but if we observe the typical patterns from companies and startups, mostly learning and understanding the key technology elements, and an unstoppable willingness to adopt. That brings us to *enablement*, the key element for adoption. For many years, most organizations could not leverage powerful AI-enabled technologies. That was a privilege reserved for just a few companies and research centers—a bit of an AI aristocracy with important entry barriers for innovation and competition. This is changing though, in many ways thanks to cloud computing.

Over the last two decades, public clouds such as Amazon Web Services (AWS), Google Cloud Platform (GCP), IBM, Oracle, and Microsoft Azure (*https://oreil.ly/c5Q1h*) have enabled companies around the world to obtain infrastructure capabilities and, depending on the use case, access to very advanced services. In recent years, areas such as big data, AI, and security were the superstars, and the key reasons for adopters to move to the cloud and leverage aaS (as-a-service) capabilities, along with potential financial and scalability reasons (*https://oreil.ly/oXxPn*).

Since 2022, generative AI capabilities have suddenly taken the stage. For example, Microsoft Azure incorporated Azure OpenAI Service (*https://oreil.ly/XVU1A*), a cloud-based platform as a service (PaaS) with enterprise-grade capabilities to leverage generative language, code, and image features (more on this later). This was the first and most advanced option for AI adopters, with a key competitive advantage from OpenAI's technologies. But you, my avid reader, probably know this already. And that's why you're here, looking for a way to apply generative AI by using pre-built models that can be easily customized and integrated via APIs (application programming interfaces) with all the security and moderation advantages a company may need.

Now it's time to dig into how to use Azure OpenAI and other Microsoft services to design, build, and integrate cloud native solutions that will solve actual business needs, with clear business cases, that will enable you to deliver high-quality services to your clients and users. If you are here, you certainly understand the cloud advantage, but you need some additional pieces of knowledge and guidance. That's what this book is about—actual AI *democratization* (illustrated in Figure I-1) for the whole innovation ecosystem. You are (or will be) part of it. Let's use this book to get you on board.

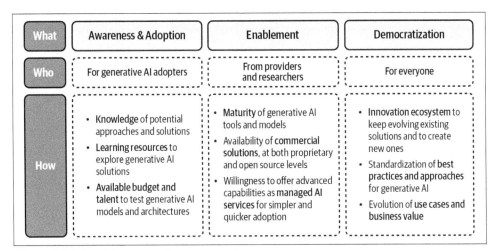

What	Awareness & Adoption	Enablement	Democratization
Who	For generative AI adopters	From providers and researchers	For everyone
How	• **Knowledge** of potential approaches and solutions • **Learning resources** to explore generative AI solutions • **Available budget and talent** to test generative AI models and architectures	• **Maturity** of generative AI tools and models • Availability of **commercial solutions**, at both proprietary and open source levels • Willingness to offer advanced capabilities as **managed AI services** for simpler and quicker adoption	• **Innovation ecosystem** to keep evolving existing solutions and to create new ones • Standardization of **best practices and approaches** for generative AI • Evolution of **use cases and business value**

Figure I-1. The ultimate AI democratization

This book is an applied guide that contains the technology "building blocks" (managed services that deliver specific value and interconnect with other applications, within an end-to-end AI architecture) related to the implementation of Azure OpenAI–enabled applications. This means you will be learning about technical settings, but also business-related topics, such as return on investment (ROI) and responsible AI.

Last but not least, the reading experience will be complemented with several expert interviews in Chapter 7. Generative AI and Azure OpenAI are rapidly evolving topics, so I want this book to become a living resource for your next professional projects.

CHAPTER 1

Introduction to Generative AI and Azure OpenAI Service

This first chapter covers the fundamentals of artificial intelligence (AI) as a way to contextualize the new developments with generative AI. It includes some technology-agnostic topics that will be useful for any kind of implementation, but it focuses on Azure OpenAI Service as the key building block to enable cloud-native application development with generative AI.

What Is Artificial Intelligence?

This section focuses on the historical evolution of AI technologies and related use cases as a way to demystify what AI actually looks like, and to connect traditional approaches with new generative AI techniques and capabilities.

Let's start with its origins. The term "AI" was coined during the 1950s. Concretely, Professor John McCarthy defined artificial intelligence in 1955 as "the science and engineering of making intelligent machines" (*https://oreil.ly/hir0l*). It is also fair to say that Professor Alan Turing previously introduced the notion of thinking machines. In 1956, Dartmouth College hosted the Summer Research Project on AI conference, with a group of participants from the most relevant universities and companies. That conference was led by Prof. McCarthy and other renowned researchers, and it was the beginning of the AI area of research. In the time since, there have been multiple cycles of hype, disappointments due to unrealistic expectations (periods often referred as AI winters due to reduced funding and general interest for AI topics), renovated expectations, and finally vast commercialization of AI-enabled solutions such as personal assistant speakers, intelligent autonomous vacuum cleaners, etc.

That said, AI has evolved a lot during the last two decades, but the reality is that initially it was mainly and only adopted by some of the biggest companies, such as Microsoft (no, not necessarily for their famous Clippy (*https://oreil.ly/0iNuM*)!), Google, Amazon, Uber, and other technology unicorns. That first wave of adoption created a great baseline so they could offer these same capabilities as managed cloud services to other AI adopters out there, which gave them a clear competitive advantage. This started the stage of data and AI democratization we are currently experiencing, where smaller companies are developing or leveraging AI-enabled services, and those solutions are already part of our day-to-day.

Before going into the details, let's take a step back and analyze the context of what artificial intelligence is today, and what it means for companies and individuals.

Current Level of AI Adoption

The term "AI adoption" describes how organizations around the world are either implementing AI systems or leveraging AI-enabled tools from other companies. Each company's level of adoption really depends on several factors, such as technology maturity, type of organization (big or small companies, public administration, startups, etc.), geography, etc. McKinsey indicates that the level of AI adoption in 2022 (from their state of AI report (*https://oreil.ly/6GDdZ*)) was 50% from all its respondents, with an interesting increase at the international level, and an even more significant increase for developing countries. Additionally, they also estimate that generative AI could add to the global economy (*https://oreil.ly/4L3JC*) the equivalent of $2.6 trillion to $4.4 trillion annually.

In addition, Boston Consulting Group defined (*https://oreil.ly/mrLCw*) the level of success and AI maturity as a combination of internal adoption plus the knowledge of AI within the organization, with only 20% of organizations being actual pioneers in terms of AI adoption. Last but not least, Gartner predicts (*https://oreil.ly/b-x4K*) that by 2025, 70% of enterprises will identify the sustainable and ethical use of AI among their top concerns, and 35% of large organizations will have a Chief AI Officer who reports to the CEO or COO.

These figures show that even if the level of global adoption is increasing, there are still differences in how companies are using AI and how successful they are. The next sections will showcase multiple examples of AI-enabled systems, at both the technology and use case levels.

The Many Technologies of AI

There are different ways to define artificial intelligence, but the reality is that there is not only one single technology under the umbrella of AI. Let's explore the main AI technologies:

Machine learning (ML)

A type of AI that relies on advanced statistical models that learn from past data to predict future situations. Take a simple use case of classifying fruits based on their existing pictures. To describe an apple to the system, we would say it is somewhat round in shape and that its color is a varied shade of red, green, or yellow. As for oranges, the explanation is similar except for the color. The algorithm then takes these attributes (based on past examples) as guidelines for it to understand what each of the fruits looks like. Upon being exposed to more and more samples, it develops a better capacity to differentiate oranges from apples and gets better at correctly identifying them. There are plenty of ML models depending on the kind of algorithm and type of task, but some relevant examples are decision forests, k-means clustering, regressions, and support vector machines (note: if you want to explore this family of AI models, take a look at the Microsoft ML Algorithm Cheat Sheet (*https://oreil.ly/T7JG9*), which explains the type of tasks for different models and their data requirements).

Deep learning (DL)

Deep learning can be defined as a subset of machine learning, with models that rely on algebra and calculus principles. The differentiating character of deep learning is that the algorithm uses a neural network to extract features of the input data and classify it based on patterns to provide output without needing manual input of definitions. The key aspect here is neural networks. The idea of neural networks comes from the fact that they mimic the way the brain functions, as a multilayer system that performs mathematical calculations. Layered with multiple levels of algorithms designed to detect patterns, neural networks interpret data by reviewing and labeling its output. If we consider our fruit example, instead of having to provide the attributes of what each fruit looks like, we have to feed many images of the fruits into the deep learning model. The images will be processed, and the model will create definitions such as the shapes, sizes, and colors.

Natural language processing (NLP)

NLP combines computational linguistics (rule-based modeling of human language) with statistical, machine learning, and deep learning models. These kinds of models were initially available only in English (e.g., BERT from Google AI), but the current trend is to create local versions or multilanguage models to support others like Spanish, Chinese, French, etc. That said, NLP has undergone a tremendous evolution in the last 20 years. NLP algorithms used to be task-specific, but modern architectures have allowed them to better generalize to different tasks and even to gain emerging capabilities that they were not trained for. From a Microsoft Azure perspective, both Azure OpenAI Service and Azure AI Language (*https://oreil.ly/b191_*) resources rely on NLP models.

Robotic process automation (RPA)

This is a set of technologies that replicates the manual interactions of human agents with visual interfaces. For example, imagine you are working in HR and you need to do the same task every week, which could be checking some information related to the employees via an internal platform, then filling out some information, and finally sending a customized email. RPA tools are easy to implement, reduce wasted time, and increase internal efficiencies, so employees can focus on added value tasks and avoid monotonous work.

Operations research (OR)

Operational research is a very important area, often included as part of the family of AI technologies, and very related to ML and the previously mentioned reinforced approaches. The University of Montreal defines operations research (*https://oreil.ly/u_H5h*) as "a field at the crossroads of computer science, applied mathematics, management, and industrial engineering. Its goal is to provide automated logic-based decision-making systems, generally for control or optimization tasks such as improving efficiency or reducing costs in industry."

OR usually relies on a set of variables and constraints that guide some sort of simulation that can be used for different kinds of planning activities: managing limited healthcare in hospitals, optimizing service schedules, planning energy use, planning public transit systems, etc.

These are the main categories of AI technologies, but the list can change depending on the interpretation of what AI means. Regardless of the details, it is important to keep in mind these technologies as a set of capabilities to predict, interpret, optimize, etc. based on specific data inputs. Let's see now how these different AI technologies apply to all sorts of use cases, which are likely to leverage one technology or combine them depending on the implementation approach.

Typical AI Use Cases

Regardless of the level of technical complexity, there are many different kinds of AI implementations, and their usefulness usually depends on the specific use cases that organizations decide to implement. For example, one organization might say, "we would like to get automatic notifications when there is a specific pattern from our billing figures" and develop some basic anomaly detection model, or even a basic rule-based one, and this could be considered an AI. Others will require more advanced developments (including generative AI), but they will need to have a business justification behind it.

Before we explore the technical and business considerations for an adopter company, here are some examples of AI-enabled applications:

Chatbots

You're likely very familiar with chatbots—those little friends that are embedded into websites—as well as automated phone bots that allow companies to automate their communication and customer support. They are based on NLP/ linguistic capabilities that allow them (with different levels of success) to understand the intent of what a client wants or needs, so they can provide them with an initial answer or hints to find the final answer. They also reduce the burden on support folks to answer initial requests, as chatbots can analyze, filter, and dispatch cases depending on the topic. The main advantage is automation and scalability of business activities (i.e., doing more with less), but there are challenges related to how efficient chatbots are for complex tasks and information. That said, chatbots are exponentially evolving with the arrival of generative AI, going from traditional rule-based engines to dynamic assistants that can adapt to the context of the discussion.

Computer vision systems

Image detection and classification applications that rely on DL technologies to analyze images and videos. For example, personal devices such as laptops and smartphones rely on this kind of technology to unlock them with an image of your face. Computer vision also supports advanced video analytics for a variety of applications.

Fraud detection

Widely used by financial institutions, AI can help detect unusual patterns that may indicate some sort of misuse of financial assets, such as credit cards. This could be a card translation from a remote country, unusual purchases, repetitive attempts to get money from an ATM, etc. These AI-enabled systems rely on different kinds of technologies (NLP, behavioral analysis, etc.) and make the surveillance more scalable, allowing humans to focus only on critical cases.

Voice-enabled personal assistants

Integrated via smartphones, speakers, cars (check out the amazing case of Mercedes with Azure OpenAI (*https://oreil.ly/yR55l*)), TVs, and other kinds of devices, these personal assistants enable interaction with human users by simulating conversation capabilities. It is widely used to reduce the accessibility barrier (i.e., it uses voice and does not require visual, writing, and reading capabilities) and allows users to free their hands while activating features such as apps, music players, video games, etc. There are also privacy concerns related to these systems, as they can act purely in a reactive manner, or "listen" continuously to human discussions.

Marketing personalization

The actual rainmaker for big companies such as Google and Meta. The ability to first understand the features related to a user (their age, location, preferences, etc.) and to connect that with the business goals of companies advertising their products and services is the key feature of modern online business. Marketing departments also use AI to segment their customer base and adapt their marketing techniques to these different segments.

In-product recommendations

Companies such as Netflix and Amazon have in-product recommendations based on their understanding of user needs. If someone looks for sports equipment, Amazon can recommend related products. It is the same for TV shows and movies on Netflix and other streaming platforms—they're able to make recommendations based on what you've watched previously. Everything is based on customer data and it relies on relatively complex AI models that we will explore later.

Robots

Examples include the Roomba vacuum cleaner, the incredible creations from Boston Dynamics (*https://oreil.ly/eVmm5*) that can even dance and perform complex tasks, the humanoid Sophia (*https://oreil.ly/RjtE9*), etc.

Autonomous vehicles

This type of system is equipped with different sets of advanced technologies, but some of them leverage AI techniques that allow cars to understand the physical context and adapt to dynamic situations. For example, these vehicles can autonomously drive with no need for a human driver, and they can make decisions based on different visual signals from the road and other cars. Tesla's Autopilot (*https://oreil.ly/-3AK_*) is a great example of this.

Security systems

This includes both cyber and physical security. As with fraud detection, AI helps security systems spot specific patterns from data and metrics, in order to avoid undesired access to precious resources. For example, Microsoft Copilot for Security (*https://oreil.ly/ISrdc*)detects hidden patterns, hardens defenses, and responds to incidents faster with generative AI. Another example would be AI-enabled cameras that can spot specific situations or objects from the video images.

Online search

Systems such as Microsoft Bing, Google Search, Yahoo, etc. leverage massive amounts of data and customized AI models to find the best answers to specific user queries. This is not a new concept, but we have seen how this kind of system has evolved a lot during recent years with the new Microsoft Copilot (*https://oreil.ly/NofXj*) and Google Gemini (*https://oreil.ly/Zv5lb*) apps. Additionally, we will see some examples for generative AI and web search applications in Chapter 3.

Predictive maintenance
   A very relevant case for industrial applications, this leverages different types of data to anticipate situations where machinery and industrial equipment may need maintenance before having specific issues. This is a perfect example of understanding past data to generate predictions, and it helps businesses avoid potential problems and approach maintenance activities in a proactive way.

Obviously, these applications can be transversal or specific to different industries (e.g., agriculture, healthcare), but they rely on the same technology pieces. Now that you understand them and their typical applications, let's focus on how AI models can learn, as this will be relevant for the general generative AI topic of this book.

Types of AI Learning Approaches

As humans, we start to learn when we are babies, but the way we do it will depend on the process we follow. We can learn by ourselves, based on our own positive or negative experiences. We can also learn from the advice of adult humans, who previously learned from their own experience; this can help us accelerate our own learning process. AI models are very similar, and the way to leverage previous experiences (in this case data and models) depends on the type of AI model learning approach, as you can see in Figure 1-1.

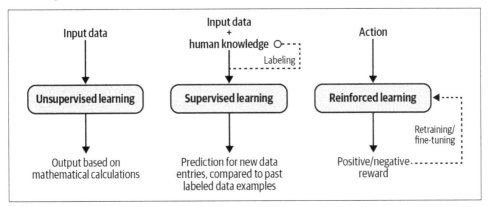

Figure 1-1. AI model learning categories

Let's walk through each approach in the figure:

Unsupervised learning
   This is based on unsupervised techniques that don't require human data annotation or support for the AI models to learn. This type usually relies on mathematical operations that automatically calculate values between data entries. It doesn't require any sort of annotation, but it is suitable for only specific types of AI

models, including those used for customer segmentation in marketing. The king of unsupervised techniques is what we call "clustering," which automatically groups data based on specific patterns and model parameters.

Supervised learning

Supervised learning is a very important type of learning for AI implementations. In this case, AI models use not only the input data, but also knowledge from human experts (subject matter experts, or SMEs) who can help AI understand specific situations by labeling input data (e.g., What's a picture of a dog? What's a negative pattern?). It usually requires some sort of data annotation, which means adding additional information (e.g., an extra column for a table-based dataset, a tag for a set of pictures). In general, this is a manual process and getting it right will impact the quality of the AI implementation, as this is as important as the quality of the dataset itself.

Reinforced learning

Last but not least, we have reinforced learning (RL) methods. Without getting too into the weeds with technical details, the main principle is the ability to simulate scenarios, and to provide the system with positive or negative rewards based on the attained outcome. This kind of learning pattern is especially important for generative AI, because of the application of *reinforcement learning from human feedback* (RLHF) to Azure OpenAI and other models. Concretely, RLHF (*https://oreil.ly/RCdKb*) gets retrained based on rewards from human feedback (i.e., reviewers with specific topic knowledge). We will explore the details in Chapter 3, because RLHF is highly relevant to the creation of Azure OpenAI models.

There are different ways in which models learn, depending on the internal architecture, the type of data sources, and expected outcomes. For the purposes of this book, it is important to differentiate and understand the high-level differences, as we will be referring to some of them in the context of generative AI.

Generative AI is here to stay, and Azure OpenAI Service is already a key factor for adoption and democratization. Let's now explore the fundamentals of generative AI, to understand how it works and what it can do for you and your organization.

About Generative AI

The term "generative AI" refers to the field of artificial intelligence that focuses on creating models and systems that have the ability to generate new content, such as images, text, music, videos, diagrams, etc.

As you may already know, this term has gained a lot of relevance in recent years, but it is not new. We can talk about probabilistic models in the 1990s, such as latent variable models and graphical models, which aimed to capture and generate data distribution. Also, recent advancements in deep learning, specifically in the form of generative adversarial networks (GANs) and variational autoencoders (VAEs), have significantly contributed to the popularization and advancement of generative AI.

The term "generative AI" has gained momentum as researchers, companies, and practitioners begin to explore the potential of these techniques to generate realistic and creative outputs. The result is now obvious, as AI encompasses a wide range of applications and techniques, including image synthesis, text generation, music generation, etc. Obviously, this is an evolving field and both academia and industry continue to innovate.

As you can see in Figure 1-2, the generation capability can be seen as an extension of other existing types of AI techniques, which are more oriented to either describe, predict, or prescribe data patterns, or to optimize specific scenarios. Advanced AI techniques, including OR and generative AI, allow adopters to go from "only insights" to automated decision making and actions.

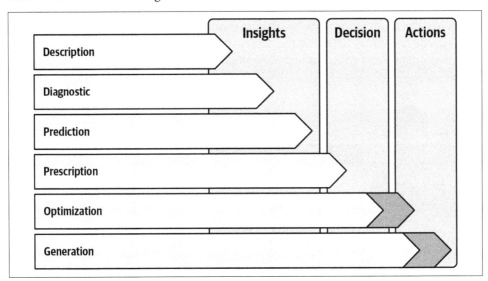

Figure 1-2. Types of AI capabilities

From a technical point of view, these models work in a very particular way. Instead of "just" predicting a certain pattern for a data entry (e.g., forecasting the ideal insurance premium for a specific client), they generate several outcomes to a specific instruction. The interaction with the generative AI model happens in a question-answer fashion, and this includes both direct instructions from humans (based on natural language instructions) and automated actions.

The term "prompt engineering" has emerged more recently in the context of NLP and the development of language models. While there isn't a specific origin or a definitive moment when the term was coined, it has gained popularity as a way to describe the process of designing and refining prompts to elicit desired responses from language models.

Prompt engineering involves carefully crafting the instructions or input provided to a language model to achieve the desired output. It includes selecting the right wording, structure, and context to guide the model toward generating the desired response or completing a specific task. There are ongoing efforts to develop systematic approaches for designing effective prompts, fine-tuning models for specific tasks, and mitigating biases or undesired behaviors in language generation.

From the previously mentioned question-answer dynamic, as you can see in Figure 1-3, *prompt* is the question, and the answer is called *completion*. The term "completion" in the context of NLP and language models refers to the generation or prediction of text that completes a given prompt or input, and it became more widely used as larger and more powerful models like OpenAI's GPT were developed. In summary, the term "completion" in language models emerged from the evolving field of language modeling, reflecting the ability of models to generate or predict text that fills in or completes a given context or prompt.

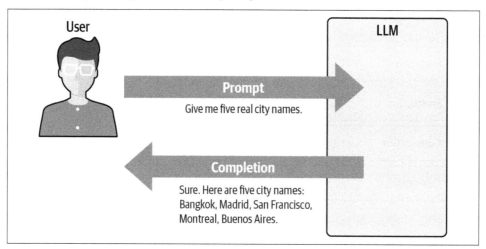

Figure 1-3. Prompts and completions

Generative AI is a new kind of artificial intelligence, and its main advantage for wide adoption is the ability to enable communication between users and the generative AI models via natural language prompts and completions. That's a game changer, but let's see now the main kind of capabilities we can get from these models.

Primary Capabilities of Generative AI

It is true that language and text-based information are a key aspect of generative AI. However, language-based prompts can serve other purposes. Companies and researchers are working on several streams:

Language
> Besides the core ChatGPT-type functionality, with questions and answers between the AI model and the human user, there are other related tasks that rely on linguistics but go a step further. What if you can use language as the creation catalyst for:

> *Code*
>> Technically, a programming language is just that…a language. LLMs are good at handling English or Spanish, but they are also great at understanding and generating code, and handling Java, Python, or C++ as they do any other spoken language. This may not be intuitive, but it makes sense to treat coding languages as any other language. And that's what generative AI does.

> *Melodies*
>> Based on musical notes, LLMs can generate melodies as they generate regular sentences. The potential of generative AI in this area is still unexplored, but it shows promising results for music creation.

> *Lyrics*
>> Another example of linguistics, lyrics can be built based on specific criteria explained via prompt, in which the users can specify the type of words, inspiration, style, etc.

Image
> The principle behind image creation is surprisingly intuitive: writing down the description (with simple natural language) of a potential image, to include it as part of the "prompt," then waiting for the generative AI engine to return one or several results matching that prompt, based on its own interpretation of previously consumed images. This kind of capability is very interesting for creative and marketing activities, where human pros can leverage image generation tools as a source of inspiration. A good example of this is Microsoft Designer (*https://oreil.ly/oIRon*), or the image creator capabilities of Microsoft Copilot.

Audio
> Imagine a technology that allows you to record your own voice for a few minutes, and then reproduce and replicate it for whatever purpose you want. Some sort of scalable voice licensing that leverages audio data to detect patterns and then imitate them. There are systems that can even generate music and other

sounds (for example, with Microsoft Copilot integration with Suno's AI-enabled music creation (*https://oreil.ly/5ltEG*)).

Video

As with image generation, the input can be a prompt describing specific scenes with different levels of detail, for which the model will deliver a video scene according to these details. A good example would be OpenAI Sora.

Others

Generative capabilities are not limited to only these formats and types of data. Actually, there are generative AI applications to create synthetic data, generate chemical compounds, etc.

These are just some of the capabilities that generative AI offers. They are fairly impressive, but certainly not the last step of the new AI era, as there are very relevant actors making sure that's the case. Let's see who the main contenders are next.

Relevant Industry Actors

While this book focuses on Azure OpenAI Service, which is related to both Microsoft and OpenAI, it is important to understand the competitive landscape for generative AI. As you already know, this field is witnessing significant advancements and competition. Researchers and organizations are actively working to develop innovative models and algorithms to push the boundaries of generative AI capabilities. Here are some examples of relevant actors accelerating the competition:

OpenAI (https://oreil.ly/xSlss)

Probably the most important actor of the generative AI wave. The company has created both proprietary tools such as ChatGPT, and other open source projects such as Whisper (*https://oreil.ly/9si-P*)). OpenAI's origins can be traced back to December 2015 when it was founded as a nonprofit organization by Elon Musk, Sam Altman, Greg Brockman, Ilya Sutskever, John Schulman, and Wojciech Zaremba. Their mission (*https://oreil.ly/yRGrR*) is to ensure that artificial general intelligence (AGI) benefits all of humanity.

OpenAI initially focused on conducting research and publishing papers in the field of artificial intelligence to foster knowledge sharing and collaboration. In 2019, OpenAI created a for-profit subsidiary called OpenAI LP to secure additional funding for its ambitious projects. The company's objective is to develop and deploy AGI that is safe, beneficial, and aligned with human values. They aim to build cutting-edge AI technology while ensuring it is used responsibly and ethically. They have democratized access to different kind of AI models:

- *Conversational GPT models*, with their well-known ChatGPT application (*https://oreil.ly/HUWak*), which relies on AI language models. It is based on the GPT (generative pre-trained transformer) architecture, which is the foundation of state-of-the-art language models known for their ability to generate human-like text and engage in conversational interactions. ChatGPT is designed to understand and generate natural language responses, making it well-suited for chat-based applications. It has been trained on a vast amount of diverse text data from the internet, allowing it to acquire knowledge and generate coherent and contextually relevant responses.

- *Generative AI models* for text (GPT-4o (*https://oreil.ly/c2NvZ*), GPT-4 (*https://oreil.ly/0SY9B*), and others), code (Codex (*https://oreil.ly/ZAbMD*)), images (DALL·E 3 (*https://oreil.ly/C9seS*)), and videos (Sora (*https://oreil.ly/ppSjf*)). Some of these models are available, as we will see in Chapter 3, via Azure OpenAI Service.

- *State-of-the-art speech-to-text models*, such as Whisper (*https://oreil.ly/9si-P*), available as an open source repository, but also as an OpenAI paid API (*https://oreil.ly/DbmUg*). Additionally, Whisper models are available via Microsoft Azure (*https://oreil.ly/qKUO5*).

Microsoft (https://oreil.ly/lYMby)

Along with OpenAI, the other key actor and one of the earliest adopters of generative AI technologies, thanks to the multimillion dollar investment in OpenAI and the partnership between both companies (*https://oreil.ly/hvKP2*). Besides Azure OpenAI Service (the main topic of this book, which we will explore deeply in upcoming chapters), Microsoft has adopted LLMs as part of their technology stack to create a series of AI copilots for all their productivity and cloud solutions, including Microsoft Copilot. Also, they have released the small language models (SML) Phi-2 (*https://oreil.ly/FW-xG*) and Phi-3 (*https://oreil.ly/vQTnL*), setting a new standard for the industry from a size/performance point of view. We will explore more details in upcoming chapters, but the company strategy has become AI-first, with a lot of focus on generative AI and the continuous delivery of new products, platforms, features, and integrations.

Hugging Face (https://oreil.ly/CGiU7)

Hugging Face is a technology company specializing in NLP and machine learning. It is known for developing the Transformers library, which provides a powerful and flexible framework for training, fine-tuning, and deploying various NLP models. Hugging Face's goal is to democratize and simplify access to state-of-the-art NLP models and techniques. It was founded in 2016 by Clément Delangue and Julien Chaumond. Initially, the company started as an open source project aiming to create a community-driven platform for sharing NLP models and resources. Their Hugging Face Hub is a platform for sharing and accessing pre-trained models, datasets, and training pipelines. The hub enables users to easily download and integrate various NLP resources into their own applications, making it a valuable resource for developers and researchers. In addition to their open source contributions, Hugging Face offers commercial products and services. Their models are available via Azure AI thanks to the corporate partnership between both companies (*https://oreil.ly/eR8a0*).

Meta (https://oreil.ly/aHn9W)

Formerly known as TheFacebook and Facebook, Meta is a multinational technology company that focuses on social media, digital communication, and technology platforms. It was originally founded by Mark Zuckerberg, Eduardo Saverin, Andrew McCollum, Dustin Moskovitz, and Chris Hughes in 2004. In recent years, they have created a very powerful organizational AI structure with relevant AI researchers, and meaningful open source AI contributions. They have released several models, including their most recent LLMs Llama 3 (*https://oreil.ly/Mfau4*) and CodeLlama (*https://oreil.ly/GBRM1*), an interesting data-centric option with good performance (based on industry benchmarks) and lower computing requirements than other existing solutions. The latest models are also available (*https://oreil.ly/hpI6k*) via Microsoft Azure, with new features (*https://oreil.ly/zvAg9*) to fine-tune and evaluate them via Azure AI Studio, as part of the exclusive Meta-Microsoft partnership that positions Microsoft Azure as the preferred cloud provider (*https://oreil.ly/ehdf3*) for Meta's models.

Mistral AI (https://oreil.ly/C4PM4)

A French company specializing in artificial intelligence. It was founded in April 2023 by researchers who previously worked at Meta and Google DeepMind. Mistral AI focuses on developing generative language models and stands out for its commitment to open source software, in contrast to proprietary models. Their Mixture of Experts (MoE) models are setting the standard for smaller language models, and are available via the Azure AI model catalog (*https://oreil.ly/t-MkN*), including the Mistral Large (*https://oreil.ly/SU0PT*) model.

Databricks (https://oreil.ly/l9hDi)

A data intelligence platform (available as a native service on Microsoft Azure (*https://oreil.ly/7P_jM*)) that has released their own LLMs, including an initial open source model called Dolly 2.0, trained by their own employees, and the first open source LLM for commercial purposes. In 2024, they released new DBRX models (*https://oreil.ly/XBH44*) (base and instruct versions), also available via the Azure AI model catalog (*https://oreil.ly/WITi2*).

Google (https://oreil.ly/39CFk)

Google is another key competitor and one of the most relevant AI innovators. Its Google Cloud Platform (GCP) introduced new AI-powered features in Google Workspace and G-Suite, and Google Cloud's Vertex AI platform is used to build and deploy machine learning models and AI applications at scale. Like Microsoft

Azure, Google Cloud offers tools that make it easier for developers to build with generative AI and new AI-powered experiences across their cloud, including access to low-code generative AI tools. Finally, Google released Gemini (*https://oreil.ly/FZ8NN*) (formerly known as Bard) as their alternative to OpenAI's ChatGPT and Microsoft Copilot.

NVIDIA (https://oreil.ly/mwSlg)
A pioneer in generative AI that offers a full-stack platform that enables innovation and creativity for solving complex challenges. Their platform includes accelerated computing, essential AI software, pre-trained models, and AI foundries. From a Microsoft point of view, there is a growing partnership between both companies, including the availability of their generative AI foundry service on Microsoft Azure (*https://oreil.ly/Ge8X7*), and the inclusion of NVIDIA AI models (*https://oreil.ly/OPGhp*) in the Azure AI model catalog.

Anthropic (https://oreil.ly/SmS4F)
An AI company founded by former OpenAI employees. They also have their own ChatGPT-style bot called Claude (*https://oreil.ly/AeNhS*), which is accessible through a chat interface and API in their developer console. Claude is capable of a wide variety of conversational and text processing tasks while maintaining a good degree of reliability and predictability. Their Claude models (*https://oreil.ly/df896*) are available via APIs.

Amazon Web Services (AWS) (https://oreil.ly/CaxMP)
AWS took some time to release generative AI–related products, but they recently announced their AWS Bedrock platform, a foundational AI service to directly connect to generative AI models. They offer their own models, and others from third parties such as Cohere or Anthropic.

IBM (https://oreil.ly/z0XDj)
IBM announced their new WatsonX platform, which includes their own model catalog, a lab/playground environment, and API-enabled integrations.

Cohere (https://oreil.ly/rDW3b)
An LLM-first company, with their own offering of language models, and their Coral productivity chatbot, which works as a knowledge assistant for companies.

You can see in Figure 1-4 the exponential evolution of the generative AI market with a timeline of new models by company, especially after ChatGPT released in 2022, with a 2023 full of model and platform releases.

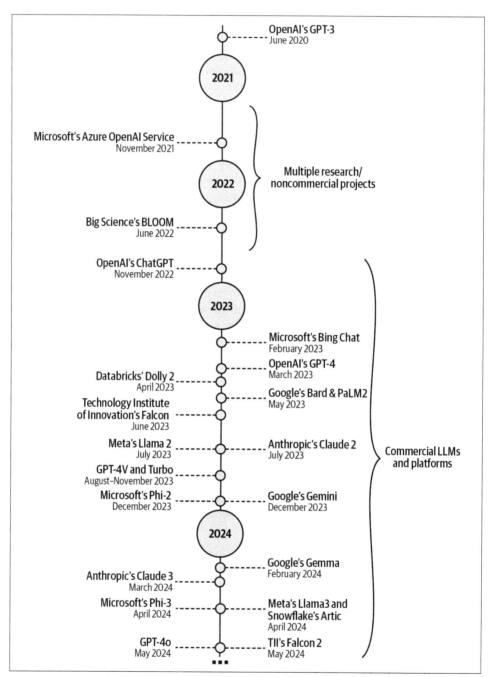

Figure 1-4. Simplified generative AI timeline

This timeline is a highly simplified version of the advancements and releases from different open source teams and other companies. For more details, both the State of AI Report (*https://oreil.ly/UwMhc*) and the Stanford AI Index Report (*https://oreil.ly/GDYK7*) contain plenty of details about research and commercial models, as well as other relevant actors we haven't mentioned here. The list of generative AI innovations will certainly evolve during the coming months and years, and future implementations of existing models like Meta's Llama 3 and OpenAI's GPT-4 and GPT-4o (*https://oreil.ly/3GPA5*) will likely focus on the efficiency of the models.

Now, let's see why generative AI is a special kind of artificial intelligence, and explain a new concept called foundation models, which is the key differentiator when comparing to traditional language models.

The Key Role of Foundation Models

There are several reasons generative AI is a total disruption. The perception of a never-seen level of performance is one of them. The ability to interact using plain language to send our instructions and to interpret the results is another one. However, one of the fundamental aspects for generative AI to deliver the value we see nowadays is the notion of *foundation models*.

Foundation models are base models pre-trained with a vast amount of information (e.g., LLMs) that are able to perform very different tasks. This is something new as traditional AI/NLP models focus on unitary tasks, one specific model per task (e.g., language translation).

For example, Azure OpenAI models such as GPT-4 and GPT-4o can do plenty of things by leveraging one single model. They can perform diverse tasks related to a specific generative capability, such as text/language, and help you analyze, generate, summarize, translate, classify, etc., all with only one model. In addition to that, if the models are able to handle different kinds of inputs at the same time, like text and image, they qualify as *multimodal models* (e.g., GPT-4V (*https://oreil.ly/kDBF5*)). You can see the main differences in Figure 1-5.

This flexible approach provides multiple options for the development of new use cases, and you will see later (in Chapters 2 and 3) how Azure OpenAI facilitates the configuration, testing, and deployment of these foundation models. But what does it represent in terms of AI disruption? Let's see first one of the fundamental reasons why generative AI and companies such as OpenAI got so much attention in recent years.

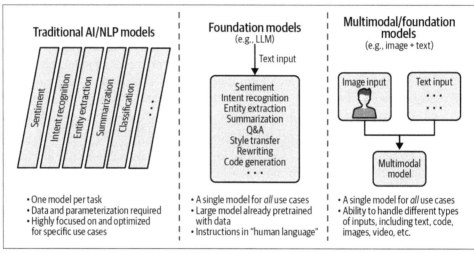

Figure 1-5. Traditional AI versus foundation models

Road to Artificial General Intelligence

Before we dig into the core part of this book, it's important to contextualize all these innovations within the general state of artificial intelligence, and the current discussions on *artificial general intelligence* (AGI) due to the unexpected capabilities of GPT-4 and other LLMs.

You may remember some cinematographic references to what a lot of people imagine as artificial intelligence—Skynet, Ultron, *I, Robot*, etc. All of them showed some sort of superior intelligence, usually represented by strong and dangerous humanoid robots that evolve over time, and that plan somehow to replace or even destroy the human race. Well, even if it is not the purpose of this book to show a naive vision of what AI and its capabilities are, we will start by demystifying and clarifying the current level of development of artificial intelligence, so everyone can understand where we are and what the realistic expectations of an AI system are. For that purpose, here are three types of AI depending on their scope and level of intelligence:

Narrow AI

The current type of capabilities that AI systems and technologies are offering. Basically, this is an AI that can get a relatively big sample of past data, and then generate predictions based on that, for very specific tasks, for example, detecting objects from new images, recognizing people from audio voices, etc.

General AI (or artificial general intelligence)

The next goal for AI researchers and companies. The idea is to generalize the training process and the knowledge it generates for AI and leverage that within other domains. For example, how can we make an AI-enabled personal assistant aware of the changing context? And then adapt previous learnings to new situations? This is not 100% feasible today, but likely to happen at some point.

Super AI

The kind of artificial intelligence that movies and books are continuously showing. Its capabilities (cognitive, physical, etc.) are far superior to humans, and it can in theory surpass them. However, this kind of super intelligence is currently a futuristic vision of what an artificial intelligence could be. It's still not feasible and probably will not happen in the upcoming years or even decades (this opinion will be different depending on who you ask).

Bringing this back to the topic of generative AI, current discussions focus on the current stage or type of artificial intelligence. But the real question is, are we still talking about narrow AI? Are we getting closer to general AI? It is a fair question given the new level of performance and flexibility of foundation models to perform a variety of tasks. Regardless of the answer (which can go from the technical to the philosophical), reality is that generative AI in general, and Azure OpenAI Service in particular, are delivering capabilities we never dreamt about before.

There was an early analysis of the GPT-4 model (*https://oreil.ly/rhEVW*) capabilities from the Microsoft team that explored this relation between the foundation models, and talks about "close to human-level performance" and an "early version of an AGI system." Also, companies like OpenAI have declared the pursuit of AGI (*https://oreil.ly/vTgyJ*) as one of their main goals.

We have covered all the fundamentals related to generative AI topics, including evolution from traditional AI, recent developments, and ongoing discussions around performance and the impact of generative AI. Let's now explore the details of Azure OpenAI Service, with special focus on the story behind it and the core capabilities.

Microsoft, OpenAI, and Azure OpenAI Service

Microsoft, one of the main technology incumbents, and OpenAI, a relatively young AI company, have collaborated and worked together in recent years to create impressive technologies, including AI supercomputers and LLMs. One of the main aspects of this partnership is the creation of Azure OpenAI Service (*https://oreil.ly/oZT0k*), the primary reason for this book, and a PaaS cognitive service that offers an enterprise-grade version of the existing OpenAI services and APIs, with additional cloud native security, identity management, moderation, and responsible AI features.

The collaboration between companies became more famous in 2023, but reality is that it had several stages with very important milestones at both the technical and business level:

- It started in 2019, when Microsoft announced a $1 billion investment in OpenAI to help advance their AI research activities and to create new technologies.
- In 2021, they announced another level of partnership to build large-scale AI models using Azure's supercomputers.
- In January 2023, they announced the third phase of their long-term partnership through a multiyear, multibillion dollar investment to accelerate AI break-throughs to ensure these benefits are broadly shared with the world.

Obviously, every step of this partnership has deepened the level of collaboration and the implications for both companies. The main areas of work are as follows:

Generative AI infrastructure
Building new Azure AI supercomputing technologies to support scalable applications for both OpenAI and Microsoft generative AI applications, and porting existing OpenAI services to run on Microsoft Azure.

Managed generative AI models
Making Microsoft Azure the preferred cloud partner for commercializing new OpenAI models via Azure OpenAI Service, which for you as an adopter means that any OpenAI model is available via Microsoft Azure, as a native enterprise-grade service in the cloud, in addition to the existing OpenAI APIs (*https://oreil.ly/v-HE1*).

Microsoft Copilot products
As we will see in the following pages, Microsoft has infused AI into their product suite by creating AI-enabled copilots that help users perform complex tasks.

Also, Azure OpenAI Service is not the only Microsoft AI service, and it is part of the Azure AI Suite (shown in Figure 1-6), which includes other PaaS options for a series of advanced capabilities that can colive and interact to create new AI-enabled solutions.

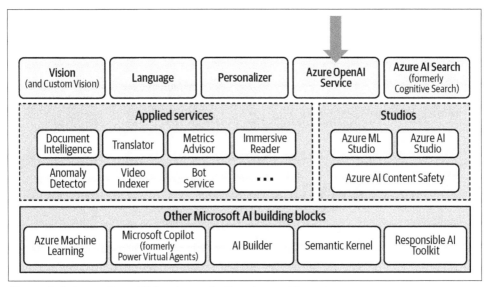

Figure 1-6. Azure OpenAI Service and other Azure AI services

We will refer to some of these building blocks in Chapters 3 and 4, as most of these services interact seamlessly with Azure OpenAI Service, depending on the envisioned solution architecture. But this is a highly evolving field, and Figure 1-7 shows the timeline of key Azure OpenAI breakthroughs (*https://oreil.ly/5zqx_*) in recent months and years.

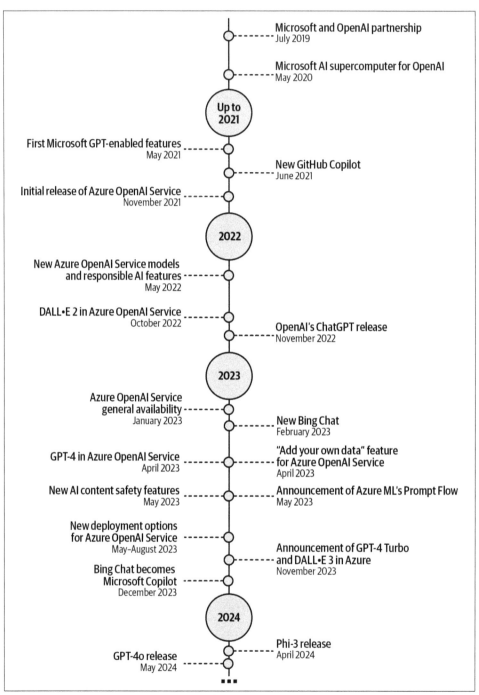

Figure 1-7. Azure OpenAI Service timeline

If you want to understand more about the origins of the partnership and the initial developments, this podcast episode (*https://oreil.ly/uGSH_*) with Microsoft's CTO Kevin Scott and cofounder (and former CEO) Bill Gates is very interesting and explains how everything started.

The Rise of AI Copilots

As part of its AI-enabled offerings, Microsoft is promoting the concept of *AI copilots*. They are personal assistants equipped with Microsoft's AI, OpenAI's GPT models, and other generative AI technologies, designed to assist users in their tasks and goals, but not to replace humans and their jobs. Copilots work alongside users, providing suggestions, insights, and actions based on AI. Users always have control and the choice to accept, modify, or reject the copilot's output. From a visual point of view, copilots are usually on the right side of the screen, and Microsoft has included them in several solutions:

GitHub Copilot
> An AI-powered pair programmer (*https://oreil.ly/KanxU*) that helps developers write better code faster. It suggests whole lines or entire functions right inside the editor, based on the context of the code and comments. GitHub Copilot is powered by GPT-4 (previously enabled by OpenAI Codex (*https://oreil.ly/ZAbMD*), now deprecated), a system that can generate natural language and computer code. GitHub Copilot is the original case and the first copilot of the Microsoft suite.

Bing Chat/Microsoft Copilot
> A conversational AI service (*https://oreil.ly/gI9u1*) that helps users find information, get answers, and complete tasks on the web. It uses GPT models that can produce natural language responses based on user input. Users can chat with Bing Chat using text or voice on browsers or the Bing app. This is the first search engine to incorporate generative AI features for chat-based discussion, now rebranded as Microsoft Copilot.

Microsoft 365 Copilot
> An AI-powered copilot (*https://oreil.ly/EQmLe*) for work that helps users unleash their creativity, improve their productivity, and elevate their skills. It integrates with Microsoft 365 applications such as Word, Excel, PowerPoint, Outlook, Teams, and Business Chat. It also leverages LLMs such as Azure OpenAI GPT-4 to generate content, insights, and actions based on natural language commands.

Windows Copilot

An upgraded AI assistant for Windows 11 (*https://oreil.ly/uJSZC*) that helps users easily take action and get things done. It integrates with Bing Chat, as well as with Windows features and third-party applications. Users can interact with Windows Copilot using natural language commands.

Fabric and Power BI Copilot

A generative AI interface for Microsoft Fabric (*https://oreil.ly/Ipshc*), the lakehouse platform, and Power BI, for automated reporting.

Security Copilot

An AI-enabled security solution (*https://oreil.ly/aKBXf*) that helps users protect their devices and data from cyber threats. It uses AI to detect and prevent malware, phishing, ransomware, and other attacks. It also provides users with security tips and recommendations based on their behavior and preferences.

Clarity Copilot

A feature that incorporates generative AI into Microsoft Clarity (*https://oreil.ly/5MgnN*), an analytics tool that helps users understand user behavior on their websites. It allows users to query their Clarity and Google Analytics data using natural language and get concise summaries. It also generates key takeaways from session replays using AI.

Dynamics 365 Copilot

A feature that brings next-generation AI (*https://oreil.ly/AVM6q*) to traditional customer relationship management (CRM) and enterprise resource planning (ERP) solutions. It helps users optimize their business processes, improve customer engagement, and increase revenue. It leverages LLMs such as OpenAI's GPT-4 to generate insights, recommendations, and actions based on natural language commands.

Others

Power Platform Copilot, Microsoft Designer (software as a service [Saas] for visual design with a generative AI prompt interface), and the new Copilot Studio (*https://oreil.ly/iq_fU*) for low-code gen AI implementations.

Summarizing, Microsoft has released a series of AI copilots for their product suite, and the reality is that Azure OpenAI Service is the key piece to *creating your own copilots*. We will analyze different building blocks of an AI copilot for cloud native applications (e.g., new terms such as plug-ins and orchestrators), but you can see in Figure 1-8 an adapted version of the "AI Copilot" layered architecture (*https://oreil.ly/jGrqE*) that Microsoft presented during Microsoft Build 2023.

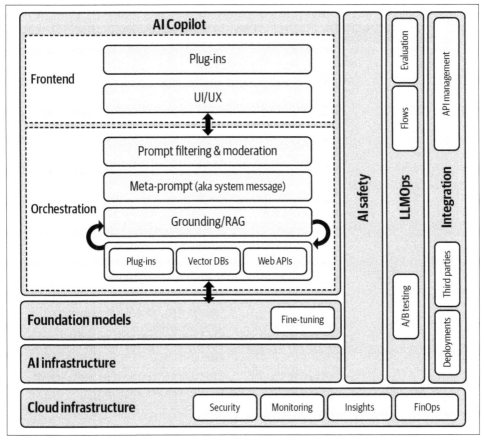

Figure 1-8. The modern AI copilot technology stack (source: adapted from an image by Microsoft)

As you can see in the figure, the AI infrastructure and foundation models are just part of the equation. Both a cloud native architecture and specific generative AI pieces are required to develop AI copilots for your existing and new applications, and that's exactly what we will cover in Chapters 2, 3, and 4. But before that, let's explore the high-level capabilities and typical use cases of Azure OpenAI.

Azure OpenAI Service Capabilities and Use Cases

We will focus now on the core capabilities and potential use cases of Azure OpenAI–enabled systems, before going into architectural and technical considerations. Keeping in mind the flexible nature of foundation models, it is easy to imagine the multiple applications of Azure OpenAI models. Let's explore the main capabilities in Table 1-1 (there are more, but you can use this as a baseline for your initial use ideation), aligned with those we have previously seen in this chapter.

Table 1-1. Main Azure OpenAI Service capabilities and use cases

Type		Capability and illustrative example	
Language	Content generation/analysis	Text generation	Automatic creation of SMS with dynamic formats and content
		Topic classification	Detect book topics based on their content, for automatic labeling
		Sentiment analysis	Detect sentiment from social media reviews to detect pain points
		Entity extraction	Find key topics from specific information
		Call to APIs	Generate an API call and integrate it with other systems
		Subject matter expert documents	Creation of role-based documentation based on books or repositories
		Machine translations	On-demand website translation
		Technical reports	Generation of reports based on databases and other information
		Agent assistance	Step-by-step, dynamic blueprints for customer agents
	Summarization	Book summaries	Summarization of long documents (e.g., books) with specific format and sections
		Competitive analysis	Extraction of key factors from two companies for competitive analysis
		Social media trends analysis	Summarization of keyword trends and connection with online news
		Reading comprehension	Reformulation of key topics with a simpler language
	Search	Internet results	Semantic search for internet topics
		Social reviews search	Detailed search of specific topics from social reviews on the internet
		Knowledge mining	Extraction of knowledge from different sources, from the same topic
		Document analysis	Search of key topics and other related terms for a specific document
	Automation	Claim management	Automatic structuration of text-based information to send it as a JSON file
		Financial reporting	Quarterly reporting based on social media summarization, figures from databases, and automation of the final report and its distribution
		Automatic answers to clients	Automatic voice-enabled answers, or chatbot discussions for Level 1 support

Type	Capability and illustrative example	
Coding	Natural language to coding language	Generating a Java loop, based on natural language instructions
	Coding recommendations	Live coding recommendations from the development tool
	Automatic comments	Automatic comment generation based on written code
	Refactoring	Automated code improvements
	Code translation	Translation from one programming language to another
	SQL queries in natural language	Database queries in natural language
	Code review	AI-enabled pair review
	Pull request info	Automated pull request comments
	Text JSON-ization	Conversion of plain text into JSON file with specific parameters
Image	Creative ideation	Random image generation related to a specific topic
	Podcast and music playlist images	Image generation based on podcast transcript or music lyrics
	Content syndication	Material for partner-enabled marketing
	Hyper-personalization	Visual customization based on user context
	Marketing campaign personalization	Visuals for marketing campaigns, based on user segment, topic, etc.

These are just a few examples of how to use the multiple capabilities of Azure OpenAI Service models. They can be combined with other services, and the models may also evolve, so don't discard scenarios for audio or video generation.

Regardless of the type of capability and use case, Azure OpenAI Service can provide support to different kinds of scenarios:

Completion

Completions are used to generate content that finishes a given prompt. You can think of it as a way to predict or continue a piece of text. Completions are often useful for tasks like content generation, coding assistance, story writing, etc.

Chat

Chat scenarios are designed to simulate a conversation, allowing back-and-forth exchanges with the model. Instead of giving a single prompt and getting a continuation, users provide a series of messages, and the model responds to them in kind. Chat scenarios (like those powering ChatGPT) are useful for interactive tasks, including but not limited to tutoring, customer support, and of course, casual chatting.

Embeddings

We will explore the notion of embeddings by the end of Chapter 2, but they basically allow us to consume specific knowledge from documents and other sources. We will leverage this sort of capability in several Chapter 3 scenarios.

The dynamic behind all these examples is the same. Azure OpenAI is a PaaS that works based on cloud consumption. Unlike other cloud services or APIs that bill their capabilities based on a number of interactions, Azure OpenAI (and other commercial LLM platforms) measure service usage based on a new concept called "tokens." Let's see what this is about.

LLM Tokens as the New Unit of Measure

In general terms, cloud and SaaS providers use very diverse ways to bill their services, from fixed monthly fees and usage tiers with volume discounts to very granular units of measure such as characters, words, or API calls.

In this case, generative AI has adopted the notion of *tokens*, which is a set of words or characters (*https://oreil.ly/Vy9ny*) in which we split the text-based information. The tokens unit is used for two purposes:

- For *consumption*, to calculate the cost of the configuration and interactions with the Azure OpenAI models. Any API call, prompt (text request) sent to the model, and completion (answer) delivered by Azure OpenAI follows this unit. The service pricing (*https://oreil.ly/7Gmq6*) is based on cost per 1,000 tokens, and it depends on the model type (GPT-3.5 Turbo, GPT-4, GPT-4o, DALL·E 3, etc.).

- For *capacity*, at both the model and service levels:

  — *Token limit*, which is the maximum input we can pass to any Azure OpenAI model (and generative AI models in general). For example, GPT-3.5 Turbo offers two options with a 4K and 16K token limit, and GPT-4, GPT-4 Turbo, and GPT-4o reach 128K. This is likely to evolve in the coming months and years. For updated information, visit the model availability (*https://oreil.ly/BI5Ue*) page and check the "Max Request (Tokens)" column.

  — *Service quotas*, which means the maximum capacity at a certain resource, configuration, and usage level for any Azure OpenAI model. This is also evolving information, and it is available via official documentation (*https://oreil.ly/wwpp8*) and the Quota section (*https://oreil.ly/ONn5Q*) from Azure OpenAI Studio. These limits are important for any deployment plan, depending on the type of application (e.g., if we are planning to deploy a service for massive business-to-consumer [B2C] applications). Also, there are recommended best practices (*https://oreil.ly/Dv9qf*) to handle these limitations.

The specific amount of tokens depends on the number of words (other providers calculate tokens based on characters, instead of words), but also on their length and language. The general rule is 1,000 tokens is approximately 750 words for the English language, but OpenAI explains the specific way (*https://oreil.ly/tMYF_*) to calculate tokens depending on the case. Additionally, you can always use Azure OpenAI Playground or OpenAI's tokenizer (*https://oreil.ly/DDQHG*) to calculate a specific token estimate based on the input text.

Conclusion

This first chapter was a mix of intro-level information related to AI and generative AI and a preliminary introduction to Azure OpenAI topics, including recent developments, primary capabilities, typical use cases, and its value as an AI copilot enabler for your own generative AI developments.

Depending on your background, this information may be just a 101 introduction, but the concepts behind the Azure OpenAI Service, even if they are new and include some new terms, can be as simple as it looks—a managed PaaS that will allow you to deploy your own cloud native, generative AI solutions.

In Chapter 2, we will analyze the potential scenarios for cloud native development, their connection with Azure OpenAI, and the architectural requirements that will help you prepare everything, before even implementing your Azure OpenAI–enabled solutions. As with this chapter, if you already have some preliminary knowledge of cloud native and Azure architectures, you may read it as a way to connect the dots and understand the specifics of these topics adapted to generative AI. If you are totally new to the topic, feel free to read the content and explore any external resource that may support your upskilling journey. We're just getting started!

CHAPTER 2
Designing Cloud Native Architectures for Generative AI

Cloud native architecture is a way of designing and building applications that can take advantage of the cloud's unique capabilities and constraints. Cloud native applications are typically composed of microservices that run in containers, orchestrated by platforms like Kubernetes, and use DevOps and continuous integration and continuous deployment (CI/CD) practices to enable rapid delivery and scalability. Cloud native architectures are at the core of the generative AI era.

Organizations such as the Cloud Native Computing Foundation (CNCF) (*https://oreil.ly/dUsAO*) are great catalysts of cloud native best practices and community development. Their goal is to be "the vendor-neutral hub of cloud native computing, to make cloud native universal and sustainable." CNCF is a great source of information and learning material for these topics. Another great resource is the twelve-factor app (*https://oreil.ly/AFEgd*), a public methodology for building cloud native applications.

As part of the cloud native movement, there are several projects and communities oriented to the use of cloud native architecture to enable scalable, reliable, and robust AI systems. They often require large amounts of data, complex algorithms, and specialized hardware to perform tasks such as image recognition, natural language processing, or recommendation systems. This is not always possible with traditional IT architecture patterns (e.g., monolithic applications (*https://oreil.ly/TrFNL*)).

The need for cloud native architecture for AI systems arises from the following reasons:

System performance

AI systems need to process large volumes of data and run complex computations in a fast and efficient manner. Cloud native architecture enables AI systems to leverage the cloud's elastic resources, such as compute, storage, and network, to scale up or down according to demand. It also allows AI systems to use specialized hardware, such as graphics processing units (GPUs) or tensor processing units (TPUs), that are optimized for AI workloads.

Agility

AI systems need to adapt to changing business requirements, user feedback, and data quality. Cloud native architecture enables AI systems to deploy new features, models, or updates quickly and reliably using DevOps and CI/CD practices. It also allows AI systems to experiment with different architectures, algorithms, or parameters using techniques such as A/B testing or canary deployments.

Innovation and integrability

AI systems need to leverage the latest advances in AI research and technology. Cloud native architecture enables AI systems to access the cloud's rich ecosystem of AI services, tools, and frameworks that offer state-of-the-art functionality and performance. It also allows AI systems to integrate with other cloud services, such as data analytics, Internet of Things, or edge computing, that can enhance the value and intelligence of AI systems.

The most important areas for cloud native are described by CNCF as CI/CD, DevOps, microservices, and containers, as shown in Figure 2-1.

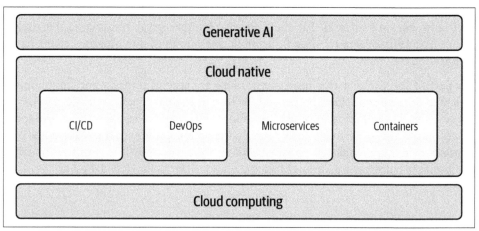

Figure 2-1. Cloud native building blocks for generative AI (source: adapted from an image by CNCF)

These four areas are relevant to generative AI applications:

CI/CD
Enables a streamlined and automated process for integrating code changes, building, testing, and deploying AI models and applications, and facilitates faster iterations and reduces time to market for generative AI developments.

DevOps
Combines the principles and practices of DevOps for AI technologies to improve the development, deployment, and operations of AI systems, and facilitates the integration of generative AI into the overall software development lifecycle. It also ensures reliable monitoring, logging, and feedback loops, enabling quick identification and resolution of issues in generative AI systems.

Microservices
Allows complex generative AI systems to be broken down into smaller, independent services, which enables modular development and deployment of different components of the AI system. It also enhances scalability and flexibility, as individual microservices can be developed, deployed, and scaled independently.

Containers
Offers a lightweight and portable way to package and deploy generative AI models and applications, and enables easy scaling, replication, and orchestration of generative AI workloads.

Cloud native architecture is a key enabler for developing advanced, intelligent AI systems that can deliver high performance, agility, and innovation on the cloud platform. In this chapter, we will explore how to prepare a cloud native architecture for an AI-enabled system that leverages Azure OpenAI Service, regardless of the kind of application you are planning to develop. Let's start by digging into some typical scenarios for AI cloud native development.

Modernizing Applications for Generative AI

This book focuses on the development of new cloud native applications with Azure OpenAI Service and the rest of the Microsoft Azure stack. However, there may be scenarios in which a company tries to leverage these capabilities for their existing applications. Let's compare both scenarios and see the approaches:

New cloud native applications
Designed from scratch using containerization (*https://oreil.ly/U0o9G*) and a microservices architecture, enabling scalability, resilience, and elasticity. They leverage the four areas previously mentioned, and they make the deployment and maintenance of generative AI applications a bit simpler.

Existing apps

Likely require migration or modernization. This means they'll either be migrated to the cloud, or modified to align with cloud native principles, such as breaking down a monolithic architecture into microservices or introducing containerization. The modernization process involves step-by-step upgrades, addressing scalability, resilience, and fault tolerance, and adopting DevOps practices gradually.

Learning Microsoft Azure (O'Reilly) by Jonah Carrio Andersson lays out some different strategies, and Microsoft's modernization guide (*https://oreil.ly/5Sm8X*) describes the process for migrating and modernizing existing on-prem/monolithic applications to the cloud, with specific cloud native features. Figure 2-2 illustrates the different levels of cloud modernization.

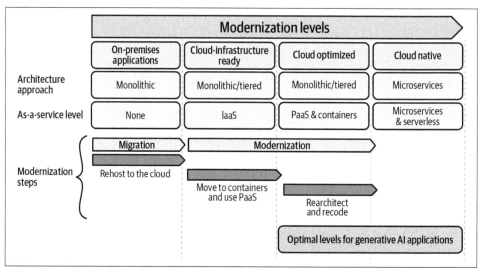

Figure 2-2. Cloud native modernization levels moving toward generative AI (source: adapted from an image by Microsoft)

Based on the modernization steps, there are different levels of maturity that range from existing on-premises applications to full cloud native ones. This is relevant for implementations with Azure OpenAI Service, as a native cloud-enabled PaaS, because new and existing applications will need some level of cloud readiness before integrating generative AI capabilities. Think of this as the way the rest of the application blocks connect with Azure OpenAI Service in a cloud-enabled way, with native and simple integrations.

The levels of maturity are as follows:

Cloud infrastructure–ready applications
> With this migration strategy, you simply transfer or relocate your existing on-site applications to an infrastructure-as-a-service (IaaS) environment. While the structure of your applications remains largely unchanged, they are now hosted on virtual machines in the cloud. This straightforward migration method is commonly referred to as "lift and shift" within the sector, but it only gets a portion of the cloud value you can get from managed PaaS/SaaS services.

Cloud-optimized applications
> At this stage, without making major code changes or redesigning, you can tap into the advantages of running your application in the cloud using contemporary technologies like containers and other cloud-managed services. This enhances your application's flexibility, allowing for quicker releases by optimizing your business's DevOps practices. This enhancement is made possible by tools like Windows containers, rooted in the Docker Engine. Containers address the challenges posed by application dependencies during multistage deployments. In this maturity framework, you have the option to deploy containers on either IaaS or PaaS, leveraging additional cloud-managed services such as database solutions, caching services, monitoring, and CI/CD workflows.

Cloud native applications
> This migration approach typically is driven by business needs and targets modernizing your mission-critical applications. At this level, you use cloud services to move your apps to PaaS computing platforms. You implement cloud native applications and microservices architecture to evolve applications with long-term agility, and to scale to new limits. This type of modernization usually requires architecting specifically for the cloud, and even writing new code (or rewriting it), especially when you move to cloud native application and microservice-based models. This approach can help you gain benefits that are difficult to achieve in your monolithic and on-premises application environment.

The last level is the end goal for optimal generative AI–enabled applications, but any of these levels (especially the last two) would be "good enough" for any application to "connect" to Azure OpenAI Service. The rest of the chapter will focus on new cloud native applications, but if you plan to leverage Azure OpenAI Service for existing applications, please start by evaluating them and analyzing the next migration or modernization steps towards AI adoption.

Now, let's focus on the key advantages of cloud native, and the key Azure-enabled building blocks that will allow you to build your Azure OpenAI solutions.

Cloud Native Development with Azure OpenAI Service

Part of the idea behind cloud native architectures is to split code development into different pieces called microservices, so all modules communicate based on a functional flow, without being part of the same technical block. This has a series of advantages, not only for Azure OpenAI–enabled development, but any cloud native implementation. We can imagine several reasons to leverage a microservices architecture:

Modular and granular AI functionality

In AI applications, different tasks such as data preprocessing, feature extraction, model training, inference, and result visualization may be involved. By implementing each of these functionalities as separate microservices, the AI system becomes more modular and granular. This allows developers to focus on building and maintaining individual services, making it easier to understand, develop, test, and deploy specific AI components. This also allows reusability of components as there might be certain cleaning pipelines or even models that could be used for different applications within the same company. Last but not least, it supports team specialization depending on the task (e.g., model output processing tends to be an integration or data engineering task, while model implementation a data science one).

Scalability and performance optimization

AI workloads can vary in intensity, with some tasks requiring more computational resources than others. By breaking down an AI application into microservices, each service can be scaled independently based on its specific resource needs. This scalability ensures efficient resource utilization and improved performance. For example, model training and inference services can be scaled independently to handle varying workloads, providing better response times and overall system performance.

AI algorithm lifecycle management

AI applications often require experimenting with different algorithms, models, or data sources to achieve the desired outcome. With microservices, developers can easily swap out or update individual AI services without affecting the rest of the system. This flexibility enables rapid prototyping, experimentation, and iteration with different AI approaches, facilitating the discovery of the most effective algorithms or models for specific tasks. Also, certain systems might run algorithms in parallel to obtain a better result by selecting the best answers of those algorithms.

Integration with external services

Microservices architecture promotes loose coupling and well-defined APIs, making it easier to integrate AI services with external systems, tools, or services. This allows AI functionality to be leveraged across different applications, domains, or platforms. For instance, an AI service for NLP can be exposed via an API and utilized by multiple applications or integrated into a chatbot or customer support system.

Now, if we think about generative AI–enabled applications with Azure OpenAI Service, the goal is to structure the end-to-end architecture in a way that makes sense and connects the "AI pieces" to both backend elements (code, cloud resources), and frontend interfaces (one or several, depending on the application), as you can see in Figure 2-3.

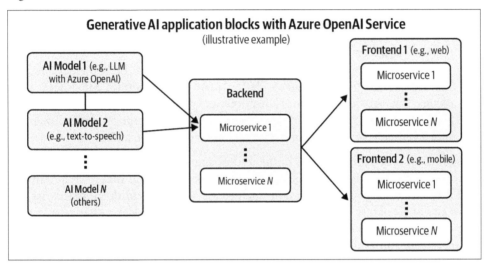

Figure 2-3. Microservice-enabled AI development

All the involved elements need to be interoperable, replaceable, and available. For that purpose, organizing the building blocks in microservices is key. The next two sections look at the containerization and serverless approaches. Let's discuss their role as cloud native enablers.

Microservice-Based Apps and Containers

Cloud native development approaches leverage the power of the cloud, by choosing the right way to develop and to deploy applications. They rely on containerization, which often refers to Docker-type containers, and Kubernetes orchestration. As they are both based on international standards (e.g., the Open Container Initiative [OCI] (*https://oreil.ly/JKa4L*)), cloud native applications are usually portable and scalable to different public and private cloud providers.

For Microsoft Azure, the key managed containerization services are Azure Kubernetes Service (AKS) (*https://oreil.ly/ymIkj*) and Azure Red Hat OpenShift (ARO) (*https://oreil.ly/SXs9T*). While both are managed Kubernetes services offered by Microsoft, there are some key differences:

AKS (https://oreil.ly/YqfZ3)
A managed Kubernetes service provided by Microsoft Azure, utilizing native Kubernetes technology. It offers a fully managed Kubernetes cluster on Azure infrastructure and focuses on providing a streamlined and simplified Kubernetes experience on Azure. It provides essential Kubernetes features, including scaling, load balancing, and deployment management. AKS integrates well with other Azure services and provides native Azure resource management and monitoring capabilities. You can find pricing information online (*https://oreil.ly/OoChO*).

ARO (https://oreil.ly/mM0MD)
A joint offering between Microsoft and Red Hat, built on the Red Hat OpenShift (*https://oreil.ly/AftCs*) Container Platform. ARO incorporates Kubernetes technology but provides additional features and integrations from the OpenShift platform. It provides a more comprehensive and enterprise-focused platform with additional security, compliance, and management capabilities.

In summary, they differ in terms of the underlying technology, vendor, and platform features. The choice between AKS and ARO depends on the specific requirements and preferences of your organization, such as the need for additional enterprise features and any existing investments or partnerships with Red Hat. Other related services you may want to explore are Azure Container Apps (*https://oreil.ly/QDzs2*) and Azure Arc for Kubernetes (*https://oreil.ly/X5vd_*) (for hybrid cloud scenarios).

Now that we have explored the containerization options in Azure, let's understand the notion of serverless and its relevance for microservice-based implementations.

Serverless Workflows

An alternative or complementary option is the serverless approach. Serverless computing is a cloud computing model that allows developers to build and run applications without the need to manage underlying infrastructure. It is particularly beneficial for AI workloads, including generative AI, as it provides a scalable and cost-effective solution.

In serverless architecture, developers focus on writing code for specific functions or tasks, known as serverless functions, with Azure Functions (*https://oreil.ly/Gm-h9*) being the native Microsoft option. These functions are executed in containers that are managed and scaled automatically by the cloud provider, as you can see in Figure 2-4. This eliminates the need for developers to provision and manage servers, making it easier to deploy and maintain AI applications.

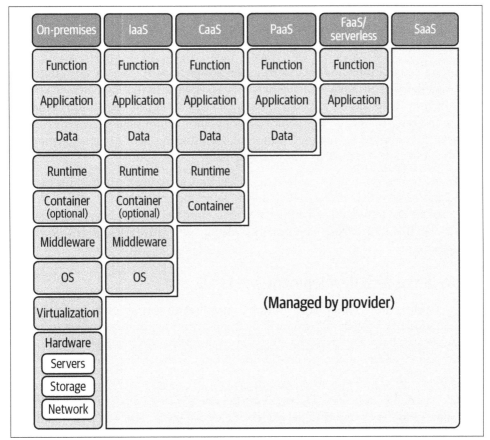

On-premises	IaaS	CaaS	PaaS	FaaS/ serverless	SaaS
Function	Function	Function	Function	Function	
Application	Application	Application	Application	Application	
Data	Data	Data	Data		
Runtime	Runtime	Runtime			
Container (optional)	Container (optional)	Container			
Middleware	Middleware				
OS	OS				
Virtualization			(Managed by provider)		
Hardware Servers Storage Network					

Figure 2-4. Managed cloud–as-a-service levels

Much like other cloud native elements, one of the key advantages of serverless for AI workloads is scalability. Generative AI models often require significant computational resources, especially when training large models or generating complex outputs. Serverless platforms automatically scale resources on demand, allowing AI applications to handle fluctuations in workload without manual intervention. This scalability enables efficient resource utilization and cost optimization, as developers pay for only the actual compute resources used during execution.

Another advantage of serverless computing is its event-driven nature. Serverless functions are triggered by specific events, such as HTTP requests or messages from message queues. This event-driven architecture is well-suited for AI workloads that require real-time or asynchronous processing. For example, generative AI applications can be triggered by user interactions or scheduled tasks, allowing them to generate outputs on demand or periodically. Additionally, serverless can be used to perform actions within a generative AI pipeline. For that purpose, Azure Logic Apps (*https://oreil.ly/Qvt6X*) can be used to trigger orchestration and workflows, and it has integration with other Microsoft 365 and Azure services, which can be useful in triggering generative AI pipelines or events.

There are some limitations related to serverless platforms, such as execution time limits, memory constraints, and deployment package size limits. However, techniques like function composition, caching, and parallel execution can help improve the efficiency and responsiveness of generative AI applications running on serverless architectures. Fine-tuning resource allocation and optimizing data processing pipelines can also contribute to better overall performance.

In general terms, you will be combining a PaaS such as Azure OpenAI, plus containerized and/or serverless pieces, depending on your implementation approach. We will now explore the web development part of your applications, to get an initial idea of the services that Azure OpenAI leverages to deploy generative AI–enabled web-based applications.

Azure-Based Web Development and CI/CD

Now, let's focus on development building blocks that go beyond core AI capabilities. As a cloud native practitioner, you will likely split your application code into several pieces. As you have already seen, those blocks are microservices that could contain backend and frontend modules (mobile applications, websites, intranets, etc.).

The interesting part comes when you discover you can host web-based applications directly via Azure App Service. Azure App Service is a PaaS, a fully managed service that allows adopters to build, deploy, and scale web applications and APIs without the need to manage underlying infrastructure. It supports various programming languages and frameworks and enables web, mobile, and API app development, as well as workflows (Logic Apps), CI/CD, and monitoring, while offering simple integration with the whole Microsoft Azure suite.

Overall, Azure App Service simplifies the process of building, deploying, and scaling web applications and APIs in the Azure cloud. It offers a robust and feature-rich platform that enables developers to focus on application development while benefiting from the scalability, availability, and management capabilities provided by the Azure platform.

You will see in Chapter 3 how Azure OpenAI offers simple deployment options that leverage Azure App Service to create chat-based applications with preexisting templates.

If you want to dive deeper into any of these topics, please visit the following links:

- Application hosting: Azure App Service Overview | Microsoft Learn (*https://oreil.ly/moBFz*)
- GitHub for CI/CD: Deploy to App Service Using GitHub Actions | Microsoft Learn (*https://oreil.ly/Z9EBe*)
- YouTube video: How to Deploy Your Web App Using GitHub Actions | Azure Portal Series (*https://oreil.ly/dSe0R*)

We will now cover the fundamentals of the Azure portal, mostly for readers with no or low Azure experience, as a way to help you understand how to search, configure, and deploy Azure OpenAI and other related services. If you have already worked with Azure and its portal, you may skip this section.

Understanding the Azure Portal

The Azure portal is a web-based UI provided by Microsoft Azure that allows users to manage and interact with their Azure resources. It serves as a central hub for accessing and managing various Azure services and functionalities, including Azure OpenAI Service. The portal provides a visually appealing and intuitive interface that simplifies the management and monitoring of Azure resources (Figure 2-5).

Figure 2-5. Azure portal: main interface

As you can see in Figure 2-5, it includes a customizable dashboard that provides an overview of your Azure resources, recent activities, and personalized tiles for quick access to frequently used services.

The navigation pane on the left side of the portal allows you to access different categories of Azure services, including Compute, Storage, Networking, Security + Identity, AI + Machine Learning, and more. You can see the sequence in Figure 2-6.

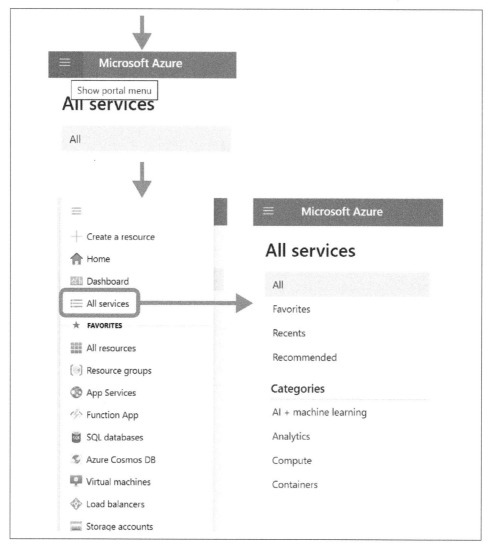

Figure 2-6. Azure portal: left panel

Also, clicking on a specific category expands a menu with subcategories and services within that category. You can actually find Azure OpenAI Service within the AI + Machine Learning category (Figure 2-7).

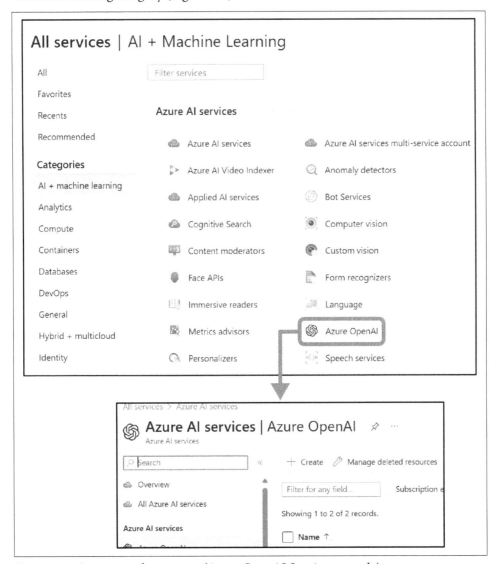

Figure 2-7. Azure portal: resources (Azure OpenAI Service example)

Alternatively, the Azure portal offers a search bar at the top, allowing you to quickly find services, resources, or documentation. As you can see in Figure 2-8, you can search by keywords or use the natural language query to locate specific functionalities or resources within Azure. Basically, you can find Azure OpenAI by just typing it there.

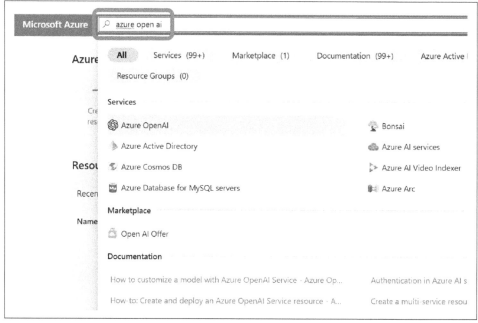

Figure 2-8. Azure portal: search (Azure OpenAI Service example)

Each Azure service has its own dedicated blade, which is essentially a panel that provides detailed information and management options for that service. If you choose Azure OpenAI from either the search engine or the left panel, you will enter your resource details (Figure 2-9). Basically, you are able to create new resources for Azure OpenAI, or manage those previously deployed. If you choose Create, you can see the required information to deploy a new Azure OpenAI Service.

Figure 2-9. Azure portal: resource details (Azure OpenAI Service example)

You can find details related to your subscription, geographic region preferences, the unique name chosen for your Azure resource, and the pricing tier. (Tiers are the level of pricing based on estimated usage; for now there is only one option for Azure OpenAI, called "Standard S0." Any update should be available via the official pricing page (*https://oreil.ly/7Gmq6*), and the Azure calculator (*https://oreil.ly/2SQ4C*).)

In addition to managing individual resources, the Azure portal allows you to create resource groups (*https://oreil.ly/J2LMM*) to logically organize and manage related resources together. This is an interesting feature, and a recommended best practice to group the required resources for your generative AI implementations with Azure, including Azure OpenAI Service and others we will need for our projects.

If you haven't created an Azure account before, the first step is to create a free one (*https://oreil.ly/WVIm2*). It usually includes credits with a value of USD $200 for initial experimentation. It requires a corporate email for the specific account and payment information.

We will explore the details of generative AI implementation approaches with Microsoft Azure in Chapter 3, but the idea behind the Azure portal is to facilitate the deployment, management, and maintenance process of the different resources required to create these architectures, regardless of the type of service. Deploying any Azure services from the Azure portal involves several steps, so remember the high-level process:

1. *Sign in to the Azure portal.*
   Open a web browser, navigate to the Azure portal, and sign up with your Azure account credentials.

2. *Create a resource.*
   To deploy an Azure service, you need to create a resource. A resource represents a service or component in Azure, such as a virtual machine, a storage account, or a database. Click on the "Create a resource" button in the Azure portal.

3. *Select a service.*
   In the resource creation wizard, you'll see a list of available Azure services. Choose the service you want to deploy by browsing through the categories or using the search bar.

4. *Configure the resource.*
   Once you've selected a service, you'll be taken to a configuration page where you can specify the settings for the resource. The options available depend on the specific service you're deploying. Fill in the required information, such as resource name, region, pricing tier, and any other relevant settings.

5. *Review and create.*

   After configuring the resource, review the settings to ensure they are correct. You can also enable additional features or add-ons if available. Once you're satisfied, click the "Review + Create" button.

6. *Validation and deployment.*

   Azure will validate the configuration settings and check for any potential issues. If everything is in order, click the "Create" button to initiate the deployment process.

7. *Monitor the deployment.*

   Azure will start provisioning the resources based on your configuration. You can monitor the deployment progress in the Azure portal. Depending on the service, the deployment may take a few minutes to complete.

8. *Access and manage the deployed service.*

   Once the deployment is finished, you can access and manage the deployed service through the Azure portal. You can view its properties, make changes to its configuration, monitor its performance, and perform other administrative tasks as needed.

This is the process for most of the Azure resources, but there are other deployment methods such as Azure Resource Manager templates (*https://oreil.ly/TZXTy*), API-enabled resource orchestration (*https://oreil.ly/jezRs*), Azure Bicep (*https://oreil.ly/aZOxZ*), Terraform on Azure (*https://oreil.ly/Wi9xy*), or command-line tools such as Azure CLI (*https://oreil.ly/Mm4N1*) or Azure PowerShell (*https://oreil.ly/22BEd*), all of them for more advanced admin/technical users. Feel free to explore them if you want to learn more.

For Azure OpenAI Service, you can always visit the official resource deployment guide (*https://oreil.ly/hSPh3*), which summarizes the steps we just walked through. Other information you may want to review before deploying the service includes the main product page (*https://oreil.ly/MDBhf*), the previously mentioned pricing guide (*https://oreil.ly/7Gmq6*), the service availability by geographic region (*https://oreil.ly/tYnCe*) (for example, if you deploy the service from the European Union, you may want to use a closer region, such as West Europe in Amsterdam, for better latency, performance, and maybe pricing), and the general documentation (*https://oreil.ly/3oNQU*).

Now that you know how to use the Azure portal, and the key information about the Azure OpenAI Service deployment process, let's analyze some important considerations at the model and general architecture levels. This will be key to creating the end-to-end implementations we will see in Chapter 3.

General Azure OpenAI Service Considerations

Now that we have explored the notion of cloud native development with Azure, and the fundamentals of the Azure portal for Azure OpenAI Service, let's go deeper into the different AI models that are available and the high-level architectures so you can know how to make sense of the Azure-enabled generative AI offerings.

Available Azure OpenAI Service Models

Most cloud-enabled PaaS resources from any public cloud, including those from Microsoft Azure, leverage native endpoints and APIs as a way to connect and to consume their models. This is the case for Azure OpenAI Service and the rest of the Azure AI Services we have seen in this chapter.

Also, there are visual elements such as Azure AI Studio (*https://oreil.ly/PCMD3*) and Azure ML Studio (*https://oreil.ly/kdZhY*) (not to be confused with Azure OpenAI Studio (*https://oreil.ly/LWQO1*), which we will explain and leverage in Chapter 3) that provide access to different proprietary and open source AI/foundation models. This includes a model catalog to leverage the curated selection of models, including those from Azure OpenAI, Meta, and Hugging Face (e.g., the Hugging Face Hub in Azure (*https://oreil.ly/96mAx*), announced by both Microsoft and Hugging Face during Microsoft Build 2023). This also allows us to test and deploy those models in a very simple way.

As you can see in Figure 2-10, if you visit the Studio page (*https://oreil.ly/kdZhY*), you will get access to your existing workspaces, or you will be able to create a new one if it is your first time connecting to the studio.

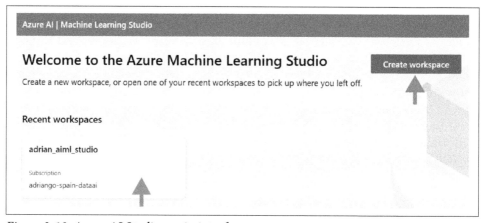

Figure 2-10. Azure AI Studio: main interface

If you access the workspace, you will see the same kind of visual interface we reviewed earlier in this chapter. In Figure 2-11, the left panel for the workspace menu offers all options related to data, models, endpoints, required resources, etc. For the sake of simplicity, we will focus on two main features: the model catalog (*https://oreil.ly/BYkuc*), and later in Chapter 4, the prompt flow functionality.

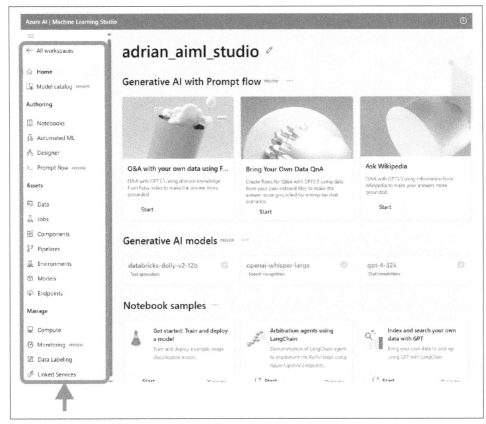

Figure 2-11. Azure AI Studio: left panel

If you choose the model catalog option and search "Azure OpenAI" or click directly on the tile as shown in Figure 2-12, you will get access to the updated list of available Azure OpenAI models.

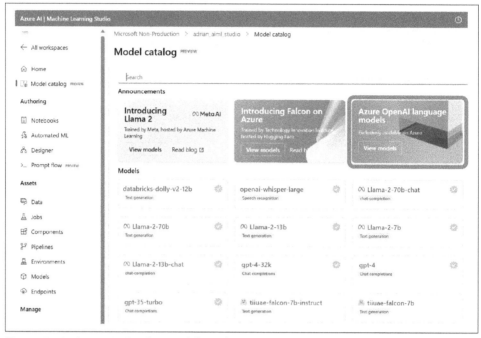

Figure 2-12. Azure AI Studio: model catalog

The models in Figure 2-13 are those available at the time of writing, but depending on when you check the catalog, you will likely find these and/or others. An alternative way to check all the available models at the moment is to use the List API (*https://oreil.ly/bk7Zd*).

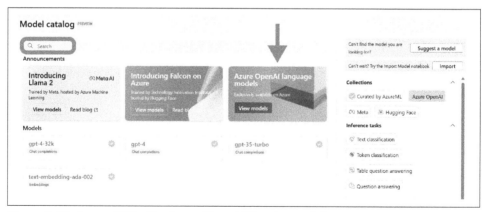

Figure 2-13. Azure AI Studio: Azure OpenAI Service models

Now, keeping in mind the evolving nature of the availability of Azure OpenAI models, explore the key model families and some examples of specific models that you will leverage for your generative AI projects. This will certainly change over time, but it is a good beginning.

Azure OpenAI Service splits its capabilities into different *model families*. A model family typically associates AI models by their intended task, such as natural language understanding, code generation, or image synthesis. Some of the most popular Azure OpenAI model families are as follows:

Language-related models
> Popular language-related models include the following:

> *GPT-3.5 Turbo and GPT-3.5 Turbo Instruct*
>> Models that improve on previous GPT-3 versions and can understand and generate natural language and code. There are several versions with different context length limits, including those for 4K and 16K tokens, which is the measure of the maximum text input.

> *GPT-4, GPT-4 Turbo, GPT-4o*
>> Models with better performance (and higher cost) than 3.5 Turbo, which can handle more complex tasks and generate more accurate and diverse outputs. They can also handle bigger text inputs (which we usually define as "context") than their predecessors.

> *Speech*
>> There are other options in Azure, but Azure AI Studio includes the speech-to-text Whisper model (*https://oreil.ly/9si-P*) from OpenAI (i.e., by typing "whisper" and selecting the model). It is not directly available from Azure OpenAI Studio, but it can be integrated with the rest of GPT models to create voice-to-text scenarios.

Other models
> Other popular models include the following:

> *Codex for programming code*
>> A series of models that can understand and generate code, including translating natural language to code. The reality is that Codex was initially a separate model, but after some time OpenAI added its capabilities to the regular GPT-3.5 Turbo and GPT-4 language models. This means the same models handle both natural language and programming code.

DALL·E for images

A series of models that can generate original images from natural language. This is the model behind tools like Bing Create (*https://oreil.ly/YwDy-*) and Microsoft Designer (*https://oreil.ly/oIRon*), and it is directly available from Azure OpenAI Studio, as we will see in Chapter 3.

It is important to differentiate the different model families and their specific capabilities to understand which ones we will use for our generative AI projects. Also, the trade-off of different Azure OpenAI models depends on the use case and the available budget. Generally speaking, more capable models like GPT-4o can handle more complex tasks and generate more accurate and diverse outputs, but they also consume more resources and incur higher costs. We will explore several scenarios in Chapter 3 that can work with all these GPT models. You can also explore the whole set of OpenAI models, including some deprecated ones that are still traced via OpenAI's documentation (*https://oreil.ly/SG-fe*).

Besides all these functionalities, one of the key features for LLM-enabled systems is *embeddings*. This is a general term related to NLP and LLMs. Embeddings are a way of representing data in a multidimensional space. They are often used to capture the semantic meaning of words, images, or other types of data. For example, in Figure 2-14, an embedding model can map a word to a vector of numbers, such that words with similar meanings have similar vectors. This means we can connect pieces of information that are not directly connected, but that may have a mathematical or linguistic connection (e.g., several knowledge bases from companies of the same sector, internal and external sources, etc.).

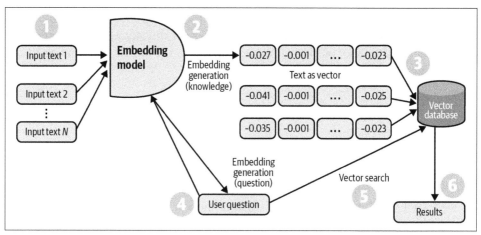

Figure 2-14. Embedding model

This example illustrates the typical *generation and search process*:

1. We collect different data inputs (PDFs, text files, URLs, etc.) to create our knowledge base. This is a simplified view as sources are previously processed to extract the text-based information. We will see options for this such as official accelerators and Azure AI Document Intelligence in Chapter 3.

2. We leverage the Embeddings API (*https://oreil.ly/bhgTY*) to generate the embeddings from diverse sources. We can use a basic API call with the text input that returns the generated vectors.

3. The generated vectors/embeddings are stored in a vector database. We will explore several database options in Azure in Chapter 3.

4. After the generation process, we can assume end users will want to search for specific topics or information that will be included as part of the different data inputs we have collected and vectorized. For that purpose, we will use the same embeddings API to generate the embeddings of the questions itself (note: we need the same embedding model for both knowledge and questions).

5. The vector database will support search functions. This means we will use the vectorized user questions as input to find information from the vector database that contains our knowledge base.

6. If there are related topics, the search function will return a Top-k variety of results that we can use to generate the answer (either by directly printing the results or by passing them as input for a chat-based scenario).

The embeddings use cases available in Azure OpenAI Service are as follows:

Text similarity
A set of models that provide embeddings that capture the semantic similarity of pieces of text. These models are useful for many tasks such as clustering, regression, anomaly detection, and visualization.

Text search
A set of models that provide embeddings that enable semantic information retrieval over documents. These models are useful for tasks such as search, context relevance, and information retrieval.

Code search
A set of models that provide embeddings that enable finding relevant code with a query in natural language. These models are useful for tasks such as code search and relevance.

At a technical level, the recommended model option for embeddings with Azure OpenAI Service is called "Ada"; this is an improved and more cost-effective (*https:// oreil.ly/6m7SL*) model than its predecessors. This is pretty useful to increase the knowledge scope of Azure OpenAI, by consuming information from PDFs, websites, text files, etc.

As previously mentioned, embeddings generation is based on a very simple API call/ response dynamic, and the specific details on how to generate embeddings for a given source are available in the official documentation (*https://oreil.ly/2cxWx*), as well as the specific context length limits (*https://oreil.ly/SQSGw*) (e.g., 8K tokens for Ada version 2). Generating embeddings is as simple as calling the embedding API with the desired text input you want to vectorize. For example, in Python:

```
import openai
openai.api_type = "azure"
openai.api_key = YOUR_API_KEY
openai.api_base = "https://YOUR_RESOURCE_NAME.openai.azure.com"
openai.api_version = "2023-05-15"

response = openai.Embedding.create(
    input="Your text string goes here",
    engine="YOUR_DEPLOYMENT_NAME"
)
embeddings = response['data'][0]['embedding']
print(embeddings)
```

The output of this would be a numerical representation, where each number in the list corresponds to a dimension in the embedding space. The exact values will depend on the specific model and its training data, but it could look like this:

```
[0.123, 0.456, 0.789, ..., 0.987]
```

We have completed the review of Azure OpenAI models and their capabilities. While we will cover the details of project examples and architectures in Chapter 3, the next section will explore general architectural building blocks for Azure OpenAI–enabled implementations, as well as general cloud infrastructure topics.

Architectural Elements of Generative AI Systems

Azure-based architectures rely on a series of interconnected services that can communicate with each other for a specific purpose. In this case, Azure OpenAI plays a crucial role to enable interactions between any customer-side application, but we rely on more building blocks to build our generative AI solutions. In Figure 2-15, you can see the main building blocks of an Azure OpenAI–enabled (simplified) architecture.

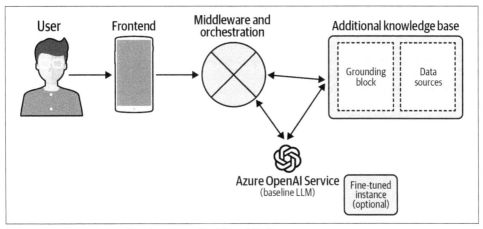

Figure 2-15. High-level architecture building blocks

Let's take a look at these pieces in a little more detail:

Application frontend
Any app-side element that leverages generative AI capabilities.

Middleware/orchestration
We will explore this element in Chapter 3, but the orchestration piece basically allows us to connect different Azure OpenAI skills with other relevant services. Also, the middleware can include API management and other topics that we will see in Chapter 3.

Azure OpenAI Service
For text-based skills, such as explaining the answer to a complex question, for both completion and chat-based scenarios.

Additional knowledge base
This is a combination of the core data sources (databases, blob storage, etc.) and knowledge extraction elements such as embeddings, Azure Cognitive Search, Bing Search, etc. For now, we will define them as "grounding blocks," but we will see the details in Chapter 3.

If you develop an application that leverages Azure OpenAI and other Azure services, and that implementation is part of a bigger data/AI-enabled platform, the end-to-end architecture might start to look something like Figure 2-16.

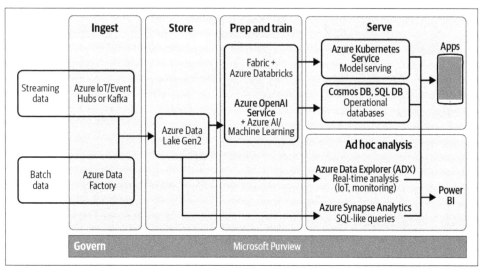

Figure 2-16. End-to-end Azure platform (including Azure OpenAI Service)

In this case, Azure OpenAI Service is just part of a bigger end-to-end that includes data sources, integration processes, SQL/NoSQL databases, containerization, analytics, etc. The final setup depends on the structure of the platform itself, but this is a good overview to understand where Azure OpenAI sits for any data and AI implementation with Microsoft Azure.

If you want to learn more about Azure-enabled architectures and the details of all these cloud services, please check out *Learning Microsoft Azure* by Jonah Carrio Andersson. Also, the main reference for architecture is the official Microsoft Architecture Center (*https://oreil.ly/0jzik*) for specific Azure OpenAI scenarios (*https://oreil.ly/y-gPD*). You may want to bookmark this resource as the Microsoft teams continuously update the content with new visual architectures and explanations, including some examples with Azure OpenAI Service.

Another interesting architecture you can explore is the Azure OpenAI Landing Zone reference architecture (*https://oreil.ly/xLs8X*), which includes end-to-end cloud considerations, including core infrastructure topics such as identity and security, monitorization, cost management, user and API management, FinOps, etc. This is a very rich and complete overview of what an enterprise-grade implementation would include, beyond the core generative AI capabilities.

Last but not least, don't forget to explore the CNCF Cloud Native AI Whitepaper (*https://oreil.ly/qd4lq*) from the AI Working Group (*https://oreil.ly/8k0bc*), which includes technology building blocks, techniques, and cloud native resources for generative AI topics.

Conclusion

As you can see, cloud native architectures are valuable for generative AI development, as they seamlessly integrate with Azure OpenAI and other Azure services. We will explore different implementation approaches in Chapter 3, but all of them rely on the capabilities and key building blocks discussed here. As an adopter, you may face situations where you will need to optimize existing applications so they can incorporate generative AI capabilities (as we reviewed in the modernization section), but you will also have the opportunity to develop new Azure OpenAI–enabled applications from scratch. In this case, leveraging containerization, serverless, and PaaS pieces will help you design well-architected and scalable architectures and solutions. Depending on your current level of knowledge, it will be important for you to understand the cloud fundamentals behind Microsoft Azure and specific services for development, APIs, and Kubernetes container orchestration.

Chapter 3 will focus on different alternatives for enhancing your Azure OpenAI applications with specific company knowledge, as well as the main features and interfaces that you will leverage for your next projects. It also includes new terms that we briefly explored in this, such as vector database and orchestration. Let's continue.

Implementing Cloud Native Generative AI with Azure OpenAI Service

This chapter will focus on the implementation of generative AI architectures with Microsoft Azure and Azure OpenAI models, always aiming to present all available options, and minimize the required development, integration, and usage cost, while accelerating the operationalization. For that purpose, I've included a series of best practices and typical architectures that will allow you to choose the best building blocks for your specific scenarios.

We will include the most relevant Azure OpenAI implementation approaches, based on existing features and repositories that will continue evolving, improving, and including new functionalities. I've included URLs to the original documentation because they are continuously updated with new features, so these links will allow you to explore any details you need. Most of them rely on official accelerators from Git-Hub repositories, and projects that you will be able to follow and/or fork. But before getting into the details, let's explore some fundamental topics that will help you understand the full extent of what a generative AI with Azure OpenAI Service means.

Defining the Knowledge Scope of Azure OpenAI Service– Enabled Apps

Generative AI applications on Microsoft Azure are not only for regular ChatGPT-type applications. They are advanced architectures that rely on diverse technology pieces, including the core infrastructure (servers, GPUs (*https://oreil.ly/y5mXm*), etc.) required to run generative AI models, and that allow adopters to create conversational applications and search engines, develop and integrate new AI copilots into their applications, customize customer attention, etc.

From an Azure OpenAI point of view, we are talking about a managed service that includes advanced functionalities that will allow you to implement *different levels of knowledge*, depending on the desired scope of your applications, and based on default capabilities and specific adjustment and customization techniques. By levels of knowledge, we mean something that goes beyond the initial scope of the LLM and its massive dataset (e.g., adding new information for an internal company application, based on its own data). Some of the options to adjust that knowledge include the following:

Baseline LLM

Azure OpenAI's language models are trained on enormous datasets containing billions of words. These datasets are carefully curated to include a wide range of topics, genres, and writing styles. The size and diversity of the training data helps the models develop a broad understanding of human language. The specific details of the training data have not been disclosed, but it includes text data from a variety of sources, including books, articles, websites, and other publicly available written material. Additionally, the training process (RLHF) includes human reviewers who help annotate and curate the data, flagging and addressing potential biases or problematic content. Feedback loops with reviewers are established to continuously improve and refine the models. One of the key advantages of the enterprise-grade Azure OpenAI service is that your data is only yours (*https://oreil.ly/qA5Ok*) and is not used by anyone to retrain models. The end-to-end process is explained in OpenAI's public paper (*https://oreil.ly/2uFNS*) titled "Training language models to follow instructions with human feedback," and their official GPT model card, shown in Figure 3-1.

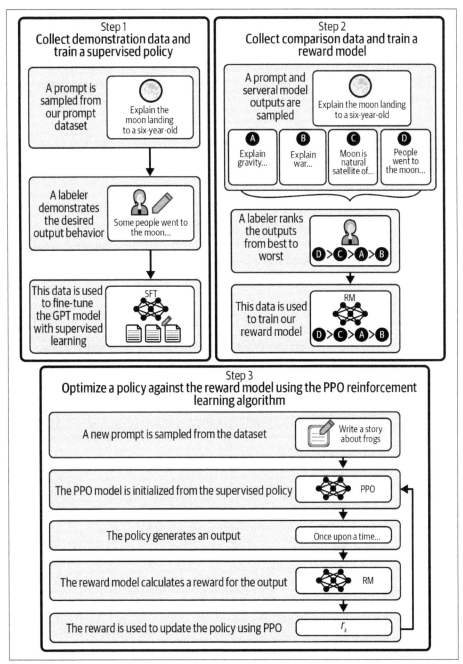

Figure 3-1. The ChatGPT training process (source: adapted from an image by OpenAI (https://oreil.ly/9Lt-2); Creative Commons 4.0 license (https://oreil.ly/YGKJ5))

Additional knowledge (grounding)

You can provide the LLMs with some additional context or knowledge, making them specific to the activity scope of the developed system. This could go from setting the topic of discussion for a chatbot to specifying URLs that are related to the topics we want to include. There are different ways to implement this grounding:

Fine tuning

Using small knowledge bases or private data to retrain the LLM with new additional information. Available via Azure OpenAI Service, it's a good option to adjust the knowledge scope of the LLM, but a less cost-efficient option (as we will explore in Chapter 5 when we calculate the cost of the Azure OpenAI–enabled implementations). In reality, there are very few use cases that require fine-tuning, because it updates the weights of the models but does not necessarily make the model more factual with respect to the data it was fine-tuned for. Most use cases can be achieved through retrieval-augmented generation (RAG).

RAG, embeddings-based retrieval

Based on Microsoft's definition (*https://oreil.ly/QlN0L*), embeddings are:

> representations or encodings of tokens, such as sentences, paragraphs, or documents, in a high-dimensional vector space, where each dimension corresponds to a learned feature or attribute of the language. Embeddings are the way that the model captures and stores the meaning and the relationships of the language, and the way that the model compares and contrasts different tokens or units of language. Embeddings are the bridge between the discrete and the continuous, and between the symbolic and the numeric, aspects of language for the model.

RAG, index-based retrieval

The ability to index existing files so we can locate them when interacting with the LLM engine. Microsoft defines indexes (*https://oreil.ly/iJSKP*) as:

> crawlers that extract searchable content from data sources and populate a search index using field-to-field mappings between source data and a search index. This approach is sometimes referred to as a "pull model" because the search service pulls data in without you having to write any code that adds data to an index.

RAG, hybrid search

As the result of combining grounding techniques, hybrid search (*https://oreil.ly/c2W8A*) leverages both embedding-based retrieval in combination with index-based retrieval to unlock some of the most powerful techniques.

Other grounding techniques

Other techniques include contextualization (providing information about topics and/or specific URLs to define a reduced knowledge scope) and live internet results to complement the LLM information and include external sources.

As you can see in Figure 3-2, all these elements contribute to the creation of an extended knowledge domain from regular LLMs, based on internet and private data. The rest of this chapter will focus on different techniques to implement them with Azure OpenAI and other Microsoft services.

Summarizing, any generative AI architecture or approach will depend on the knowledge domains and levels we require for the end solutions. If our application can rely on (just) the LLM, which already contains a massive amount of information, then we can implement the model with no additional building blocks. On the other hand, if we need to add specific information from other sources (including PDFs, text documents, websites, databases, etc.), then we will leverage the so-called fine-tuning and grounding techniques.

Let's now explore the available interfaces and tools for you to create new applications with Azure OpenAI Service. You will understand the key building blocks before moving into a step-by-step guide of the most relevant implementation approaches.

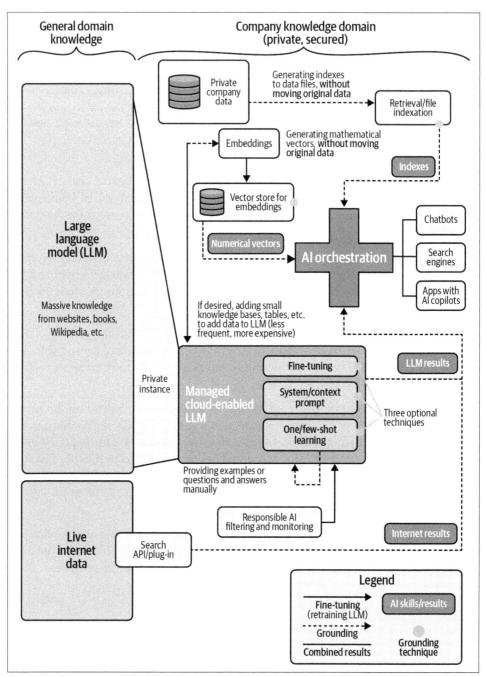

Figure 3-2. Knowledge scope for generative AI

Generative AI Modeling with Azure OpenAI Service

One of the key adoption factors that encourages people to use Azure OpenAI is the availability of different visual and code-based interfaces that you can leverage while using the service. In this section we will explore them as well as how to use these interfaces depending on your generative AI implementation approach.

 Initially, Microsoft released Azure OpenAI Service with "Gated General Availability," meaning that any organization willing to use the service had to *complete a detailed application form* to explain the potential use cases and guarantee good usage of the platform. Microsoft's goal was to validate that any application enabled by Azure OpenAI was always aligned with their responsible AI approach (*https://oreil.ly/QsuYY*) and the intended use (*https://oreil.ly/7ojQP*) of the platform. If you are getting started with Azure OpenAI Service, check first if you still need to apply for access (*https://oreil.ly/MDBhf*) and prepare the required information for the application form (*https://oreil.ly/dp14y*).

Azure OpenAI Service Building Blocks

Before diving into the "how to," let's explore the available building blocks for any Azure OpenAI practitioner to prepare and deploy new solutions. Essentially, there are two primary components for the Azure OpenAI Service: the *visual interfaces* that allow users to test, customize, and deploy their generative AI models and the *development interfaces* that enable the exploitation and integration of those advanced capabilities with any application.

Both elements are complementary and great assets for any kind of adopter, as they require a relatively low level of AI knowledge to make them work. For example, *citizen users* (hybrid technical-business profiles that are not very technical, but that understand the principles of generative AI and have some knowledge of prompt engineering, can use the visual playground, or leverage Microsoft Copilot Studio) and *regular developers* are great candidates for the development platforms.

Visual interfaces: Azure OpenAI Studio and Playground

As with any other Azure AI service (*https://oreil.ly/TDoRH*), Azure OpenAI includes the notion of a "Studio" (i.e., Azure OpenAI Studio) (*https://oreil.ly/LWQO1*) that makes the interaction with generative AI models very simple, by providing an intuitive UI that facilitates service deployments and leverages existing Azure OpenAI APIs without any code required from the user perspective.

Azure OpenAI Studio includes access to all available models (*https://oreil.ly/BI5Ue*) (by type and geographic region), predefined prompting scenarios and examples, and several applications called *playgrounds*. The Azure OpenAI Playgrounds are different apps within Azure OpenAI Service, which include (as you can see in Figure 3-3) a customizable ChatGPT type of instance (*Chat*), other GPT language models for non-chat scenarios (*Completion*), a playground to connect AI models with your data (*Bring your own data*), and one for image generation applications with OpenAI's DALL·E models.

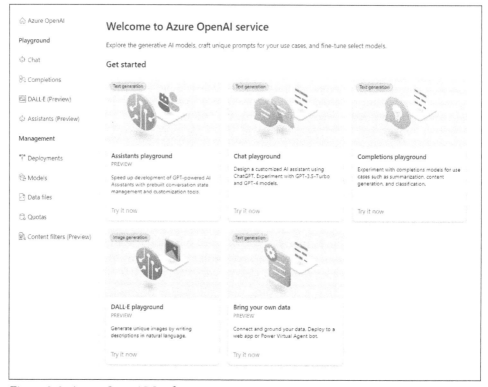

Figure 3-3. Azure OpenAI Studio

You can access each playground (and their related management features) from the left panel of the studio, or visit them directly by following the URLs included here:

Chat playground (https://oreil.ly/FRU9K)
>This includes both the conversational Chat playground with the features and settings (*https://oreil.ly/K_fjL*) required to create a private ChatGPT implementation, and the bring your own data (represented as one of the playgrounds in Azure OpenAI Studio) functionality that I will explain later in this section. The Chat playground (shown in Figure 3-4) leverages the Chat Completion API (*https://oreil.ly/ZJOLp*).

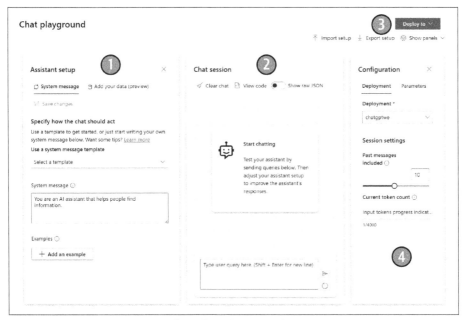

Figure 3-4. Azure OpenAI Studio: Chat playground

As indicated in Figure 3-4, the main tiles and features of the Chat playground comprise the following:

1. Assistant setup

This area is located on the left side of the screen and allows users to configure the chatbot's behavior. Users can choose from templates or create their own custom system messages. This section helps users define how the chatbot should act and respond to user queries:

System message

A type of meta-prompt (*https://oreil.ly/OmKQO*) (i.e., a prompt that sets the by-default context of the discussion) to guide the AI system's behavior. It can be used to introduce the system, set expectations, provide feedback, or handle errors. One important thing to remember is that even if there is no token limit for this message, it will be included with every API call, so it counts against the overall token limit/context length (*https://oreil.ly/BI5Ue*) of the model.

Examples

This area is located at the bottom-left corner of the screen. You can add examples to the bot intelligence, so it learns the proper way to answer specific questions. It's a good option when we don't need to fully retrain a model, for example, when you need to add a couple of topics from your company's knowledge base and you want to define the best way to answer. From the official description: "Add examples to show the chat what responses you want. It will try to mimic any responses you add here so make sure they match the rules you laid out in the system message."

2. *Chat session*

This area is located in the middle of the screen and serves as the main interaction point between you and the chatbot. You can type your queries here and the chatbot will respond accordingly. The chat session allows you to test the chatbot's performance and make adjustments to the assistant setup as needed, as well as import and export bot configurations, or get the result as a JavaScript Object Notation (JSON) file (*https://oreil.ly/LZJH4*).

3. *Deploy to*

This option allows you to deploy your chatbot to a specific platform or environment. Azure OpenAI Studio allows direct deployments to both Azure Web Apps (*https://oreil.ly/TtlXr*) and Microsoft Copilot Studio (*https://oreil.ly/YV0SN*). We will explore these deployment options later in this chapter.

4. *Configuration*

This area is located in the top-right corner of the screen. It provides options for you to access deployment and session settings. Users can also clear the chat history and manage parameters related to the chatbot's deployment:

Deployment

To handle session-level configurations, such as the Azure OpenAI deployment resource you want to use (e.g., you may have several for different geographic regions), as well as the memory of the session, which will impact how many interactions the system can remember when getting new questions:

Deployment instance

You will select one option, from the resources you have previously deployed (*https://oreil.ly/-4D4f*) (if you haven't, you will need to create one before using Azure OpenAI Studio), based on the geography and model needs you may have.

Past messages included and current token count

Session-level parameters you may want to adjust for the specific test you do via the Chat playground. These parameters will be gone when you finish the playground session, except if you deploy an application (we will see the deployment options in a couple of sections).

Parameters

This right panel includes all technical settings that will allow you to configure the expected output message, including the level of creativity versus determinism of the answer:

Max response

This parameter helps you set a limit on the number of tokens per model response. The max response is measured in the number of tokens, and it is shared between the question (including system message, examples, message history, and prompt/user query) and the model's response.

Temperature

This parameter and the Top-p parameter are direct alternatives to control the AI model's randomness. Lowering the temperature means that the model will produce more repetitive and deterministic responses. Increasing the temperature will result in more unexpected or creative responses. Try adjusting temperature or Top-p, but not both.

Assistants playground (https://oreil.ly/S4KFy)

Released in 2024 (*https://oreil.ly/MdxvG*), the Assistants playground is visually similar to the Chat playground, but it includes:

- The ability to handle conversation threads, by using the "thread ID" parameter that converts the chat discussion into a stateful application that keeps context and memory. You can see the details in Azure OpenAI's Assistants API specification (*https://oreil.ly/ErRd6*).
- Other functionalities such as the API call log, the Code Interpreter (*https://oreil.ly/3jSFV*), and function calling (*https://oreil.ly/2R7Pz*).

Keep in mind that this is a relatively new option, but the official documentation (*https://oreil.ly/HH4hH*) includes the detailed steps for creation and management of assistant files. Keep an eye on and bookmark this URL to follow any news and technical resources.

Completions playground (https://oreil.ly/zJYtL)

As we reviewed in Chapter 1, the completion skill is (along with chat and embeddings models) one of the core concepts for NLP and modern LLMs. Completion focuses on unitary interactions for all kinds of text-based requests (with no need for memory between interactions, as you may need for chat-based applications in which the model keeps the discussion context). It leverages the Completions API (*https://oreil.ly/Uczv9*). As shown in Figure 3-5, the Completions playground allows you to type a prompt, or choose from a series of examples. It also includes the same kind of setting parameters that we reviewed in the Chat playground.

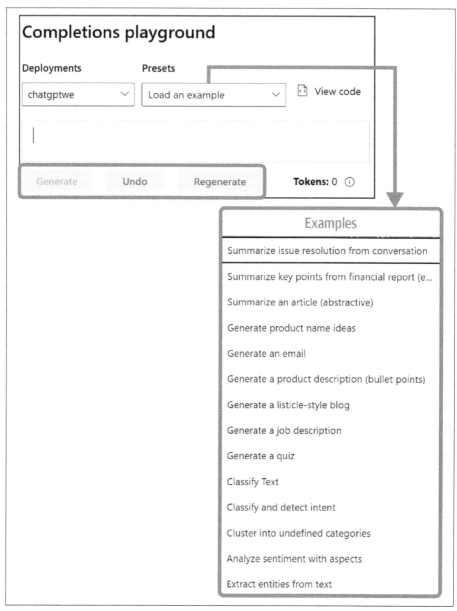

Figure 3-5. Azure OpenAI Studio: Completions playground

You can generate an answer (completion), and even regenerate it to obtain a totally new output. If you choose one of the examples from the drop-down menu, you will see an automatic prompt appear and the corresponding completion, highlighted as in Figure 3-6.

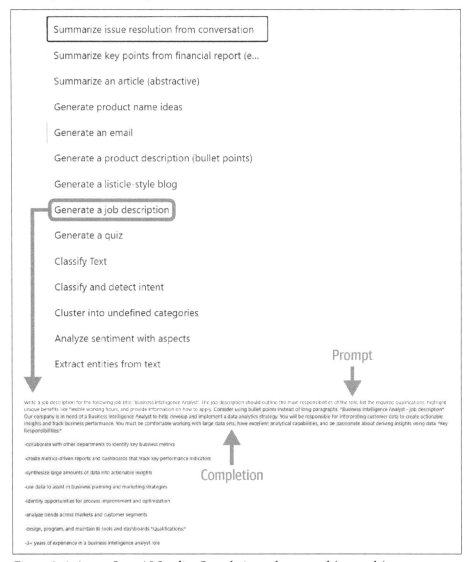

Figure 3-6. Azure OpenAI Studio: Completions playground (example)

Summarizing, you may use chat for multistep scenarios where you need to maintain a sequence of interactions with the AI model, while completions can be used for specific unitary cases. As you will see later, these two playgrounds are just visual interfaces that consume existing Azure OpenAI completion (*https://oreil.ly/ Uczv9*) and chat (*https://oreil.ly/ZJOLp*) APIs.

Bring your own data playground

Even if Azure OpenAI Studio shows this feature as a separate playground, it is technically part of the Chat playground. To access this functionally, you can either use the Chat playground's Assistant setup and select the "Add your data" tab or go directly to the "Bring your own data" tile of the Studio (Figure 3-7). For both cases, the result will be the same.

Once you reach this point, the sequence of steps is pretty simple. As you can see in Figure 3-8, the system will allow you to select your own sources of data, to combine their knowledge with the baseline LLM. That knowledge can come from PDF files, text-based documents, slides, web files, etc. In this case, besides the Azure OpenAI resource previously deployed, the bring your own data functionality will leverage other resources such as Azure Data Lake Gen2/Azure Storage, to save the files, and Azure Cognitive Search, to index the files. Azure Cognitive Search offers a vector search functionality based on the Embeddings API (*https:// oreil.ly/imKOS*)) that I will explain by the end of the chapter. Finally, you can always check the official documentation (*https://oreil.ly/z_iRM*) to follow the latest updates for this Azure OpenAI feature, as it is a quickly evolving one due to the continuous incorporation of new functionalities.

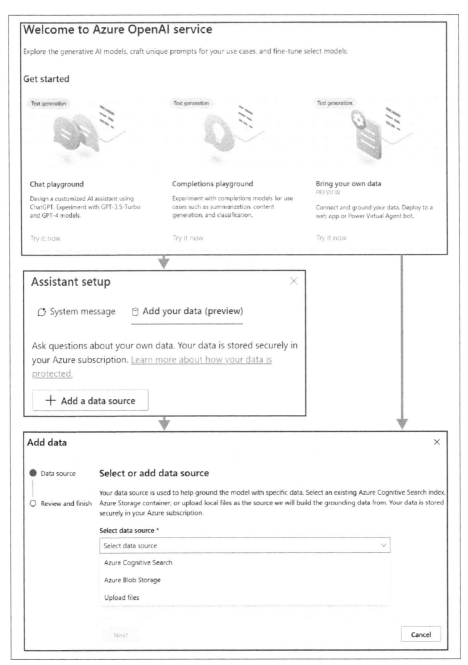

Figure 3-7. Azure OpenAI Studio: Bring your own data

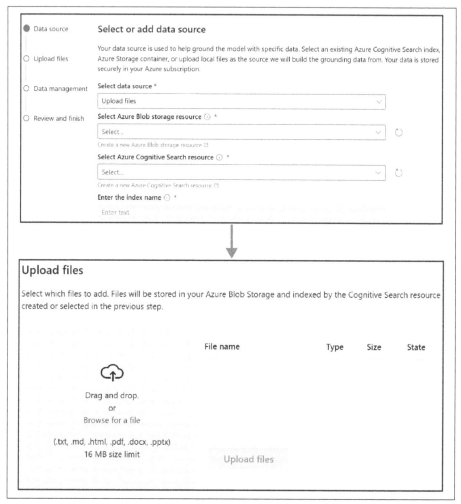

Figure 3-8. Azure OpenAI Studio: Bring your own data source details

DALL·E playground (https://oreil.ly/r4h7Y)

The last playground tile provides direct access to the generative AI DALL·E models (versions 2 and 3) from OpenAI. This is a text-to-image model that allows you to create new images from just text-based descriptions. Imagine describing a place or a scene and getting a visual representation in the form of images that are freshly created on demand. This means they didn't exist previously and that you can integrate this capability into your solutions and combine it with the rest of the language. The DALL·E playground (shown in Figure 3-9) leverages the Image Generation API (*https://oreil.ly/bm-7a*).

Figure 3-9. Azure OpenAI Studio: DALL·E playground

As shown in Figure 3-9, relevant aspects of the playground include the following:

1. *Playground*

    The DALL·E playground is visually simple—a prompt field and the results (image) below. It's similar to the structure of the Bing Create application (*https://oreil.ly/YwDy-*), but with the option to deploy the DALL·E model for your own development.

2. *Settings*

    The settings panel offers you the option to choose the number of images you want to generate and the image size.

3. *Album*

    The album section showcases all past image experiments, offering you the option to review previously created images, generate new ones, etc.

Besides the different playgrounds, you can also explore the left-side *Management* panel shown in Figure 3-10, which include options such as deployments, models, data files, quotas, and content filters.

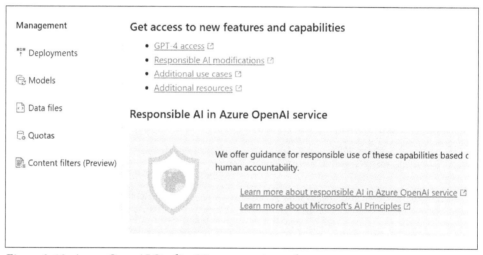

Figure 3-10. Azure OpenAI Studio: Management panels

Let's explore the most important features:

Deployments (https://oreil.ly/PGocU)

    Allows you to deploy any specific model instance available in the geographic region (*https://oreil.ly/XZnCX*) of your Azure OpenAI resource and to visualize those that you previously deployed (Figure 3-11).

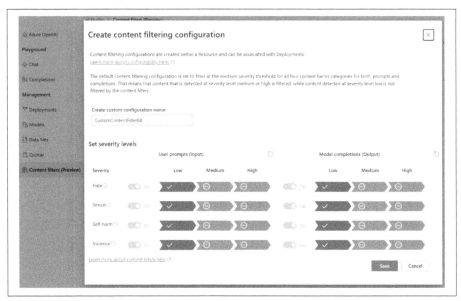

Figure 3-11. Azure OpenAI Studio: deployments

Content filters (https://oreil.ly/Bpsud)
> For responsible AI moderation. Each filter from those in Figure 3-12 (e.g., hate, sexual, self-harm, and violence topics for both prompts and completions, with different levels of filtering) can be applied to the deployments, and those deployments will include the content filter for each chat or completion implementation. We will explore this feature in Chapter 4, as part of the responsible AI measures for generative AI implementations.

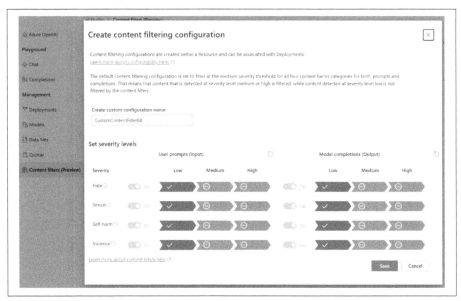

Figure 3-12. Azure OpenAI Studio: content filters

Models (https://oreil.ly/oC3Hj)
> This option shows the available Azure OpenAI models (*https://oreil.ly/XZnCX*), related to the specific geographic region of the chosen deployment.

Data files (https://oreil.ly/2TZwW)
> This file management feature allows you to prepare the dataset for fine-tuned implementations (*https://oreil.ly/FDMr1*). We will explore more about fine-tuning later in this chapter.

Quotas (https://oreil.ly/ONn5Q)
> The quota panel shows the usage quotas (*https://oreil.ly/bEN4D*) related to different models and geographic regions. It also helps you request a quota increase (*https://oreil.ly/iiysu*) if you need more. Alternatively, and I will explain this in Chapter 6 as part of the pricing and estimation exercise, you have an option to hire dedicated capacity, by leveraging the so-called provisioned throughput units (PTU) for Azure OpenAI (*https://oreil.ly/KCC6K*), which are reserved instances with performance and service availability benefits.

We will explore some of these functionalities later in this chapter and in Chapter 4, as they will all be relevant, depending on the type of Azure OpenAI implementation you plan to utilize. Now, let's see what you can do to deploy these models via Azure OpenAI Studio.

Deployment interfaces: Web apps and Microsoft Copilot agents

As mentioned in this chapter, the Chat playground includes some easy-to-use deployment options. They are not available for the rest of the playgrounds, but they can simplify the preliminary deployment of Azure OpenAI models for internal testing and use purposes, without any coding required. These no-code deployments can incorporate the specific knowledge from the bring your own data functionality. There are two possibilities:

Web apps with Azure App Service (https://oreil.ly/moBFz)
> The first available deployment option, which you can use with or without the "bring your own data" feature activated. As we discussed in Chapter 2, App Service is the Azure option to deploy native web apps; it allows integrations with both external and internal systems and web development with a variety of programming languages. From Azure OpenAI Studio and its Chat playground, you can simply "Deploy to" and then configure your deployment (see Figure 3-13).

Figure 3-13. Azure OpenAI Studio: web app deployment

As shown in Figure 3-13, configuration options include the following:

Choosing the web app
You can create a new App Service resource directly from this feature (in that case, you will need to define the "app name" that will be part of your web app URL), or choose an existing one if you have previously deployed via Azure portal's App Service panel (*https://oreil.ly/dPLy2*).

Pricing plan
To select the preferred pricing tier (*https://oreil.ly/IdDXQ*) for the web app.

Chat history
A functionality that allows the web app users to recover their previous interactions (*https://oreil.ly/-yyQg*) with chat. It relies on Cosmos DB (Azure's NoSQL database) (*https://oreil.ly/-yyQg*), which obviously adds cost to the existing Azure OpenAI and App Service resources.

Once you have selected all these options, you can click on Deploy. You will need to wait around 10 minutes for all the resources to be deployed, then you will be able to launch your web app from the studio, or by typing the URL *https://<app-name>.azurewebsites.net*. The look and feel will be something like the interface you see in Figure 3-14.

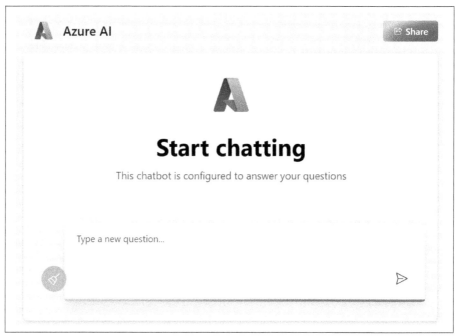

Figure 3-14. Azure OpenAI Studio: web app interface

The UI of the new app will contain a regular chatbot setup, with options to share and check previous discussions on the top-right side of the window. You can also customize the visual aspect of the application (*https://oreil.ly/BVUkG*) by using the official source code (*https://oreil.ly/MeBin*), and deploy it programmatically, with Azure App Service and using your preferred programming language, instead of leveraging Azure OpenAI Studio.

Bots with Microsoft Copilot Studio (formerly Power Virtual Agents [PVAs]) (https://oreil.ly/YV0SN)

This option is available for Chat playground implementations that include the "bring your own data" feature. That means that if you don't add extended knowledge from PDFs or other documents, the Chat playground won't include Microsoft Copilot Studio/PVA as a deployment option in the top-right corner in Figure 3-15.

Figure 3-15. Azure OpenAI Studio: Copilot deployment

How to handle PVAs is outside of the scope of this book, but you can explore the detailed instructions from the official documentation (*https://oreil.ly/Qi9J3*) that show how to use PVAs with Azure OpenAI for the *generative answers* feature. This option is available for only certain geographic regions, so you will need to validate if your deployments with Azure OpenAI models show the PVA deployment option in the Chat playground. If this is not the case, you may want to deploy new models in other regions.

Summarizing, these visual interfaces can help you leverage Azure OpenAI models in a simple manner. They provide an intuitive way to launch the Azure OpenAI APIs in just a few clicks. However, you will need code-based tools to implement the other advanced architectures you will see later in this chapter. Let's now explore those APIs and other development kits so you can leverage everything that Azure OpenAI Service has to offer.

Development interfaces: APIs and SDKs

In addition to all the previously explored interfaces, one of the key enablers for integrating Azure OpenAI with existing or new applications is the ability to consume the preconfigured models as regular endpoints. From a development point of view, we can call those models by using the APIs and related software development kits (SDKs) and pass any input and configuration parameters within the code. This section covers the main pieces you need to know—the *Azure OpenAI Service REST APIs*, including the official API reference documentation (*https://oreil.ly/qH3FL*), with specific details for chat, completions, embeddings, and other deployments. There is also an official repo (*https://oreil.ly/mbA1v*) with the full specifications. There are general APIs that will help you with the configuration and deployment of Azure OpenAI services, while the service APIs help you consume the models to bring the AI capabilities to your generative AI applications.

The main APIs you need to know and their high-level call details are as follows:

General management APIs (https://oreil.ly/xkqqk)
> For Azure AI service account management (including Azure OpenAI), with tasks such as account creation, deletion, listing, etc.

APIs for model-related information (https://oreil.ly/Y7VMR)
> To obtain the list of available Azure OpenAI models and information about their specific capabilities and the model lifecycle (including potential deprecation details).

Completions (https://oreil.ly/Uczv9)
> The required API for nonchat language scenarios. This and other APIs are versioned by using the "YYYY-MM-DD" date structure for `api-version`, and you will need to copy the resource name and deployment-ID from the Azure OpenAI model you previously deployed (remember the step-by-step process from the Azure portal, in Chapter 2). To create a completion resource, the POST operation is:

```
POST https://{your-resource-name}.openai.azure.com/openai/deployments/
   {deployment-id}/completions?api-version={api-version}
```

The request and response dynamic follows this structure, with the prompt parameter the input for the model to generate a specific completion, and a series of optional parameters (*https://oreil.ly/Uczv9*) such as `max_tokens` (the limit of tokens for the expected answer) or the number `n` of expected completions/answers.

Request:

```
curl https://YOUR_RESOURCE_NAME.openai.azure.com/openai/deployments/\
   YOUR_DEPLOYMENT_NAME/completions?api-version=YYYY-MM-DD\
   -H "Content-Type: application/json" \
```

```
    -H "api-key: YOUR_API_KEY" \
    -d "{
        \"prompt\": \"The best thing in life\",
        \"max_tokens\": 5,
        \"n\": 1
    }"
```

Response:

```
{
    "id": "cmpl-4kGh7iXtjW4lc9eGhff6Hp8C7btdQ",
    "object": "text_completion",
    "created": 1646932609,
    "model": "gpt-35-turbo-instruct",
    "choices": [
        {
            "text": ", is eating burgers with a milkshake",
            "index": 0,
            "logprobs": null,
            "finish_reason": "length"
        }
    ]
}
```

The answers (completions) contain the finish_reason parameter. finish_rea
son defines why the model stopped generating more information; for most cases
this will be due to max_tokens, which stops the model once it reaches the limit.
However, there is another option that we will explore in Chapter 4 that stops the
model due to what we call *content filters*.

Chat completions (https://oreil.ly/ZJOLp)
Dedicated API for chat scenarios (and the only supported one for future model
versions), including the configuration parameters we previously reviewed with
the Chat playground. This includes input parameters we discussed for the Azure
OpenAI Playground, such as temperature and max_tokens. There is one important parameter for chat messages, known as the ChatRole (*https://oreil.ly/WLv1g*).
This allows you to split the interactions based on different roles:

System
Helps you set the behavior of the assistant.

User
Provides input for chat completions.

Assistant
Provides responses to system-instructed, user-prompted input.

Function
Provides function results for chat completions. We will explore this concept
later in this chapter, after we cover the different Azure OpenAI APIs.

The sequence for a typical chat scenario follows these steps:

1. *Resource creation*

   Using a similar structure to what you have seen in a regular completion API call (including the date as the API version). The regular POST operation for chat completion is:

   ```
   POST https://{your-resource-name}.openai.azure.com/openai/deployments/
       {deployment-id}/chat/completions?api-version={api-version}
   ```

2. *System message*

   This is how you set the context of the chat engine, by defining the scope of the discussion, allowed or forbidden topics, etc. The system message is also called the context prompt or *meta-prompt*. The `messages` parameter (*https://oreil.ly/vFEYS*), along with the `role` subparameter (*https://oreil.ly/y5HFq*), is the place where you will define your system message, using:

   ```
   {
     "messages": [
       {
         "role": "system",
         "content": "the context and system message to add to your chat"
       }
     ]
   }
   ```

3. *User-assistant interaction*

   This leverages the same `messages` parameter, with the *user* and *assistant* roles. The structure for both roles is similar to what we have discussed for the system message, and the response includes the same `finish-reason` parameter that will give you a hint about the result (i.e., if the completion has finished due to the `max_tokens` assigned to the answer, or if there is a filtering reason due to negative topic detection).

Image generation (https://oreil.ly/bm-7a)

The API call to generate images based on text-to-image DALL·E models. As with the visual playground, the input parameters include the text-based prompt, and two optional inputs such as the number n of desired images (if you don't include it, the system will generate only one image), and the size (by default 1024×1024, with alternative 256×256 and 512×512 options). The POST operation to create an image generation resource is:

```
POST https://{your-resource-name}.openai.azure.com/openai/\
    images/generations:submit?api-version={api-version}
```

Here is an example of a curl (command-line tool for downloading and uploading files from various protocols and servers) (*https://oreil.ly/xApmg*) request:

```
curl -X POST \
  https://{your-resource-name}.openai.azure.com/openai/deployments/\
  {deployment-id}/images/generations?api-version=2023-12-01-preview \
  -H "Content-Type: application/json" \
  -H "api-key: YOUR_API_KEY" \
  -d '{
        "prompt": "An avocado chair",
        "size": "1024x1024",
        "n": 3,
        "quality": "hd",
        "style": "vivid"
      }'
```

The end-to-end process includes three different steps:

1. *Request* the image generation (via POST operation (*https://oreil.ly/kPf-m*)), which helps you pre-generate the images based on the text-based input prompt. It returns an operation ID that you will leverage for the next step.

2. *Get* the result of the image generation (GET operation (*https://oreil.ly/lxX0B*)), which allows you to recover the pre-generated images for the specific operation ID.

3. *Delete* the previously loaded images (DELETE operation (*https://oreil.ly/5UfTB*)) from the server, for the specific Azure OpenAI resource, and the existing operation ID. If you don't use this option, the images will be automatically deleted after 24 hours.

Speech to text (https://oreil.ly/hKakE)

Based on the Azure OpenAI Whisper model (*https://oreil.ly/SJNcT*), these APIs allow you create transcriptions from audio pieces, for a variety of languages and accents, with great performance and the possibility to combine it with other Azure OpenAI models. You can specify the input audio file, language, discussion style, output format (by default a JSON file), etc. This Azure OpenAI speech-to-text (S2T) feature has a limitation of 25 MB for the input audio file, but you can leverage the batch transcription mode of Azure AI Speech (*https://oreil.ly/NnMTz*) (not Azure OpenAI, but the Azure AI Speech services for voice ↔ text features (*https://oreil.ly/-HLPL*)) to transcribe bigger files. The POST operation looks similar to the previous APIs:

```
POST https://{your-resource-name}.openai.azure.com/openai/deployments/
  {deployment-id}/audio/transcriptions?api-version={api-version}
```

The corresponding curl request (illustrative example):

```
curl $AZURE_OPENAI_ENDPOINT/openai/deployments/MyDeploymentName/\
  audio/transcriptions?api-version=2023-09-01-preview \
  -H "api-key: $AZURE_OPENAI_KEY" \
  -H "Content-Type: multipart/form-data" \
  -F file="@./wikipediaOcelot.wav"
```

Embeddings (https://oreil.ly/imKOS)

This API call allows you to generate embeddings from specific text inputs, from some of the architectures you will see in this chapter. The model and its specific input length will depend on model availability (*https://oreil.ly/gvAHr*) at the time of your implementation. The POST operation is similar to the previous ones, and the dynamic is as simple as requesting the embeddings (*https://oreil.ly/xFJTh*) for a text input and obtaining a JSON response (*https://oreil.ly/yYCuU*) with the generated embeddings, for you to store (we will see several vector store/database options by the end of the chapter) and leverage them later:

```
POST https://{your-resource-name}.openai.azure.com/openai/deployments/
    {deployment-id}/embeddings?api-version={api-version}
```

And the corresponding curl example:

```
curl https://YOUR_RESOURCE_NAME.openai.azure.com/openai/deployments/\
    YOUR_DEPLOYMENT_NAME/embeddings?api-version=2023-05-15\
    -H 'Content-Type: application/json' \
    -H 'api-key: YOUR_API_KEY' \
    -d '{"input": "Sample Document goes here"}'
```

Fine-tuning (https://oreil.ly/1pqcT)

As we reviewed at the beginning of this chapter, one of the implementation options includes the ability to fine-tune pre-built models with your specific, available information. We will see more details later in this chapter, but for now keep in mind that if you choose this option, there is a specific set of APIs that you can leverage to create, manage, explore, and delete new fine-tuning "jobs." Also, you will handle your own input files for the fine-tuned models.

Other relevant APIs

Other relevant APIs include the following:

Bing Search (https://oreil.ly/2yZuu)

The Bing Search API allows you to leverage Microsoft Bing's search engine for your own development. You can extend the capabilities of your Azure OpenAI–enabled implementations with live search functionalities.

Form Recognizer (currently known as Azure AI Document Intelligence) (https://oreil.ly/vxtJA)

This helps you transform information from forms and images into structured data. It includes advanced optical character recognition (OCR) functionalities that will support your Azure OpenAI development with specific data sources such as PDF or DOC files.

Azure AI Search (previously known as Azure Cognitive Search) (https://oreil.ly/ wp6r8)

> One of the most important elements for RAG architectures, for both vectors and index approaches.

In addition to these APIs, there is an Azure OpenAI library for .NET developers (*https://oreil.ly/9XMBN*) and the OpenAI library for Python (*https://oreil.ly/-cwGH*), which essentially replicates the features of the official API for a .NET development environment. It provides an interface with the rest of the Azure SDK ecosystem, and it facilitates the connection to Azure OpenAI resources or to non–Azure OpenAI endpoints.

This set of visual and development interfaces are your toolkit for most of the Azure OpenAI implementations out there. They are rapidly evolving, but the links to the official documentation will help you access updated information any time. Now, before moving on to the implementation approaches, let's take a look at a powerful feature that will enable your generative AI systems to interact with other external APIs: function calling.

Interoperability features: Function calling and "JSONization"

The Azure OpenAI function calling (*https://oreil.ly/bQdsv*) option is a way to leverage language models to generate API calls and structure data outputs based on a specific target format. Technically, it is one of the options within the Chat Completion API— the function (*https://oreil.ly/WLv1g*) chat role. You can see several samples (*https://oreil.ly/0nhYM*) on how to use this functionality, but it essentially relies on the following steps:

1. Calling the Chat Completions API, including the functions (based on the official FunctionDefinition format (*https://oreil.ly/5Q-8c*)) and the user's input

2. Using the model's chat response to call your API or function

3. Calling the Chat Completions API again, including the response from your function, to get a final response

This is a relatively new functionality, so you can expect some feature improvements over time. You can always check the official documentation (*https://oreil.ly/UAYNH*) to get the latest details and advice. Additionally, you can also explore the JSON mode (*https://oreil.ly/Fi3-l*) for Azure OpenAI, as it allows you to get a JSON object from the Chat Completions API answer, a powerful feature for interoperability purposes.

This completes the first part of this section. You have learned about the knowledge domains, how to leverage different building blocks to improve and increase the level of knowledge of your generative AI solutions, and the availability tools you will use for implementation. Now, we will move to the next part of this chapter, in which we will explore some of the most relevant development approaches, based on the industry's best practices. Let's get started.

Potential Implementation Approaches

There are several ways to implement generative AI applications with Azure OpenAI Service. The type of implementations you use will mostly depend on your specific use case, as well as the technical and financial context for adoption. This means there are situations where the most expensive option is not always the best, or other options may have limitations, such as when we don't have specific data besides our website, etc. Let's explore the primary implementation types, based on the customization levels of Figure 3-16.

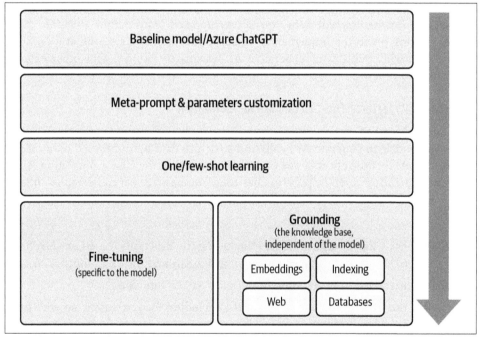

Figure 3-16. Implementation approaches with Azure OpenAI Service

As you can see from the figure, you can customize a model by preparing a good meta-prompt, adjusting technical parameters, providing one or a few "shots" as examples to guide the model, and implementing fine-tuning and/or grounding techniques. The next sections will go into the details of how to do all of this.

Basic Azure ChatGPT instance

A basic, private GPT type of instance is the simplest kind of implementation, and one of the most popular Azure OpenAI cases nowadays. When companies want to have a private "ChatGPT" for their employees, this is the answer. It keeps your own data safe and private and deploys the instance within your own cloud infrastructure. It's one of the favorite options for internal use with employees.

The deployment process is relatively simple:

1. Within your Azure OpenAI Studio, deploy a GPT-3.5 Turbo, GPT-4, GPT-4 Turbo, or GPT-4o model instance. This type of model is technically similar to what ChatGPT is, and it will deliver that level of performance. Remember to choose the specific geographic region that is closest to you.

2. Once you have created the resource, go to the visual playground. There, you will see a left menu with the option "Chat."

3. Once there, you can prepare the system message (*https://oreil.ly/OmKQO*) / meta-prompt to contextualize the chatbot by telling it something like "You are an AI assistant for company X, to answer questions from the employees" (internal use) or "You are an AI assistant for company X with website Y. If anyone asks something that is not related to this topic, say you cannot answer" (for clients).

4. You can also customize parameters such as the max length of the answers or the temperature of the messages, which is a metric between 0 and 1 to define the level of creativity of the model.

5. Once you have tested performance and you are ready to deploy the model, you can come back to the resource page (Azure portal) and find both the endpoint and the keys for that specific resource. That page contains examples of code to for calling the APIs.

The end-to-end architecture (Figure 3-17) is pretty simple—a pre-deployed model that we can directly consume from our applications, based on the existing endpoints and APIs.

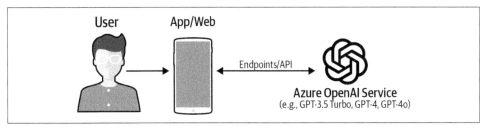

Figure 3-17. Simplified Azure ChatGPT architecture

This type of implementation is good enough for internal company cases where you don't require any customization based on private data, for example, internal chatbots for employee productivity based on general internet information, or search engines for intranet sites. For the rest of the cases where there is some custom data involved, we will explore other options. Let's dig into the first of them next.

Minimal customization with one- or few-shot learning

Besides the baseline model, and system message/meta-prompt and parameters customization, there is an option to perform *one- or few-shot learning*, which means providing the LLM with examples of discussions based on the expected output for a specific topic. This is a useful and simple option for small adjustments, and it relies on a very similar architecture to the previous one, with relatively light changes. The main difference when compared to the previous approach is the inclusion of one or few examples to guide the LLM before starting to use it (Figure 3-18).

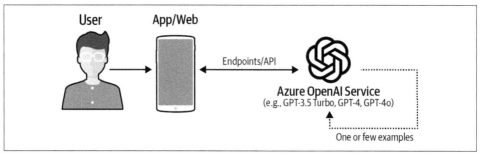

Figure 3-18. One/few-shot learning architecture

The one-shot/few-shot learning process can be achieved in several ways:

- Via APIs (code)
  - — Use the Chat Completions API with GPT-4 and other models that are designed to take input formatted in a chat-like transcript. You can provide conversational examples that are used by the model for in-context learning.
  - — Use the Completions API with the GPT-3 models, which can take a string of text with no specific format rules. You can provide a set of training examples as part of the prompt to give additional context to the model.
- Via playground (visual)
  - — Use the Chat playground to interact with GPT-4, GPT-4o, etc. You can add few-shot examples in the chat transcript and see how the model responds.
  - — Use the Completions playground to interact with the GPT-x models. You can write your prompt with few-shot examples and see how the model completes it.

Overall, all these customizations are intended to improve the performance of the model versus a regular vanilla "ChatGPT" implementation like the one we previously explored, but there are ways to retrain the model in a deeper way, like the one we will explore next.

Fine-tuned GPT models

As mentioned earlier in the chapter, there are different ways to customize an LLM to adjust its knowledge scope. Most of them rely on the orchestration/combination of the LLM with other knowledge pieces, without really combining the data sources (i.e., grounding). In this case, we will focus on the only way to "retrain" an Azure OpenAI model with custom company data: the Azure OpenAI Service fine-tuning feature (*https://oreil.ly/T0GP8*).

This approach may have some advantages for companies with very specific and valuable data intellectual property, but its cost (you will need to add hosting cost to the regular API calls for the fine-tuning process) and technical complexity will probably lead you (and most of the adopters out there) to other kinds of grounding approaches with better performance/cost balance.

Also, the fine-tuning feature relies on a very special kind of training process. It is not the regular label-based training process you can do, for example, in classification tasks with traditional AI models. We are talking about a new kind of supervised process that leverages Azure OpenAI's prompting system to inject information based on the JSON Lines (JSONL) file format (*https://oreil.ly/SdBph*).

For example, with GPT-3.5 Turbo, you will leverage the system and user roles to reeducate the model:

```
{
  "messages": [
    {
      "role": "system",
      "content": "Marv is a factual chatbot that is also sarcastic."
    },
    {
      "role": "user",
      "content": "Who wrote 'Romeo and Juliet'?"
    },
    {
      "role": "assistant",
      "content": "Oh, just some guy named William Shakespeare. Heard of him?"
    }
  ]
}
```

Other legacy models such as DaVinci require a prompt/completion format based on a question-answer logic:

```
{"prompt": "<prompt text>", "completion": "<ideal generated text>"}
{"prompt": "<prompt text>", "completion": "<ideal generated text>"}
```

This new way to inject data and knowledge allows us to reeducate the model in a very granular manner, but it is a complex way to do so. You can see the overall architecture in Figure 3-19, in which you will basically customize the model, based on a fine-tuning process that relies on specific organizational data.

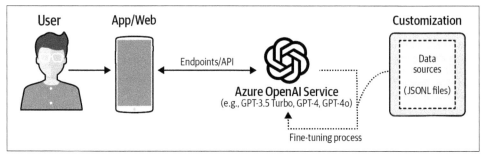

Figure 3-19. Azure OpenAI fine-tuning architecture

The steps to perform *fine-tuning* with Azure OpenAI Service are:

1. *Prepare your dataset* in JSONL format. For recent models such as GPT-3.5 Turbo, GPT-4, and GPT-4o, you will leverage the Chat Completions API structure for system and user messages.

2. Launch the *custom model wizard* from Azure OpenAI Studio, as shown in Figure 3-20, to train your new customized model.

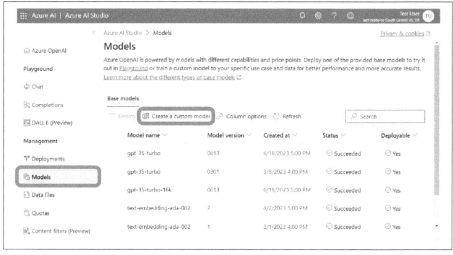

Figure 3-20. Azure OpenAI: custom model wizard

3. *Select a base model* (e.g., GPT-3.5 Turbo), choosing your training data and, optionally, your validation data to evaluate model performance. Those datasets are the JSON files you previously prepared.

4. Review your choices and *launch the training* of the new customized model. Check the status of your customized model and wait for the training to finish.

5. *Deploy your customized model* for use in an application or service, via APIs.

All these options can work depending on the type of application (*https://oreil.ly/cK_7b*) and the intended scope of the model customization. However, there are ways to combine the LLM with internal data sources, from which you can extract knowledge, and then refer to that information from the Azure OpenAI completion and chat completion models. This is what we call RAG (*https://oreil.ly/26QYs*) or grounding, and there are different ways to implement it. The next sections contain different grounding alternatives.

Embedding-based grounding

As you now know from earlier chapters, embeddings are mathematical representations of text-based information as vectors in a vector space, and an alternative and/or complement to the traditional index-based approach. These embeddings are stored and managed as mathematical vectors that represent distances between topics. This means if we are looking for information about animals and we have a vectorized knowledge base that includes animal-related topics, we can recover the Top-k answers (i.e., the most relevant "K" number of pieces of information).

You can use the Azure OpenAI embeddings API to generate vector representations of text that capture the semantic meaning and similarity of the text. Some possible use cases for embeddings are document search, text classification, clustering, or text similarity.

The end-to-end process to create and use an embedding-based system is aligned with what you have seen thus far in this chapter. From an Azure OpenAI perspective, the steps are as follows:

1. *Select the knowledge base* that contains the information that will complement the baseline LLM knowledge domain. This may include PDF, DOC, PPT, TXT, and other file formats. In Azure, you may store that information via Azure Blob Storage or Azure Data Lake Gen2. Keep in mind that if your files are similar to any general information that may be available on the internet (for example, public descriptions of industry concepts), you probably don't need to ground them. However, if you have very specific files with information on how to answer questions, or perform internal tasks, those may be good candidates for embeddings generation.

2. *Choose and deploy your database/vector store.* By the end of this chapter, you will see all available options for implementation in Azure with Azure OpenAI–generated embeddings.

3. *Prepare the input dataset.* This includes two different steps:

    a. *Extract the information* from your documents. For example, you can use Azure Document Intelligence/Form Recognizer to extract text from your PDFs with the OCR feature. You can also use other non-Azure tools.

    b. *Split the information.* For this to work, it is important to keep in mind the embeddings model token limit (*https://oreil.ly/SQSGw*) (e.g., 8K for Ada model version 2) to prepare the input without exceeding the limit (you can use OpenAI's tokenizer tool (*https://oreil.ly/DDQHG*) to understand the extent of what 8K means in terms of document length). This means you will need to make one API call for each of the limited-size blocks you have prepared before, or leverage chunking techniques (*https://oreil.ly/3DHfa*) to split and handle larger documents.

4. *Leverage the Azure OpenAI embeddings models (https://oreil.ly/gvAHr).* Use the API operations you saw earlier in this chapter and get the mathematical vectors from the API response. *Store the vectors* within the chosen vector store.

5. Any time you want to find information from your knowledge base, or if you want to leverage it from any chat or search application, you will need to *generate the embeddings of the question itself,* then perform the search against the vector search. Keep in mind that you will need to leverage the same model (e.g., Ada version 2) for both your knowledge base and the question. You can send the result of the search, with the Top-k results, to the chat or search application, directly or by including it as content for the answer of the completion.

This process is similar for other embeddings and conversation models (for example, those that are available via Azure AI Studio's model catalog and Hugging Face), and the high-level architecture includes the elements you can see in Figure 3-21: basically, the baseline Azure OpenAI model gets complemented with the internal knowledge base that contains PDFs, Word docs, etc. Instead of retraining/fine-tuning the model, we just combine it with that knowledge base so it can find similarities between the users' questions and the information contained within the data sources.

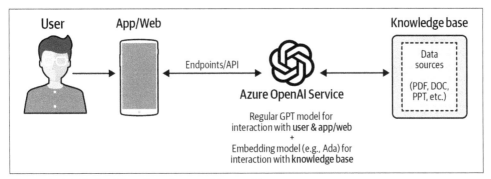

Figure 3-21. Embedding-based grounding architecture

You can find more information and code examples on how to create embeddings (*https://oreil.ly/8Duc8*) from the official Microsoft documentation (in addition to the API definitions we covered earlier in this chapter).

Additionally, there is one official Microsoft accelerator (*https://oreil.ly/iG5UU*) for this type of implementation that you can leverage during the development phase. There are several deployment and storage options. Feel free to explore the code to see the API call details.

Document indexing/retrieval-based grounding

The document indexing/retrieval-based grounding approach is an alternative to the embedding-based approach. In this case, we will not generate mathematical vectors. Instead, we will generate indexes of specific documents, so Azure OpenAI Service can find the information from those sources and include it as part of its answers. For that purpose, we will also use Azure Cognitive Search, which is a service that allows you to index, understand, and retrieve relevant data from a knowledge base or a collection of documents.

The combination of both services enables powerful chatbot applications that can communicate with users in natural language and provide intuitive and personalized interactions, based on specific data from the organization. Much like the embedding-based approach, there is an official Microsoft accelerator (*https://oreil.ly/JNWAz*) available for you to deploy your first proof of concept, in addition to a second one called GPT-RAG (*https://oreil.ly/Q5NK9*) from the Microsoft Argentina team, with some additional functionalities for bigger implementations. You can explore both to see updated details and implementation approaches with Azure OpenAI and Azure Cognitive Search. You can also see the high-level architecture of the key building blocks in Figure 3-22.

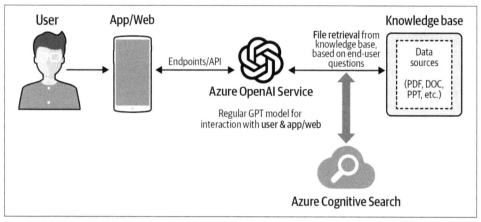

Figure 3-22. Retrieval-based grounding architecture

The main difference when compared to the embedding-based approach is that instead of generating embeddings for both the knowledge base and the user question, you will just perform a search against the Azure AI Search engine (or any equivalent, as we will explore in Chapter 4 for vector databases).

You may see this option as something a bit simpler than the embeddings approach, and a better fit for applications where you need to find the source of information (and even provide a link to the original document as part of the answer); embeddings can potentially handle bigger datasets and deliver better performance. However, it really depends on the specific dataset and its knowledge scope and file format as well as the envisioned use case, so my recommendation is for you to try both options and evaluate the one that delivers best results from a user perspective.

Hybrid search–based grounding

There are newer implementation approaches based on hybrid search techniques (*https://oreil.ly/mwZPy*). Concretely, hybrid search combines vector embeddings and doc retrieval capabilities. The hybrid search feature (*https://oreil.ly/c2W8A*) from Azure AI Search offers that combination, plus a reranking technique (*https://oreil.ly/S7b8p*) that produces the final result, with better performance than the previously mentioned grounding techniques. Now, let's explore some additional grounding options that can add more knowledge scope to your generative AI applications.

Other grounding techniques

We have explored several fine-tuning and grounding techniques, mainly based on text information from different sources. But what happens if you want to leverage other kinds of data? Or if the required information can be found only via live internet results? Here are some other grounding techniques you may want to explore:

LLM + web results

This approach relies on the Bing Web Search API (*https://oreil.ly/qud-9*) to extend the knowledge scope of Azure OpenAI Service models. As you may know, all LLMs are based on training datasets that go up to a specific date (e.g., initial Azure OpenAI models were updated with data up to 2021). If you need updated information, you can use the Bing Web Search API to find web pages, images, videos, news, etc., or use it to create a custom search instance that filters web results based on the criteria. The result from the API can then be used by Azure OpenAI to return an answer based on that information.

LLM + tabular data and/or databases

Similar to other sources, tabular data (e.g., Excel and CSV files) and regular SQL-type databases (e.g., SQL Server, Azure SQL, PostgreSQL) can be good grounding sources. You can develop what the industry calls Database Copilots to allow end users to query information without any complex SQL syntax, just natural language–based prompts. Or you can leverage it for other data exploration (*https://oreil.ly/s3snz*) topics, such as exploratory data analysis or root-case analysis.

Just as with the other previous grounding options, there is an official Microsoft accelerator (*https://oreil.ly/eFneC*) that combines these grounding techniques, with specific code samples and updated implementations.

At the end of the day, each implementation approach (baseline, fine-tuned, or grounding based) serves a different purpose, but the next section is a summarized guide for you to understand the pros and cons of each one, so you can make the most informed decision and create your generative AI applications with Azure OpenAI with the best balance of performance, cost, and technical complexity.

Approach Comparison and Final Recommendation

There is not a single right answer to the question, "Which approach should I use for my generative AI implementation?" It really depends on the use case, type and volume of available data, existing IT architectures, available budget and resources, etc. Again, there is no right answer, and the choice relies for now on experimentation and performance testing.

Table 3-1 shows the general pros and cons of the implementation approaches.

Table 3-1. Comparison of implementation approaches with Azure OpenAI Service

	Approach	Pros	Cons
1	Basic ChatGPT-type instance (vanilla, private)	• Relatively simple and quick to deploy • Good option for internal (employee) use cases • Available via Azure OpenAI's visual playground • Option to define the topic scope based on URLs, by leveraging the system message	• Lack of updated data • Very limited for client-side applications • Higher risk of model hallucination

	Approach	Pros	Cons
2	Examples with one-shot/few-shot learning	• Easy to implement • Good option to adapt system behavior based on specific pieces of knowledge from your company • Available via Azure OpenAI's visual playground	• Lack of updated data • Very limited for client-side applications • Higher risk of model hallucination
3	Fine-tuning	• Good to fine-tune an existing model with specific company data • Leverages mature product features	• Complex to prepare input data for both fine-tuning and few-shot learning • Increased cost for fine-tuned models
4	Embedding-based grounding (vectors with Azure AI Search)	• Great for customization without requiring fine-tuning • Good fit for large amounts of data • Easy use of embeddings APIs	• Requires preparation of the input data based on token limits • Need to scan files via OCR to extract content first • Initial embeddings generation cost for custom data (depending on the data scope)
5	Retrieval-based grounding (indexing with Azure AI Search, no embeddings)	• Good option for information retrieval from existing files • Indexing allows for citing sources (good for explainability) • Option to use the "add your own data" option from the Playground, for small implementations	• Potentially less performant than embeddings for large amounts of private data (to be confirmed during your preliminary experimentation)
6	Hybrid search	• More performant thanks to the combination of indexing, embeddings, and reranking of model results • Relatively feasible via Azure OpenAI Playground	• Complex, but for Azure OpenAI, no more than the regular embedding-based RAG
7	Other grounding techniques (Bing Search, databases, etc.)	• Great to add live results to the LLM, and to explore internal sources such as databases and tabular files • Updated results with no need to retrain or adjust the model	• A bit more complex (requires orchestration engines such as LangChain or Semantic Kernel) • Less documentation available for this kind of implementation

These implementation approaches have different advantages and levels of complexity. One of the key aspects is the ability to evaluate how well they perform, and how good these Azure OpenAI models are for specific questions and tasks. Let's explore all of this in the next section.

AI Performance Evaluation Methods

One of the key stages of any generative AI project is model performance evaluation. However, it is not a simple task to evaluate the performance of LLM-enabled systems, and it is not fully standardized yet. That said, you can start evaluating metrics with Azure OpenAI and Azure AI Studio, as you will see in Chapter 5 with LLMOps and prompt flow for evals.

Here is a selection of the most important metrics for generative AI evaluation:

Groundedness
Groundedness refers to how well a generative AI's responses are based on the information given or available in the input. This is a good metric to analyze how AI sticks to the facts, in order to avoid hallucinations. You can explore the new Groundedness Detection feature (*https://oreil.ly/Lk4ZI*) from the AI Content Safety Studio.

Similarity
This metric measures how much a GPT output resembles that of a human one. This is useful for human validation of the results from Azure OpenAI models.

Relevance
It measures how connected an AI's output is to the input given. It's like checking if someone's answer in a conversation is related to the question you asked.

Classification accuracy
A metric for classification tasks, between 0 and 1, that measures the output of the AI model compared to a ground truth.

Levenshtein distance
This measures how many changes, such as adding, deleting, or changing pieces, you would need to make to get from the AI's output to the expected output.

Coherence
This checks if the AI's output makes sense and follows a logical order, like checking if a story has a beginning, middle, and end, and doesn't jump around randomly.

Fluency
This measures how smoothly the AI's output reads, by checking if a written paragraph is easy to read and understand, from a linguistics and grammar point of view.

F1 score
This is a balance between the words in the model answer and the ground truth.

Other metrics
Other metrics from traditional NLP.

From an Azure perspective, you can explore the available metrics for evaluation via Azure AI Studio (*https://oreil.ly/q2S7r*) and Azure Databricks with MLFlow (*https://oreil.ly/3kONX*). Here are several ongoing initiatives from some of the main industry actors (including Microsoft and OpenAI), but you can expect more news and tools in the upcoming months and years:

- Microsoft's LLM evaluation framework (*https://oreil.ly/H6gB8*)
- Microsoft's evaluation flows (Azure AI Studio) (*https://oreil.ly/4NrIz*)
- Microsoft's documentation for LLM metrics monitoring (*https://oreil.ly/VtjxD*)
- OpenAI's Evals project (*https://oreil.ly/NgdLZ*)

Additionally, there are other families of metrics that you can use to measure and analyze performance:

Positive/negative review of answers
A manual way to both track performance and potentially reeducate the model with weighted reconfigurations (e.g., few-shot learning with the good answers). You could enable this by using a positive/negative sign in the UI and by adding a binary numeric value at the database level if you decide to store the questions and answers for review purposes (e.g., ID, question, answer, review) in a JSON file stored via Cosmos DB. For this purpose, my recommendation is to create a set of test questions, and to involve subject-matter experts during the creation of that set and during the evaluation of the system.

Traditional product analytics metrics
For example, session time, amount of re-questioning to get the best answer, overall product rating, etc. This would require tools such as Microsoft Clarity (*https://oreil.ly/2RHm1*), Pendo, Amplitude, Mixpanel, etc., connected to the cloud native app (e.g., iOS, Android, web, etc.). Alternatively, there are cloud native features such as Azure App Insights (*https://oreil.ly/HXkzL*) that can be deployed as part of the generative AI app monitoring system. Additionally, these tools can be leveraged to track performance for A/B testing experiments (for example, if we launch two different versions of the AI model with different user sets).

Conclusion

This chapter includes not only the available visual and code-based tools for your Azure OpenAI implementations, but also the recommended implementation approaches, to help you understand the differences between regular, fine-tuned, and grounded LLMs. Once again, there is not a perfect or a single way to do it. All of these approaches try to leverage the existing power of the Azure OpenAI models, and the ability to increase the knowledge scope of your applications with examples, internal data sources, live internet search, etc. In Chapter 4 we'll take a look at additional building blocks for your generative AI development.

CHAPTER 4

Additional Cloud and AI Capabilities

Generative AI applications are way more than "just a big model." As you have already seen, LLMs play a central role, but there are other relevant pieces that complement the capabilities of Azure OpenAI Service: fine-tuning via Azure OpenAI APIs or playgrounds, grounding with Azure Cognitive Search and/or Azure OpenAI embeddings, live search capabilities with Bing Search API, etc.

Additionally, we have new kinds of tools that allow us to expand the capacities of LLMs even more. A curated selection for any generative AI and Azure OpenAI adopter could include plug-ins, LMM integration, databases, and more. Let's dig into these in more detail.

Plug-ins

One of the most important new terms in AI applications is the notion of "plug-ins." We can define them as direct interfaces to advanced functionalities, interconnecting Microsoft's Azure OpenAI (or OpenAI's ChatGPT) with other systems. For example, there are plug-ins (*https://oreil.ly/MIQOJ*) from companies such as Expedia, Fiscal-Note, Instacart, KAYAK, Klarna, Milo, OpenTable, Shopify, Slack, Speak, Wolfram, and Zapier. They are external to Azure OpenAI, and their nature and business models depend on the developer companies.

Additionally, Microsoft announced in May 2023 (*https://oreil.ly/hpj1M*) its own collection of plug-ins, defining them as "standardized interfaces that allow developers to build and consume APIs to extend the capabilities of large language models (LLMs) and enable a deep integration of GPT across Azure and the Microsoft ecosystem." These plug-ins include direct interfaces to Bing Search, Azure Cognitive Search, Azure SQL, Azure Cosmos DB, and Microsoft Translator. As a developer, that means that you can connect Azure OpenAI with other Microsoft and Azure-related pieces, with minimal development and integration effort.

LLM Development, Orchestration, and Integration

There are also developer-oriented pieces that enable the combination of existing LLMs with other services, regardless of the programming language. Let's dig into some of those options now.

LangChain

LangChain (*https://oreil.ly/TpuFf*) is an open source framework that you can use to develop applications that are powered by language models. It provides various language-related utilities and tools (e.g., embeddings, pipelines, agents, plug-ins) and is one of the key components for some of the accelerators you saw earlier in Chapter 3. The official documentation (*https://oreil.ly/T5bxE*) talks about six key areas, noted in increasing order of complexity:

LLMs and prompts
> This includes prompt management, prompt optimization, a generic interface for all LLMs, and common utilities for working with LLMs.

Chains
> Chains go beyond a single LLM call and involve sequences of calls (whether to an LLM or a different utility). LangChain provides a standard interface for chains, lots of integrations with other tools, and end-to-end chains for common applications.

Data-augmented generation
> Data-augmented generation involves specific types of chains that first interact with an external data source to fetch data for use in the generation step. Examples include summarization of long pieces of text and question/answers over specific data sources.

Agents
> Agents involve an LLM making decisions about which actions to take, taking that action, seeing an observation, and repeating that until done. LangChain provides a standard interface for agents, a selection of agents to choose from, and examples of end-to-end agents.

Memory
> Memory refers to the persisting state between calls of a chain/agent. LangChain provides a standard interface for memory, a collection of memory implementations, and examples of chains/agents that use memory.

Evaluation

Generative models are notoriously hard to evaluate with traditional metrics. One new way of evaluating them is using language models themselves to do the evaluation. LangChain provides some prompts/chains for assisting in this.

The article "Introducing LangChain Agents" (*https://oreil.ly/uVska*) by Valentina Alto (*https://oreil.ly/ZTYEf*), a Microsoft AI specialist and author of *Modern Generative AI with ChatGPT and OpenAI Models* (Packt), explains an implementation example for Azure OpenAI Service with LangChain. You can also check the official integration doc (*https://oreil.ly/HGIXQ*) for LangChain and Azure OpenAI Service.

Semantic Kernel

Semantic Kernel (*https://oreil.ly/Xrcss*) is an open source SDK that helps combine Azure OpenAI Service and other LLMs with regular programming languages like C#, Java, and Python. The SDK includes features such as prompt chaining, recursive reasoning, summarization, zero-shot/few-shot learning, contextual memory, long-term memory, embeddings, semantic indexing, planning, retrieval-augmented generation, external knowledge stores, and the "use your own data" option.

The end-to-end notion of the kernel includes the building blocks you can see in Figure 4-1.

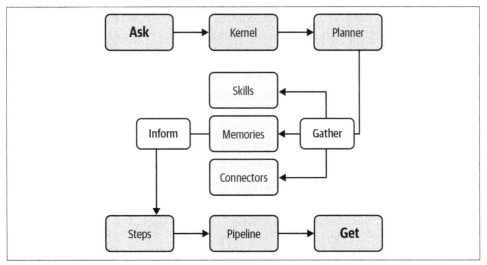

Figure 4-1. Semantic Kernel building blocks (source: adapted from an image by Microsoft (https://oreil.ly/lODC4))

Let's look at each part of the figure in more detail:

ASK

Refers to the input you present to the Semantic Kernel, which might be a question or directive in natural language. Examples include inquiries like, "Can you name the tallest mountain in the world?" or commands like, "Condense this piece of text." Semantic Kernel seeks to interpret your ASK and cater to it using its diverse capabilities.

Kernel

Represents the core processor that manages your ASK, choreographing a blend of AI services, memories, models, and add-ons to craft a response. You have the flexibility to tailor the kernel's settings and parameters as per your preference.

Planner

An intrinsic facet of the kernel, the planner ingeniously stitches functions together, formulating a strategy to address your ASK. If posed with a request like, "Compose a haiku about the moon," the planner might amalgamate functions related to topic initiation, rhyming, and poem structuring.

Gather

At this juncture of the plan, the kernel embarks on collating data from an array of outlets including AI models, memory storage, connectors, or even vast external repositories of knowledge. If you're curious about "the largest mammal on Earth," the kernel could tap into resources like Bing or Wikipedia for answers.

Skills

Epitomize the proficiency range of Semantic Kernel in addressing your ASKs, harnessing its vast components. Skills might span a spectrum from basic to intricate, contingent on the intricacy of the steps and sources utilized. Examples of skills include areas like elucidation, interpretation, crafting, categorizing, and even answering queries. Consider skills the functional "anatomy" of your AI application.

Memories

The system's capacity to store, recall, and process information derived from previous interactions, tasks, or externally acquired data. It's analogous to how human memory works but in a digital format.

Connectors

Connectors serve as bridges, enabling Semantic Kernel to interface with a spectrum of AI platforms, models, memories, or external data troves. Using connectors, one can tap into platforms like OpenAI, Azure OpenAI, or even models like ChatGPT, as well as memory systems or information havens like *Encyclopaedia Britannica*.

Inform

This phase sees the kernel apprising you of your ASK's outcome, which could be manifested as text, visuals, audio, or a specific activity. Suppose you prompt, "Illustrate a tranquil forest"; the kernel might respond by curating an image-based query and projecting the resultant picture.

Steps

Constituting the foundational blocks in the plan to address your ASK, each step might be framed as a prompt or an innate function. Prompts entail language-based directives dispatched to Azure OpenAI models. In contrast, native functions refer to standardized coding operations, often scripted in languages like C# or Python. For instance, in response to "Describe the process of photosynthesis," one step might involve a prompt pinpointing the core mechanisms, while another leverages a native function to align them in a bulleted format.

Pipeline

Essentially a series of actions initiated to address your ASK. Pipelines can either be preset or dynamically crafted by the planner. For a request like, "Pen a narrative on the evolution of technology," the pipeline could encompass stages such as outlining, crafting an intro, articulating main content, concluding, and final arrangement.

GET

Denotes an operation you can initiate on Semantic Kernel to glean details or data from its constituents. You might, for example, utilize GET to peek into the kernel's memory bank, exploring its reservoir of past insights.

Last but not least, Semantic Kernel is one of the in-house Microsoft projects for generative AI, an effort led by Dr. John Maeda, and information is available on the official GitHub repository (*https://oreil.ly/DRPCl*). Here are some additional resources if you want to continue exploring Semantic Kernel:

- Official cookbook with Semantic Kernel "recipes" (*https://oreil.ly/c-Dej*)

- LinkedIn Learning free course from Dr. John Maeda (*https://oreil.ly/TXE5e*)

- Some words from the creators (interview (*https://oreil.ly/TWIMU*) and video (*https://oreil.ly/A84pK*))

LlamaIndex

LlamaIndex (*https://oreil.ly/QZtYV*) is a data framework for LLM applications. This is another alternative for your generative AI applications with Azure OpenAI and includes both enterprise and open source (*https://oreil.ly/DOHDI*) options. It offers simplicity through a set of RAG scenarios and orchestration capabilities that combine LLM and internal data sources, and it has good traction with the developer community. Depending on how you use it, it can be an equivalent, alternative, or complement to both Semantic Kernel and LangChain.

Bot Framework

The Microsoft Bot Framework (*https://oreil.ly/ssiQu*) is a classic of the pre-ChatGPT bot era. It does not rely on Azure OpenAI Service, but some adopters are using it for specific scenario integrations (e.g, to deploy GPT-enabled projects within Microsoft Teams or other communication channels), and it includes a set of tools and services intended to help build, test, deploy, and manage intelligent chatbots:

Bot Framework SDK
A modular and extensible software development kit that allows you to build bots in C#, JavaScript, Python, or Java (*https://oreil.ly/jpXNm*). The SDK provides libraries and templates for common bot scenarios, such as dialogs, state management, authentication, etc.

Bot Framework Composer
An open source visual authoring tool that lets you create bots using a graphical interface and natural language prompts. You can use the Composer to design dialogs, skills, and answers for your bot without writing code.

Azure Bot Service
A cloud service that enables you to host your bot on Azure and connect it to various channels and devices, such as Facebook Messenger, Microsoft Teams, Skype, web chat, etc. Azure Bot Service also provides features such as analytics, debugging, security, etc.

Bot Framework Emulator
A desktop application that allows you to test and debug your bot locally or remotely. You can use the Emulator to send and receive messages from your bot, inspect the bot state and activities, and access the bot logs.

Bot Framework Connector
A service that handles communication between your bot and the channels or users. The Connector defines a REST API and an activity protocol for how your bot can send and receive messages and events.

As you can see, the Microsoft Bot Framework is a complete solution for classic bot (not LLM) scenarios, with Azure Bot Service being part of some of the official Azure OpenAI Accelerators. The full spec is available via its official GitHub repository (*https://oreil.ly/Z-meG*).

Power Platform, Microsoft Copilot, and AI Builder

Besides the SDKs and development frameworks, there are other pieces for no-code and low-code implementations. The Power Platform (*https://oreil.ly/4xSv4*) suite of tools and services helps build and manage low-code applications, automate workflows, analyze data, and build chatbots, connecting these to any AI-enabled Azure feature, including Azure OpenAI. Microsoft Copilot/Power Virtual Agents (PVAs) (*https://oreil.ly/YV0SN*) is one of the components of Power Platform that allows you to create intelligent chatbots using a low-code graphical interface. You can use PVAs to build bots that can provide answers, perform actions, and interact with users in natural language.

There are three different ways these components can interact with Azure OpenAI for no-code/low-code generative AI applications:

- By using an *Azure OpenAI connector from Microsoft Copilot/PVAs*, via Azure OpenAI APIs. An implementation example for that scenario is available online (*https://oreil.ly/5AQE8*). This is a highly manual option, but still simple to implement.

- By leveraging the Boost conversations (aka *generative answers*) feature of PVA (*https://oreil.ly/_qrYJ*). This functionality allows the bot to find and present information from multiple sources. Generative answers can be used as the primary solution in the chatbot, or as a fallback when other authored topics are unable to address a user's query.

- Besides these two bot-type applications, you can also leverage Power Platform's AI Builder component (*https://oreil.ly/0Az00*) and its integration with Azure OpenAI (*https://oreil.ly/LdRQ0*) for automation and apps. A video demo on YouTube (*https://oreil.ly/dozKD*) illustrates the implementation process.

These development building blocks are your tools to continue evolving your generative AI projects with Azure OpenAI. The list will probably grow over time, but this selection represents some of the most relevant pieces for any generative AI practitioner today. Let's now check the available vector databases for Azure-first implementations, which will enable your embedding-based projects with Azure OpenAI and allow you save the generated vectors.

Databases and Vector Stores

As previously mentioned, embeddings are a technique that generates mathematical representations of distances between topics, and that information is what we call a "vector." They have become relevant to the generative AI space because of their ability to connect information that is linguistically related. This is relevant for search engines, document retrieval during chat sessions, etc. For that purpose, we rely on a specific kind of database called a vector database (*https://oreil.ly/r8kST*), as it is better suited to store and manage this kind of information.

The main advantage of a *vector database* is that it allows for fast and accurate similarity search and retrieval of data based on its vector distance or similarity. This means that instead of using traditional methods of querying databases based on exact matches or predefined criteria, you can use a vector database to find the most similar or relevant data based on its semantic or contextual meaning. Vector databases are used to store, search, and retrieve vectors (previously generated via embedding techniques) representing documents, images, and other data types used in machine learning applications.

From an Azure OpenAI Service point of view, there are different native Azure services, or open source pieces deployable via Azure, that will serve as vector databases. Let's go through those now.

Vector Search from Azure AI Search

Vector search is a recent feature from one of the existing Microsoft Azure AI services, specifically Azure AI Search (*https://oreil.ly/-AIvZ*). This piece is part of the implementation for both embedding- and retrieval-based approaches.

Vector search (*https://oreil.ly/NAq-o*) is a new capability for indexing, storing, and retrieving vector embeddings from a search index. You can use it to enable typical cases such as similarity search, multimodal search, recommendations engines, or grounding/RAG implementations. The main differentiator (based on its creator's words (*https://oreil.ly/Rp75V*)) is the ability to enable not only classic vector search, but also "a hybrid search approach that harnesses both vector and traditional keyword scores [and] delivers even better retrieval result quality than a single search method alone," as illustrated in Figure 4-2.

	Full-text search	Pure vector search	Hybrid search
Exact keyword match	✓	✗	✓
Proximity search	✓	✗	✓
Term weighting	✓	✗	✓
Semantic similarity search	✗	✓	✓
Multimodal search	✗	✓	✓
Multilingual search	✓	✓	✓

Figure 4-2. Vector and hybrid search features with Azure AI Search (source: adapted from an image by Microsoft)

You can leverage the official documentation (*https://oreil.ly/ThbR-*) for this highly evolving technology, as well as the technical guides on how to save your previously generated vectors (*https://oreil.ly/kYtXx*) and how to perform vector queries (*https://oreil.ly/Zyfb3*) via Azure AI Search's vector search feature (*https://oreil.ly/yCCjU*).

Vector Search from Cosmos DB

Vector search is a similar vector feature from a different Azure native service, in this case Azure Cosmos DB (*https://oreil.ly/Cx4hl*), which is a managed multitype NoSQL database that supports several types of key-value, column, graph, and document formats. It includes open source options such as PostgreSQL, MongoDB, and Apache Cassandra.

The vector search feature comes from the Azure Cosmos DB for MongoDB vCore product (*https://oreil.ly/8KAtS*), which provides a fully managed MongoDB-compatible database service in Azure. The new functionality was announced in May 2023 (*https://oreil.ly/Evn2W*), and it's an alternative to the Azure Cognitive Search option. This is an option for environments where MongoDB is already part of the technology stack. You can view an additional repo with implementation samples (*https://oreil.ly/5pwnr*), and implementations with Semantic Kernel as the orchestrator (*https://oreil.ly/UXVhD*).

Azure Databricks Vector Search

As with Azure AI Search and Cosmos DB, there is another excellent native option with Azure Databricks. It offers the Databricks Vector Search (*https://oreil.ly/aWOhX*) feature, which is directly integrated into the serverless engine and into Unity Catalog (*https://oreil.ly/iVOyi*) for data and AI governance. This is a good option if you want to leverage a native end-to-end platform in Azure and connect Azure OpenAI to the vector store by leveraging diverse orchestration engines (e.g., LlamaIndex (*https://oreil.ly/9R2wP*), LangChain (*https://oreil.ly/lEpJo*)).

Redis Databases on Azure

An alternative option is Azure Cache for Redis (*https://oreil.ly/M14AR*), which is a solution to accelerate the data layer of applications through in-memory caching based on Redis open source databases. It contains RediSearch, which is a Redis module that provides full-text search capabilities. The Azure version is built on top of the Redis engine and is designed to be used with Redis Enterprise.

Similar to the previous two options, Azure Cache for Redis has evolved and incorporates a new vector search feature (*https://oreil.ly/TffQk*) that combines the power of a high-performance caching solution with the versatility of a vector database, opening up new frontiers for developers and businesses. As with Cosmos DB, this option is great for those companies already using Redis or Azure Cache for Redis as part of their technology stack.

Other Relevant Databases (Including Open Source)

There are other options available, including native and open source solutions that you can leverage via Azure:

pgvector (https://oreil.ly/MrXx1)
> For vector similarity search in Cosmos DB for PostgreSQL (*https://oreil.ly/0zLAU*) and Azure Database for PostgreSQL (*https://oreil.ly/ZoCki*), the native options for PostgreSQL (*https://oreil.ly/eicMh*) in Azure.

Elasticsearch vector database (https://oreil.ly/kBZto)
> Available in Azure OpenAI Playground, directly integrated to the On Your Data feature (*https://oreil.ly/kb6Mf*).

Neo4j (https://oreil.ly/ZeDfD)
> Enables you to implement RAG patterns with graph data. A good option to leverage the power of knowledge graphs, available in Azure (*https://oreil.ly/Yx9Sk*), including accelerators to test it out (*https://oreil.ly/Knsgw*).

Pinecone on Azure (https://oreil.ly/VVUhS)
> Available in private preview since July 2023, this allows for the deployment of a Pinecone vector (commercial, fully managed) database directly via Azure. Here is an implementation sample (*https://oreil.ly/aoRAk*) with Azure OpenAI Service and the Pinecone database.

Milvus (https://oreil.ly/evSww)
> An open source project for vector databases, available on Azure (*https://oreil.ly/pp5mc*). It is one of the main open source contenders, and a graduated project from the Linux Foundation (*https://oreil.ly/DFoM9*).

Azure Data Explorer (https://oreil.ly/jolGS)
> For vector similarity search, another vector store option to store embeddings using an Azure native service. Here is a step-by-step explanation (*https://oreil.ly/TwpP-*).

Other vector databases, for deployment via containers (not PaaS)
> Weaviate (*https://oreil.ly/p3osX*), Chroma (*https://oreil.ly/iCwUQ*), Vespa (*https://oreil.ly/tWhdm*), Qdrant (*https://oreil.ly/E37Kz*), etc.

Additionally, and even if it is not a vector store (just a library that creates an in-memory vector store), you can also explore Faiss (*https://oreil.ly/Vd9ZW*), Meta's library for efficient similarity search and clustering of dense vectors. Its Index Lookup tool (*https://oreil.ly/1IpVq*) via Azure ML Prompt Flow allows querying within a user-provided Faiss-based vector store.

Feel free to explore all these vector store and database options, and others from the OpenAI Cookbook list (*https://oreil.ly/9o2Wh*). The simplest way to start is by leveraging native services such as Azure Cognitive Search or Azure Cosmos DB, but the choice will depend on your implementation approach. Let's now take a look at some additional technology building blocks you may need for your generative AI projects.

Additional Microsoft Building Blocks for Generative AI

In addition to what we've already covered in this chapter, there are some consolidated services and ongoing research projects that we can leverage for our Azure OpenAI projects. Let's dig into a few of those.

Azure AI Document Intelligence (formerly Azure Form Recognizer) for OCR

Some of the grounding scenarios we previously analyzed rely on images and PDF documents as the main source of knowledge, in addition to the base LLM. If we want to combine the LLM's knowledge with the information from those images and PDFs, we need to extract the information from those documents in advance, and have it transformed from the source to relevant formats such as JSON or JSONL.

For PDFs, the classic technique that extracts text from the document is OCR (optical character recognition (*https://oreil.ly/f3IcI*)). This is a mature technique that recognizes every character of a document, to read and extract its information for later use.

If we want to leverage native Azure services to perform OCR tasks, there is an Azure AI service called AI Document Intelligence (previously called Form Recognizer) (*https://oreil.ly/f6YWE*). From the official website, it is "an AI service that applies advanced machine learning to extract text, key-value pairs, tables, and structures from documents automatically and accurately." This is a preliminary step before performing fine-tuning, embeddings, etc. This official article (*https://oreil.ly/2D87V*) explains the end-to-end process that combines AI Document Intelligence and Azure OpenAI Service to directly launch queries against the document.

Alternatively, the previously mentioned Azure AI Search service includes a similar OCR cognitive skill (*https://oreil.ly/SIhrW*) that works with both images (that contain text) and documents.

Microsoft Fabric's Lakehouse

This option is a must for any company looking to implement their Microsoft Azure–enabled data strategy for a lakehouse architecture: Microsoft Fabric (*https://oreil.ly/Ha1sU*). This resource could be a topic for a whole new book, but you should know that it is a platform that helps create, use, and govern data insights across an organization. As you can see in Figure 4-3, it includes data integration and science tools, data lakes, governance, and visualization elements. The relationship between Fabric and Azure OpenAI is bidirectional. Data from Microsoft Fabric can serve as a source for RAG patterns, but you can also leverage Azure OpenAI models (*https://oreil.ly/0JHzt*) within Microsoft Fabric data tools. It also contains a GPT-enabled Copilot for data analysis with natural language. If you want to learn more, you can explore the official documentation (*https://oreil.ly/hVfoG*), specific examples (*https://oreil.ly/8LFSp*), and the REST API specification (*https://oreil.ly/4JcB6*).

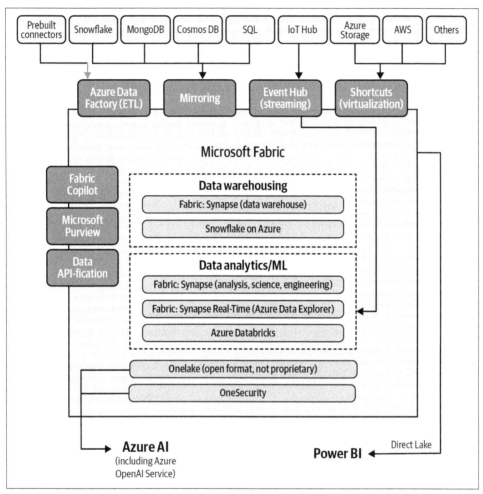

Figure 4-3. Lakehouse with Microsoft Fabric

Microsoft Azure AI Speech

Another complementary service is Azure AI Speech (*https://oreil.ly/-HLPL*), which includes speech-to-text, text-to-speech, speech translation, and speaker recognition capabilities for voice-enabled features that you can use for your Azure OpenAI–enabled applications. This is very useful for accessible interfaces where users can communicate with the generative AI engine by voice. Also, there are visual avatar functionalities (*https://oreil.ly/1aXfO*) that will help you add virtual faces to your implementations.

Microsoft Azure API Management

Azure API Management (*https://oreil.ly/4uV20*) is a transversal element that supports all your enterprise-grade Azure OpenAI deployments, allowing you to manage, balance, and monitor your different subscriptions, models, and API keys (*https://oreil.ly/w6Jht*). It is ideal for cost management and multidepartment chargeback.

Ongoing Microsoft Open Source and Research Projects

In the following we will review a selection of ongoing Microsoft research projects, all of them related to LLM development. Most of them are not production-ready building blocks, but even if they won't be used by regular generative AI practitioners, you may want to take a look and see the latest generative AI–related developments:

DeepSpeed (https://oreil.ly/4faw5)
A deep learning optimization library developed by Microsoft, designed to help researchers train large-scale models faster and more efficiently, between 10 and 100 times larger than previously possible. Additionally, DeepSpeed Chat (*https://oreil.ly/Z1ygr*) is an open system framework for enabling an end-to-end RLHF training experience to generate generative AI models at all scales.

ONNX Runtime (https://oreil.ly/0Sbqp)
A cross-platform inference and training machine-learning accelerator, intended to improve customer experiences (by providing faster model inference) and to reduce training costs. It was open sourced by Microsoft in 2019 (*https://oreil.ly/Od81D*), and is based on the ONNX open format (co-developed by Microsoft with Meta and AWS) (*https://oreil.ly/8wflB*). It includes the DirectML execution provider (*https://oreil.ly/pvwrw*), a component of ONNX Runtime to accelerate inference of ONNX models.

JARVIS/HuggingGPT (https://oreil.ly/i94HD)
A project to use LLMs as interfaces to connect different AI models from Hugging Face and others for solving complicated AI tasks.

ToxiGen (https://oreil.ly/QPTVC)
A large machine-generated dataset for hate speech detection, from Microsoft.

LLM-Augmenter (https://oreil.ly/8AKVq)
A project that aims to reduce hallucinations (i.e., LLMs delivering incorrect answers) by utilizing external knowledge for LLMs and automated feedback.

AdaTest (https://oreil.ly/655LO)
A Microsoft project to find and fix bugs in natural language/machine learning models using adaptive testing.

LoRA (Low-Rank Adaptation) (https://oreil.ly/l4klw)
Helps reduce the number of training parameters for LLMs, making this process less storage and computing intensive.

Guidance (https://oreil.ly/V7VzS)
A Microsoft project that enables control of modern language models more effectively and efficiently than traditional prompting or chaining.

PromptCraft-Robotics (https://oreil.ly/6w_-c)
A research project that aims to combine ChatGPT and robotic systems such as drones, camera-enabled robots, etc.

Gorilla LLM (https://oreil.ly/7b-nN)
A collaboration between Microsoft Research and the University of Berkeley, who have developed an LLM connected to APIs, which means that it can provide appropriate API calls for different topics including PyTorch Hub, TensorFlow Hub, HuggingFace, Kubernetes, OpenAPI, and others. A great step toward a more general kind of intelligence.

PowerProxy AI (https://oreil.ly/rkSfN)
A project that helps in monitoring and processing traffic to and from Azure OpenAI Service endpoints.

AutoGen (https://oreil.ly/YkztN)
A framework that enables the development of LLM applications using multiple agents that can converse with each other to solve tasks.

UniLM (https://oreil.ly/xokVD)
A Microsoft repo that contains a series of research papers and links to other LLM-related GitHub repositories.

LIDA (https://oreil.ly/73woE)
A Microsoft library for automatic generation of visualizations and infographics with LLMs.

"Algorithm of Thoughts" (https://oreil.ly/WDK37)
A research paper that explores potential LLM improvements with human-like reasoning techniques.

PromptBench (https://oreil.ly/X-6-Q)
A Python package for LLM evaluation.

Promptbase (https://oreil.ly/RKDGV)
A collection of best practices to obtain the best performance from LLMs.

AICI (https://oreil.ly/kseB7)
> An Artificial Intelligence Controller Interface that limits and directs output of LLMs in real time.

Olive (https://oreil.ly/JkcW3)
> A hardware-aware model optimization tool for compression, optimization, and compilation.

Phi-3 (https://oreil.ly/-octd)
> A revolutionary open source small language model (SLM) available via Azure AI Studio and Hugging Face (*https://oreil.ly/whwMD*).

Orca/Orca-2 (https://oreil.ly/PvATt)
> A Microsoft research project to specialize SLMs with domain-specific data.

PyRIT (Python Risk Identification Tool for generative AI) (https://oreil.ly/azSbW)
> A powerful framework to enable red team activities for your generative AI applications with Azure OpenAI and other LLMs.

LLMLingua (https://oreil.ly/7VUz2)
> A prompt compression method that speeds up LLM inference with minimal performance loss, making the models more efficient from a token consumption and latency perspective.

Given that generative AI is a highly evolving area, I aimed to provide you with a quick overview of what the industry is trying to achieve, in addition to the core Azure OpenAI LLM capabilities you already know.

Conclusion

This chapter is a continuation of what we covered in Chapter 3, and it includes an ecosystem of projects and technologies that you can leverage to create very advanced cloud native architectures. Most of them are additional and complementary to Azure OpenAI and required to implement some of the Chapter 3 technical approaches.

This is a highly evolving area, so consider this chapter as an initial toolbox for your generative AI practitioner journey. The next chapter will focus on the notion of LLMOps (LLM operations, an evolution of the DevOps and MLOps concepts), and how to handle production-level topics such as performance, security, and privacy. Let's explore it together.

CHAPTER 5

Operationalizing Generative AI Implementations

At this point, we have explored the evolution of generative AI and Azure OpenAI Service, the main approaches for cloud native generative AI app development, and AI architectures and building blocks for LLM-enabled applications with Azure.

In this chapter, we will explore the main considerations for going from implementation to production-level deployments. For this purpose, we will talk about advanced prompt engineering topics, related operations, security, and responsible AI considerations. All of these will contribute to a proper enterprise-grade implementation of cloud native, generative AI–enabled applications.

The Art of Prompt Engineering

Prompt engineering is one of those disciplines that has taken existing AI skills frameworks by surprise. Before OpenAI's ChatGPT, no one could imagine that the ability to interact with AI models by using just natural written language would be one of the most precious skills for companies trying to adopt, test, and deploy their generative AI systems. If there is an equivalent of the famous "Data Scientist: The Sexiest Job of the 21st Century" (*https://oreil.ly/0ZFLS*), it is prompt engineering, with powerful examples such as the prompt engineer job at Anthropic in the US (*https://oreil.ly/kNLkR*), with a base salary of $300K+.

It is also a highly evolving area. What started as a simple way to send instructions to models is becoming a sort of "art" that allows you to also contextualize, secure, and operationalize LLMs. It has a mix of technical and creative skills. Some people see similarities between prompt engineer and QA (quality assurance) skills, as they both include empathy, creativity, technical testing, planning, etc. The lingo is also new. Similar to the call-response dynamics of traditional APIs, here we talk about prompt (request) and completion (answer from the model).

Microsoft describes (*https://oreil.ly/T7PuQ*) prompt engineering as a key element to obtaining the best performance from GPT-enabled models, as models are very sensitive to the quality or shape of the prompts. Here is the official guidance for prompting techniques with Azure OpenAI Service (*https://oreil.ly/jJkyA*), both for chat (*https://oreil.ly/8SMeX*) or completion (*https://oreil.ly/1VuzR*) scenarios. Table 5-1 shows the recommended techniques in general terms.

Table 5-1. Recommended prompting techniques

Recommendation	Example
Leverage both system messages (at the beginning of the prompt to set context, instructions, etc.) *and few-shot learning* (for examples of the desired input and output) as a way to improve performance.	*Meta-prompt or system message:* "You are an AI assistant for finance topics for company X, if anyone asks about something else, please say you cannot answer."
	Few-shot examples: "If anyone asks about the price of product A, redirect to this URL."
	"If you get a question about company services, enumerate A, B, C, and D. Then ask the client to choose."
Use clear instructions, define the expected format, and leverage both positive and negative examples.	"Provide answers in two paragraphs, max 1,000 tokens."
	"Avoid talking about specific stock prices as they may be outdated. Instead, focus on enumerating trusted sources where clients can find those prices."
Adapt the prompts to multiple scenarios or subtasks, depending on the context or user input, and *use variables* as a technique to represent dynamic or unknown values in the input or output (for example, $name for username or $date for current date).	*Passing the parameters as variables for the string:* "Provide recommendations to a user who is $age years old, from $location, adapting the language to their local context. Use their name $name when providing an answer."
Apply conditional logic, as a way of using if-then statements or other logical operators to control the flow and content of the output, such as changing the tone, format, or information based on certain conditions or criteria.	"If the sentiment from the user prompts is mostly negative, use a kind, explicative, step-by-step approach."
	"If the user prompts have a friendly tone, go directly to the point. One paragraph max"
Use feedback loops by adding the model's output as part of the input for the next iteration, such as appending the output to the prompt or using it to generate new questions or instructions.	*Meta-prompt or system message:* "Answer user questions for company X, and keep in mind… <output from previous discussion> while answering. Explain the why of your reasoning."

OpenAI defines (*https://oreil.ly/gtxFR*) their own set of best practices as well to optimize prompting and get the best model performance:

Always leverage the most recent model.
This allows you to take advantage of the latest advancements and updates. Ensure you are working with the most recent iteration of the model. This does not mean to use the most powerful model, but the most recent version of each model. You can always obtain the most recent version from the official Azure OpenAI model page (*https://oreil.ly/BI5Ue*).

Incorporate instructions at the outset.
Position your instructions at the start of your prompt. Use markers like ### or """" to distinctly separate these instructions from the context.

Aim for specificity and detail.
Avoid vagueness when defining the desired context, outcome, length, format, and style.

Provide a clear output format via examples.
Examples can help guide the model toward your preferred output. For instance, Example 1, Example 2, etc.

Follow a progression by starting with a zero-shot approach.
This implies testing the model for specific questions without providing any illustrative examples. Then, proceed to few-shot scenarios, in which you provide one or several examples to the model, as LLMs can learn from their content and shape. If neither of these strategies yields the desired results, consider fine-tuning or grounding the model.

Eliminate fluffy descriptions.
Favor precision and brevity over vague, overcomplicated language to streamline your prompt and improve the model's understanding.

Specify what to do.
Rather than merely pointing out what should be avoided, clearly articulate the desired action. This positively guides the model to perform as intended.

Nudge the model with leading words in code generation.
When your task is related to code generation, "leading words" can be instrumental in guiding the model toward a specific pattern.

All of these recommendations and further recommendations (*https://oreil.ly/Xfw5-*) are oriented to reduce *generative AI model hallucination*, which is the ability (or limitation) of LLMs to create nonfactual information based on their creative ability. This is a recurring topic for all generative AI technologies, and most advanced architectures are created so that LLMs don't deliver imaginary or incorrect results. Besides

Microsoft's and OpenAI's best practices, this four-step framework can help with this problem by leveraging the best prompt engineering practices:

1. Include.

This strategy suggests including specific instructions in the prompt, such as requesting that the model not make stuff up and stick to facts. By providing clear guidelines, the AI model is more likely to generate accurate and factual content.

2. Restrict.

This approach involves limiting the output of the AI model. For example, you can choose from a confined list of options instead of allowing the model to generate free-form strings. By restricting the output, you can ensure that the generated text stays within the desired boundaries and is less likely to be based on hallucination.

3. Add chain of thought (CoT).

This strategy recommends incorporating a "chain of thought" style of instruction, such as "Solve the problem step by step." By guiding the AI model to follow a logical and structured thought process, it is more likely to produce coherent and accurate text.

4. Repeat and position.

This technique involves repeating the most important instructions in the prompt a couple of times and positioning them at the end of the prompt. This makes use of the latency effect, which means that the AI model is more likely to remember and follow the instructions that are presented last.

By implementing these strategies in prompt engineering, you can improve the quality of AI-generated text and reduce the chances of hallucination, leading to more accurate and reliable content. This is fundamental for the operationalization of generative AI in the enterprise.

As prompt engineering is a highly evolving area, I recommend you expand your knowledge with other fabulous external resources from community pros:

PromptsLab's Awesome-Prompt-Engineering repo (https://oreil.ly/ZmTev)

This repository contains hand-curated resources for prompt engineering with a focus on generative pre-trained transformers (GPT), ChatGPT, PaLM, etc. It includes papers, tutorials, blogs, videos, courses, and tools related to prompt engineering.

Lilian Weng's blog (https://oreil.ly/lIbm7)

Lilian is Head of Safety Systems at OpenAI. Her blog introduces the concept of prompt engineering, the challenges and opportunities it poses, and some examples of how to design effective prompts for different tasks.

Chip Huyen's blog (https://oreil.ly/yQ7rt)

Chip is a well-known industry expert, cofounder of Claypot AI, and the author of *Designing Machine Learning Systems* (O'Reilly). She shares some best practices and tips for building LLM applications for production, such as how to choose the right model, how to optimize the inference speed, and how to monitor the quality and reliability of the outputs.

Xavier Amatriain's blog (https://oreil.ly/3jvie)

Xavier shares his incredible wealth of knowledge with 101 (introduction and resources) (*https://oreil.ly/ZT8WB*) and 201 (advanced methods and toolkits) (*https://oreil.ly/n_unu*) articles, as well as online intro level prompt engineering training (*https://oreil.ly/jIbNt*).

DAIR.AI's Prompt Engineering Guide (https://oreil.ly/JBB67) and its related GitHub repository (https://oreil.ly/QzS_D)

Guides, papers, lectures, notebooks, and resources for prompt engineering, including a series of examples for advanced prompt engineering scenarios (*https://oreil.ly/0sWII*).

Prompt engineering is just one step in operationalizing our generative AI implementations. We will now explore other operations related to Azure OpenAI and LLMs.

Generative AI and LLMOps

If we take all the architectural, model, and prompting considerations, and we explore the envisioned workflow for an end-to-end LLM implementation, we come to the notion of *LLMOps*, a new term used to define all LLM-related operations in the enterprise. LLMOps is similar to MLOps (machine learning operations) (*https://oreil.ly/VLSZA*), which is a set of tools and best practices to manage the lifecycle of ML-powered applications.

LLMOps (*https://oreil.ly/dgVl1*) is a discipline that combines several techniques for the development, deployment, and maintenance of LLM and generative AI applications. This includes prompt engineering, but also deployment and observability topics. The operations related to AI topics are not new, but have evolved exponentially in recent years, as you can see in Figure 5-1.

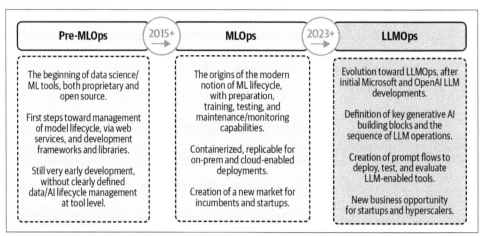

Figure 5-1. Evolution of LLMOps

This was an evolution in terms of operations complexity, but also the scalability of the methods, and the availability of commercial platforms to make them simpler:

Up to 2015

This period represents the time before the development of modern MLOps practices. During this period, proprietary tools were used for modeling and inference, but there was also a rise of open source data science tools such as Python and R. These tools allowed for more flexibility and accessibility in data science and machine learning.

2015+

The inclusion of cloud native and containerization made it a bit easier to put models into production, and to scale in a robust and more efficient manner. This period witnessed the growth of MLOps platforms, which use dockerized ML stacks and deploy them both on premises or in the cloud via Kubernetes, including manageability and monitoring features.

2023+

The beginning of the LLMOps solutions market. A promising area, but still a very new one (we will explore one of the first LLMOps tools in this chapter), focused on specific functionalities that were not part of the traditional MLOps tools. That said, existing MLOps and new LLMOps approaches share some similarities, as you can see in Figure 5-2.

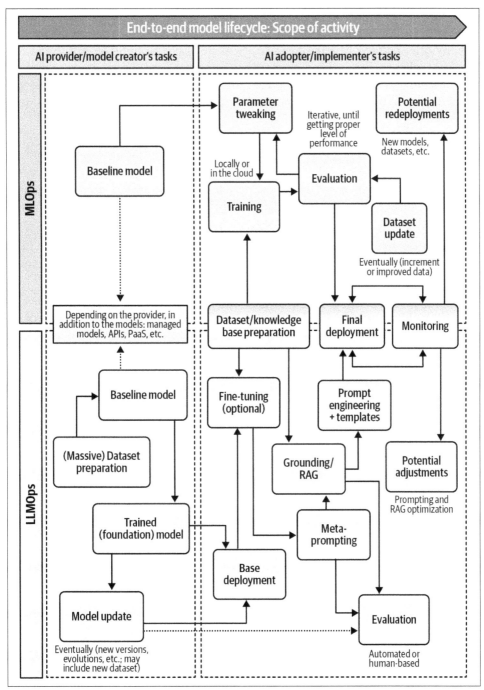

Figure 5-2. Comparison of MLOps/LLMOps and AI provider/adopter scope of activity

Summarizing, LLMOps bring a completely different split of AI model provider versus adopter activities as compared to MLOps, given the role of the pre-trained foundation models and their massive datasets. There are also clear differences in data needs (format, volume), the creation of pipelines and flows, and the methods to evaluate and monitor the results of the models. Also, some engineering tasks traditionally focused on preparing and testing ML models are evolving toward prompt engineering.

Additionally, companies such as Databricks compare LLMOps to traditional MLOps (*https://oreil.ly/Rle9o*) based on these concepts:

- LLMs can be *fine-tuned with new data* to adapt to specific domains or tasks, which reduces the amount of data and resources needed compared to training from scratch.

- LLMs can benefit from *reinforcement learning from human feedback*, which helps in improving their performance and evaluating their outputs in open-ended tasks.

- LLMs have *different performance metrics* than traditional ML models, such as BLEU (*https://oreil.ly/dWQ8D*) and ROUGE (*https://oreil.ly/SRoZf*), or any of the built-in evaluation metrics (*https://oreil.ly/gfK28*) from Azure AI Studio that we discussed in Chapter 3.

- LLMs can be *combined with other systems*, such as web search or vector databases, to create pipelines that can handle complex tasks like knowledge base Q&A, or even combined in more complex multi-agent systems (MAS) (*https://oreil.ly/CXcJI*).

Coming back to generative AI activities, it is already clear that they go way beyond simply prompt engineering activities and include additional considerations at the system and application levels. Technical LLM and prompt-related questions can be explored from many different perspectives. For example:

- From a *user experience* perspective, by anticipating customer questions and assessing model responses, and including UX designers during the generative AI app development process

- Keeping in mind *application capabilities*, including:

  — Cost, latency, and token length limitations (e.g., splitting tasks into smaller chunks)

  — Articulating instructions, orchestrating prompt flows, and shifting things back and forth between assistant and system roles

  — Adjusting model parameters such as temperature, output formats, etc.

- Combining core LLM and prompt activities with the overall *architecture design*:
  - Working with architects to address complex system requirements
  - Employing advanced patterns like RAG and rounding AI responses in enterprise data to obtain accurate answers
- Including *compliance, security, and responsibility* questions from the design phase—for example, choosing the best Azure region to guarantee data residency in EU countries, or choosing the best filtering/moderation settings at both the prompt and completion levels

In the following sections, we will explore some of these topics, and the considerations and options available from an Azure and Azure OpenAI perspective. Let's start by talking about prompt flows and pipelines.

Prompt Flow and Azure ML

Azure AI Studio and Azure ML (*https://oreil.ly/JyodR*) are enterprise-grade AI services for the end-to-end machine learning lifecycle, which includes building, testing, deploying, and managing machine learning models. They are PaaSs that include AutoML functionalities (*https://oreil.ly/i0jAV*) to leverage existing pre-built classification, regression, forecasting, computer vision, and NLP models.

With the arrival of Azure OpenAI Service to the family of Azure AI solutions, Azure ML has incorporated a new functionality called *prompt flow*. A prompt flow is a graphical representation of the data flow and processing logic of your AI application (it offers a Python library (*https://oreil.ly/_JxYW*) and a Visual Studio extension (*https://oreil.ly/FjBbh*) as well); this Azure ML feature is a development tool designed to streamline the entire development cycle of LLM-enabled applications.

Microsoft defines flows (*https://oreil.ly/AI5N-*) as executable workflows that streamline the development of your LLM-based AI application, with a comprehensive framework for managing and processing data flows. Prompt flow includes three different types of flows (*https://oreil.ly/BZRXb*):

Standard flow
This is the default flow type (*https://oreil.ly/3yWpf*) for general application development, for instruction (not chat) scenarios. You can use a variety of built-in tools to create a flow that connects LLMs, prompts, and Python tools. You can also customize and debug your flow using a notebook-like interface.

Chat flow
This is a specialized flow type (*https://oreil.ly/XlxTr*) for conversational applications. You can use the same tools as the standard flow, but with additional features for chat inputs/outputs and chat history management. You can also test and debug your flow in a native conversation mode.

Evaluation flow

This is a dedicated flow type for evaluation scenarios (*https://oreil.ly/IGZNA*). You can use this flow to measure the quality and effectiveness of your prompts and flows using built-in or custom evaluation flows. You can also compare the results of different prompt variants using charts and tables.

Regardless of the prompt type, the prompt flow platform (*https://oreil.ly/jZEeX*) focuses on the different implementation phases of Azure OpenAI and other LLMs in Azure, including the four-stage process that you can see in Figure 5-3.

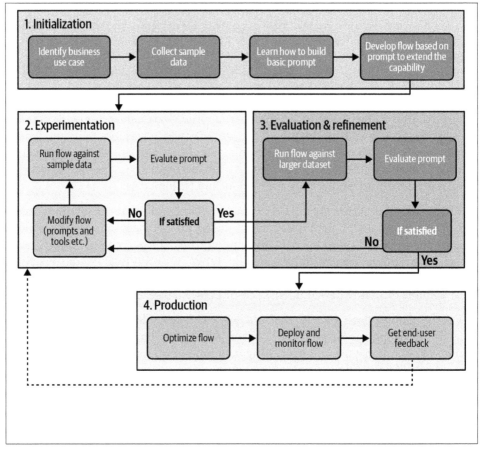

Figure 5-3. LLM prompt flow steps (source: adapted from an image by Microsoft)

Let's walk through each step:

1. *Initialization (or creation)*
   Use the prompt flow authoring canvas to design and develop your prompt flow. It connects LLMs, prompts, and Python tools in one prompt flow, and it can generate multiple prompt variants (*https://oreil.ly/MWjlS*) to adjust the LLM outputs. It also allows integration with LangChain functionalities (*https://oreil.ly/7GqOL*).

2. *Experimentation (or testing)*
   In this stage, the prompt flow testing panel helps you run and debug your prompt flow. You can see the input and output of each node in your prompt flow and their variants.

3. *Evaluation and refinement*
   In this stage, you can use the prompt flow evaluation panel (*https://oreil.ly/4NrIz*) to assess the quality and effectiveness of your prompt flow versions/variants (*https://oreil.ly/htoB5*). You can use built-in evaluation flows or create your own custom evaluation flows to measure different metrics, such as accuracy, fluency, diversity, and relevance. You can also see the results of your evaluation flows in charts and tables.

4. *Production (or deployment)*
   In this stage, you can use the prompt flow deployment panel to deploy your prompt flow (*https://oreil.ly/FPZDN*) as a real-time endpoint, for example via Azure Kubernetes Service (AKS). You can also monitor the endpoints via Azure Monitor (*https://oreil.ly/0GS-u*), troubleshoot (*https://oreil.ly/XuSsH*), and manage them using Azure AI/ML Studio's prompt flow runtimes (*https://oreil.ly/6UWqf*).

Prompt flow is a very powerful (and evolving) tool with the capability to plan and deploy prompt-based implementations. The next step is to plan security requirements for these generative AI applications.

At the time of writing this book, Microsoft released a series of functionalities (*https://oreil.ly/QdI37*) that are relevant to this and the next section, as they include performance, safety, and security capabilities:

AI-assisted safety evaluations (https://oreil.ly/GcCSo)
This powerful feature will help you create automated evaluations to systematically assess and improve your generative AI applications before deploying to production. You can check the transparency note (*https://oreil.ly/XKzEs*) to understand how and when to use them.

Prompt Shield (https://oreil.ly/KwA_D)
This functionality protects generative AI development against direct and indirect attacks. Direct attacks are those included directly in the prompt, while indirect attacks happen when the application processes information that wasn't directly authored by either the developer of the application or the user. You can learn more about Prompt Shields from the official documentation (*https://oreil.ly/_J-J9*).

Spotlighting (https://oreil.ly/P_Oz6)
A technique from Microsoft Research that leverages the system prompt (*https://oreil.ly/Wbc7V*) to protect against indirect attacks.

Securing LLMs

Creating efficient prompts and managing all required flows is key to reaching a high level of performance for enterprise-level implementations. However, companies developing generative AI applications have high security requirements to reduce any potential risk. As you can see in Figure 5-4, there are several levels of security for any LLM development with Microsoft's Azure Cloud and Azure OpenAI Service.

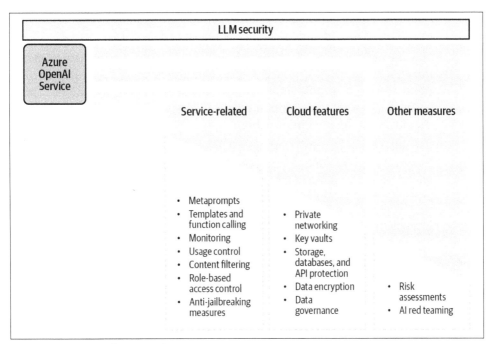

Figure 5-4. Layered approach to securing LLMs

This approach includes:

Service-level measures

Securing a generative AI implementation with Azure OpenAI starts by managing all service model-related topics, including core model performance, but also the protection of prompts, endpoints, and the APIs. Here are some ways to implement these:

- For interaction with the model, use contextualization methods via *system message/meta-prompts* to define and reduce the topic scope. This allows you to programmatically avoid prompts that are not desired by design.

- For the prompt templates we define as reusable text strings, store and protect them via databases in Azure. Regardless of the format, those databases can be securely consumed by implementing monitoring activities with Azure Monitor (*https://oreil.ly/mp1Ls*).

- For Azure OpenAI endpoints, Azure Application Gateway provides a single point of entry and load balancing (*https://oreil.ly/6plOw*) to get the responses in a fast and reliable way. An Application Gateway can function as a Web Application Firewall (WAF), providing protection against common web-based attacks, configured with a custom set of rules that match the requirements of your OpenAI application to ensure only authorized access. That said, load balancing is not supported for stateful operations like model fine-tuning, deployments, and inference of fine-tuned models.

- You can also leverage RBAC (role-based access control) with Azure OpenAI (*https://oreil.ly/YJOZv*), to decide who can access what, depending on their rights to access specific information via generative AI applications. This is useful if you want to develop internal copilots for different departments that should access different information.

- For additional security controls, such as model auditing and monitoring (*https://oreil.ly/4uV20*), Azure API Management helps grant access to the model APIs (*https://oreil.ly/sQuG_*), leveraging Microsoft Entra ID (*https://oreil.ly/EXO6A*) (Azure Active Directory) groups with subscription-based permissions, enabling request logging with Azure Monitor, and providing detailed usage metrics and key performance indicators for your models.

Other cloud-level measures

Besides the core model measures, there are other security and networking best practices that will help secure the rest of the cloud native architecture:

- Use *Azure Private Link* to connect API Management to your Azure OpenAI instances and other Azure resources such as AI Search (*https://oreil.ly/iBwcQ*). This can help protect data and traffic (*https://oreil.ly/jcELV*) from external exposure and keep them within the private network. You can use private endpoints (*https://oreil.ly/q0MUT*) to connect between different virtual networks.

- Enable *Azure Key Vault* to store the security keys and secrets (*https://oreil.ly/aTyqt*) that are used by the generative AI applications. This can help prevent unauthorized access to your data and models. Alternatively, tools like Databricks MLflow AI Gateway (*https://oreil.ly/owP_k*) can also help centralize management of LLM credentials and deployments, especially for cases that combine Azure OpenAI Service and other non-OpenAI LLMs.

- Deploy *Azure Storage* to store model training artifacts and data, and *Defender for Storage* to add an Azure-native layer of security intelligence (*https://oreil.ly/cAjUN*) that detects potential threats to storage accounts. This helps prevent malicious file uploads, sensitive data exfiltration, and data corruption. Additionally, you can leverage services such as Microsoft Sentinel and *Cloud Defender for Databases*, a security service that protects databases with attack detection and threat response (*https://oreil.ly/Xk9Q-*), or Defender for APIs (*https://oreil.ly/FPScz*), a service that offers protection, detection, and response capabilities for your APIs. All this can help ensure that your data is accessible and secure.

- Leverage by-default encryption mechanisms (*https://oreil.ly/n9bqC*) in Azure (*https://oreil.ly/zwa8V*) as a way to protect data natively at rest and in transit. More specifically, Azure OpenAI Service includes automatic ways to encrypt your data (*https://oreil.ly/aTCqC*) when it's persisted to the cloud, in order to meet organizational security and compliance commitments.

- *Govern data and manage data quality* by using Microsoft Purview (Microsoft's unified data governance solution) (*https://oreil.ly/KFNn6*) and third-party tools such as CluedIn (*https://oreil.ly/thi-L*) or Profisee (*https://oreil.ly/Y4IPx*) for master data management (MDM) and data quality. You will learn more about this topic in Chapter 7 within the book's expert interviews.

- Last but not least, there are other building blocks based on the Well-Architected Framework (*https://oreil.ly/jHwtt*) that help build an end-to-end landing zone (*https://oreil.ly/wQkFc*) for highly secured Azure OpenAI implementations.

General company-level governance measures

These may include measures such as the following:

- From a general *security management* perspective, the AI Security Risk Assessment at Microsoft (*https://oreil.ly/YzOaS*) is a process of evaluating the potential risks and vulnerabilities of AI systems, such as machine learning models, data pipelines, and deployment environments. Microsoft developed a framework and a tool to help organizations conduct AI security risk assessments and improve the security of their AI systems, and it can be leveraged for Azure OpenAI and generative AI implementations.

- From a *security testing and risk mitigation* point of view, the notion of red teaming (*https://oreil.ly/JLZeB*) defines systematic adversarial attacks for testing security vulnerabilities. Red teaming for Azure OpenAI and other LLMs (*https://oreil.ly/oDBO_*) is a practice of testing the security and robustness of generative AI systems. It involves simulating adversarial attacks on AI systems and identifying potential harms or vulnerabilities that could affect their quality, reliability, and trustworthiness. Red teaming is an important part of the responsible development and deployment of AI systems that use LLMs. Testing is done at both the LLM and application/UI levels.

Even if this three-level approach can help secure and avoid most security risks, this new area of development requires continued analysis and improvement. As with any other generative AI topics, the industry keeps updating the list of potential risks related to LLMs, and being aware of them can help reinforce your security initiatives.

The OWASP Foundation (*https://oreil.ly/WnMkm*) has elaborated a comprehensive list of the main risks and vulnerabilities often seen in LLM applications, highlighting their potential impact, ease of exploitation, and prevalence in real-world applications:

Prompt injection
This is a way of tricking an LLM by giving it clever inputs that change its behavior (for example, imagine an HR application for automated CV analysis that leverages LLMs where someone inserts a prompt in hidden text that alters the backend of the AI-enabled tool). In general, the inputs can overwrite the system prompts that guide the LLM, or even manipulate data from other sources that the LLM uses. This includes jailbreaking, a technique that exploits prompt manipulation to bypass usage policy measures in LLM chatbots, enabling the generation of responses and malicious content that violate the policies of the chatbot. All these issues can come from any part of the generative AI code, including development with pieces such as LangChain and Semantic Kernel.

Insecure output handling
This is a problem that occurs when an LLM output is not checked carefully before using it, exposing other systems to risks. The output may contain harmful content that can cause different kinds of attacks. For example, this could occur in RAG scenarios with LLMs connecting and sending insecure queries to databases.

Training data poisoning
Someone messes with the data that is used to train an LLM, making it vulnerable or biased and affecting its security, performance, or ethics.

Model denial of service
Attackers make an LLM do a lot of work that uses up its resources, making it slow or expensive. The problem is worse because LLMs need a lot of resources to run, and the user inputs are hard to predict.

Supply chain vulnerabilities
An LLM application can be compromised by using components or services that have weaknesses, leading to security attacks. The components or services may include third-party datasets, pre-trained models, and plug-ins.

Sensitive information disclosure
This can occur when an LLM accidentally reveals private data in its responses, allowing unauthorized access, privacy violations, and security breaches. It is important to clean the data and enact strict user policies to prevent this. This can also apply to meta-prompt leakage, revealing key performance information to external users.

Insecure plug-in design

This becomes an issue when LLM plug-ins have unsafe inputs and poor access control. This lack of application control makes them easy to exploit and can result in consequences like remote code execution.

Excessive agency

LLM-based systems may do things that have unintended consequences. For example, if the LLM can interface and control other systems (i.e., an AI copilot controlling some software-based functionalities for an autonomous car), it can increase the attack surface. The issue comes from giving too much functionality, permissions, or autonomy to LLM-based systems, and can impact not only the AI piece, but also the rest of the connected systems.

Overreliance

This occurs when systems or people depend too much on LLMs without supervision. They may face problems like misinformation, miscommunication, legal issues, and security vulnerabilities due to incorrect or inappropriate content generated by LLMs. It can also generate shadow IT issues, where company employees may be using LLM-enabled systems that are not part of the approved list of applications.

Model theft

This occurs when someone accesses, copies, or steals proprietary LLM models without permission. The impacts include economic losses, compromised competitive advantage, and potential access to sensitive information. Research has shown that it is even possible to re-create part of the training sets of an LLM (*https://oreil.ly/gvG-Q*).

Additionally, there are other organizations already exploring risks related to generative AI open source software (OSS) (*https://oreil.ly/8vcyo*), due to its special nature. That said, securing both closed and open models will continue to be an important area of study. Let's now analyze other legal considerations.

Managing Privacy and Compliance

Securing generative AI developments is a must, but it is just one of the key elements for company-level implementations. There are additional compliance and data privacy requirements that will impact the technology choice, including considerations such as data residency, model availability by geographic region, etc.

For that purpose, there are core features related to Microsoft Azure and the managed Azure OpenAI Service that help achieve compliance and facilitate any legal and auditing activity:

- General *data protection* mechanisms for Microsoft Azure services, which focus on the key principle (*https://oreil.ly/SfBXe*) of "giving you control over the data you put in the cloud. In other words, you control your data." This is important to leverage key security and data protection features, while keeping control of the data.

- Compliance information (*https://oreil.ly/lKBjQ*) related to all Azure-related services. This includes international regulations such as GDPR (*https://oreil.ly/hiTwi*), CCPA (*https://oreil.ly/2btT8*), HIPAA (*https://oreil.ly/Uy8hS*), etc. This guarantees that any implementation with Microsoft Azure (including Azure OpenAI) is aligned with all regulatory requirements.

- Personally identifiable information (PII) detection and document redaction (*https://oreil.ly/kFlHF*) via Azure AI Language (*https://oreil.ly/b191_*), which can enable your generative AI scenarios with a preliminary filtering of any sensitive data before creating your RAG-enabled scenario with your knowledge base. For example, this is very relevant for personal information in healthcare or finance scenarios.

- Specific advantages of *Azure OpenAI as a managed service*, when compared to other non-Azure options. Specifically:

  — *Data privacy and security*: The data sent to Azure OpenAI Service stays within Microsoft Azure and is not passed to OpenAI (the company) for predictions. Azure OpenAI Service automatically encrypts any data that is persisted in the cloud, including training data and fine-tuned models. It includes specific information about how data and prompts are handled. Refer to the official Microsoft documentation (*https://oreil.ly/1hpAO*) for any updates to this information:

    Your prompts (inputs) and completions (outputs), your embeddings, and your training data:

    — are NOT available to other customers.
    — are NOT available to OpenAI.
    — are NOT used to improve OpenAI models.
    — are NOT used to improve any Microsoft or 3rd party products or services.
    — are NOT used for automatically improving Azure OpenAI models for your use in your resource (The models are stateless, unless you explicitly fine-tune models with your training data).
    — Your fine-tuned Azure OpenAI models are available exclusively for your use.

The Azure OpenAI Service is fully controlled by Microsoft; Microsoft hosts the OpenAI models in Microsoft's Azure environment and the Service does NOT interact with any services operated by OpenAI (e.g. ChatGPT, or the OpenAI API).

— *Regional availability and private networks*: Azure OpenAI Service allows you to define the location of the models (based on specific model region availability (*https://oreil.ly/BI5Ue*)) data processing and storage for your training data, which can be important for meeting local regulations or customer preferences.

— *Responsible content filtering*: Azure OpenAI Service provides an additional layer of content filtering (*https://oreil.ly/SzGoi*) to prevent models from generating inappropriate or offensive content. At the API level, this means that the response may include `finish_reason = content_filter` (*https://oreil.ly/dQJ34*) when the content is filtered.

— *Other AI content safety features:* These included jailbreak detection (now called Prompt Shields) (*https://oreil.ly/_J-J9*), protected material detection (*https://oreil.ly/mbVoM*), and service abuse monitoring (*https://oreil.ly/hIfnG*). These advantages, plus the content filtering, help improve the quality and safety of applications that use Azure OpenAI Service.

— *Support and SLAs for reliability*: Azure OpenAI Service offers more comprehensive technical support and a service level agreement (SLA) (*https://oreil.ly/stFaz*) that guarantees high availability of the service. This can provide more confidence and peace of mind to customers who use Azure OpenAI Service for their critical applications.

— *Specific Azure OpenAI product terms* (*https://oreil.ly/9LTNj*) with data, intended use, intellectual property, and other details. This documents relevant conditions and Microsoft commitments for enterprise-grade implementations.

— Last but not least, Azure OpenAI includes custom data management options at both the data and prompt levels (which are equally considered private customer data), such as DELETE API operations, and the option to opt out (*https://oreil.ly/66UHN*) of automated prompt monitoring and filtering for harmful topics.

Now, let's continue with the last item of our generative AI operationalization topics, which focuses on existing and future regulations, as well as responsible AI practices for implementations with Azure OpenAI Service.

Responsible AI and New Regulations

One of the direct consequences of the new generative AI era was the general awareness from all society actors of the potential advantages and risks of artificial intelligence. The "AI Ethics" movements are not new, but they were mainly related to academics, AI observatories, and international associations trying to make sense of the principles that should guide what a "good AI" would be, as well as the potential negative outcomes of AI-enabled systems. Now, with the arrival of generative AI and ChatGPT, regulatory initiatives are accelerating and including new considerations for LLMs, etc. From a platform point of view, Azure OpenAI Service and Azure AI Studio have evolved and incorporated several responsible AI (RAI) measures.

This section includes contextual information (e.g., international regulations) that will be important to keep in mind while designing generative AI solutions, plus several resources that facilitate the implementation of generative AI with responsible AI approaches, including several Microsoft resources for RAI and LLMs, including Azure OpenAI Service models.

Relevant Regulatory Context for Generative AI Systems

Even if AI regulations are still a work-in-progress at the international level (at least in 2024), there are some key initiatives that will help you understand what regulators will be focusing on, especially for your generative AI development:

The European Union (EU) AI Act
> The first example of comprehensive regulation for AI systems (*https://oreil.ly/ JGDQh*), and a key reference for other international regulations (*https://oreil.ly/ x0Hi6*) (e.g., Canada's AI and Data Act, China's AI regulation). It is mainly based on several levels of risks, with specific obligations for both providers and adopters (in this case, Microsoft is the provider of your Azure OpenAI models, and you or your company are the adopters). It also includes *specific requirements for generative AI systems*. There are several levels of AI risk:

> *Unacceptable risk*
>> These are AI systems that pose a clear threat to people's safety, dignity, or rights, such as those that manipulate human behavior, exploit vulnerabilities, or enable social scoring or mass surveillance. Some exceptions may be allowed for law enforcement purposes under strict conditions and oversight. Most of your applications will never be at this level, but it is important to be aware of the "forbidden" kind of systems.

> *High-risk systems*
>> These are AI systems that have a significant impact on people's lives or the functioning of society, such as those used in health, education, employment, justice, or transport. These systems will have to meet strict requirements

before and after being deployed, such as ensuring data quality, human oversight, accuracy, security, and transparency. They will also have to be registered in an EU database.

Depending on your industry and area of activity, it will be important to align to this sort of requirement. In general, it will be a way to provide information about the details of the system, at both a performance and maintenance level.

Generative AI systems
These are specific requirements for generative AI systems, all of them relatively simple to implement with Azure and Azure OpenAI:

Disclosing content that is generated by AI
This can be easily achieved by providing a watermark for the generated content, at both the UI level and when the user copies answers from the Azure OpenAI–enabled tool.

Designing the model to prevent it from generating illegal content
This is directly related to the ability to filter inputs and outputs to avoid any kind of negative content. We will deep dive into this later in this chapter.

Publishing summaries of copyrighted data used for training
This will include the initial provider obligations (directly related to the baseline LLM), and your obligations in the case of fine-tuning or grounding with other copyrighted data.

Limited-risk systems
These are AI systems that pose little or no risk to people or society, such as those used for entertainment, leisure, or personal use. These systems will be mostly free from regulation, but will still have to comply with existing laws and ethical principles.

The AI Risk Management Framework
From the National Institute of Standards and Technology (NIST) in the United States, this framework (*https://oreil.ly/o3Y12*) is not an AI regulation per se, but it sets the field for a definition of what a trustworthy AI should be, including generative AI applications. The framework says that AI systems need to be valid and reliable, safe, secure and resilient, accountable and transparent, explainable and interpretable, privacy-enhanced, and fair with harmful bias managed. NIST has launched a specific working group (*https://oreil.ly/HRZ4D*) for generative AI topics to catch up with latest developments. This framework is part of Microsoft's commitment (*https://oreil.ly/T23SA*) to adopt best practices in their products.

Other generative AI development regulatory resources

For example, the *Association for Computing Machinery (ACM)*'s generative AI principles (*https://oreil.ly/81nar*) include considerations for generative AI models, including limits and usage, personal data, correctability, and system ownership questions.

Meanwhile, the *Global Partnership on AI (GPAI)*'s 2023 report on Detection Mechanisms for Foundation Models (*https://oreil.ly/LZaot*) focuses on the detection side of AI-generated content, and complements the transparency requirements of international regulations and frameworks. There is a similar initiative from the Partnership on AI (*https://oreil.ly/WAEgA*) for generative AI and responsible practices for synthetic media.

This list of regulations, frameworks, and recommendations will continue evolving in upcoming years, but all of them converge and include transparency and accountability questions that should be considered when developing an Azure OpenAI system. For that purpose, the next two sections include organization- and technical-level resources that you can apply to your generative AI development.

Company-Level AI Governance Resources

Microsoft has released a series of resources to guide the responsible implementation of AI systems, including generative AI, which can serve as baseline or inspiration to adapt generative AI development with Azure OpenAI to responsible approaches:

- Microsoft's Responsible AI Standard (version 2) (*https://oreil.ly/fqvjp*), which includes RAI principles, and a comprehensive document with requirements to adopt those principles (*https://oreil.ly/ACiW4*). This is the approach used at Microsoft to achieve fairness, reliability and safety, privacy and security, inclusiveness, transparency, and accountability. These principles are highly related to the regulations and frameworks we have previously analyzed, so they represent a good baseline for your generative AI implementations for the enterprise. If you want an alternative version, also oriented to generative AI, here is a list of RAI principles from LinkedIn (*https://oreil.ly/cmghy*).

- The Responsible AI Maturity Model (*https://oreil.ly/LV_Ei*), a way to analyze and evaluate the level of responsible AI maturity at your company. It includes 5 levels and 24 empirically derived dimensions. This is a good way to make sure we are setting the foundations for a generative AI aligned with future regulations.

- Specific LLM and Azure OpenAI best practices and requirements to guarantee RAI approaches, including:

  — A *four-stage methodology for responsible AI and Azure OpenAI*, adapted from the general Microsoft RAI Standard, which includes measures (*https://oreil.ly/uJiId*) to:

- *Identify* and prioritize potential harms that could result from your AI system through iterative red teaming, stress testing, and analysis.

- *Measure* the frequency and severity of those harms by establishing clear metrics, creating measurement test sets, and completing iterative, systematic testing (both manual and automated).

- *Mitigate* harm by implementing tools and strategies such as prompt engineering and content filters. Repeat measurement to test effectiveness after implementing mitigations.

- *Define and execute* a deployment and operational readiness plan.

- An *eight-step approach to responsible AI for LLMs* (*https://oreil.ly/l3zSt*), including Azure OpenAI and other open source options in Azure, such as Meta's LLaMA2. It focuses on risk mitigation, user-centric design, and additional safety measures.

- Specific *requirements for adopting Azure OpenAI*, which includes a code of conduct with forbidden use cases (*https://oreil.ly/PHCsq*), including violence, exploitation, harmful content, etc. and a transparency note with intended use cases (*https://oreil.ly/nCF82*) and adoption considerations.

- The HAX Toolkit (*https://oreil.ly/XPSKw*), which is a very good resource for your user-facing AI solutions, to support the design process and anticipate how the AI-enabled system will work and behave.

Organizational-level measures will help you align with regulations and international requirements. However, the actual implementation of countermeasures at the model level requires technical RAI tools.

Technical-Level Responsible AI Tools

These are the main tools and features you can use to guarantee that your Azure OpenAI implementations are aligned with RAI principles:

- The general RAI Dashboard (*https://oreil.ly/AP5-N*) and Toolbox (*https://oreil.ly/Z8187*), which Microsoft defines as the way to assess, develop, and deploy AI systems in a safe, trustworthy, and ethical manner, by using a collection of integrated tools and functionalities to help operationalize responsible AI in practice. The official repository (*https://oreil.ly/gnM8L*) includes tools to evaluate errors, analyze fairness, understand data dimensions, interpret models, etc.

- *Azure AI Content Safety*, which adds an extra layer of protection (*https://oreil.ly/6LWOF*) to filter out harmful inputs and outputs from the model. This can help prevent intentional abuse by your users and mistakes by the model. This safety system works by checking both the prompt and completion for your model with a group of classification models that aim to detect and stop the output of harmful content in four categories (hate, sexual, violence, and self-harm) and four severity levels (safe, low, medium, and high). The default setting is to filter content at the medium severity level for all four harm categories for both prompts and completions. You can access it:

— Directly from AI Content Safety Studio (*https://oreil.ly/C0iVp*), which allows text, image, and multimodal moderation, as well as customization and online activity monitorization. It also includes Prompt Shields for your LLM-enabled deployments.

— Via Azure OpenAI Studio's content filter (*https://oreil.ly/9W9J9*) for responsible AI moderation. Each filter can be applied to Azure OpenAI "deployments," and those deployments will include the content filter for each chat or completion implementation.

Conclusion

This chapter covered the final set of technical considerations for generative AI applications with Azure OpenAI Service. You have explored all relevant operational questions related to deploying, securing, protecting, and responsibly adopting generative AI. Remember, designing and architecting solutions with Azure OpenAI is "just" the first step (as we discussed in Chapters 2, 3, and 4). The operationalization of these generative AI applications is key for company-level implementations, where security, performance, and privacy, as well as regulations and AI ethics, are key aspects for sustainable project implementations.

Now, we will continue with a key business-related aspect of generative AI: elaborating realistic and financially sustainable business cases. This means analyzing potential projects and their expected benefit and justifying the human and technical cost by discussing ROI (return on investment) scenarios. These aspects are as relevant as the technical details we've explored thus far to successfully implementing generative AI applications in your company.

CHAPTER 6

Elaborating Generative AI Business Cases

The first five chapters of the book focused on technical aspects related to cloud native architectures for generative AI, advanced capabilities with Azure OpenAI and other Azure services, and the operationalization of generative AI in the enterprise, including topics such as LLMOps and responsible AI. In Chapter 3, we even explored detailed technical approaches that leverage different Azure resources, with recommendations depending on the project scope and type of company data.

One of the main motivations for companies to adopt Azure OpenAI, and LLMs in general, is to generate significant advantages in the form of savings by automating language-based scenarios, or to create differentiation, to offer something better than their competitors, with the potential for increased revenue.

In this chapter, we will focus on the business considerations of building a generative AI project with Azure OpenAI Service, including project planning and evaluation topics such as cost scenarios and estimations, ROI, roadmapping, etc. We will cover the key aspects that will allow any technical implementation to become a sustainable and feasible generative AI initiative.

Premortem, or What to Consider Before Implementing a Generative AI Project

One of the most interesting managerial techniques is the premortem (*https://oreil.ly/jjw4R*). A bit less known than the *postmortem* (in which we analyze a project after we have finished it), the *premortem* is done before starting the project, by assuming that it has already failed, and then trying to identify the factors that caused the failure. This is a powerful tool for generative AI and any AI project, given the complexity and uncertainty of this type of implementation, because it can include any technical or business topic as a way to identify potential risks and to create a mitigation plan.

Table 6-1 compiles a list of typical risks related to a generative AI implementation, and the following sections of this chapter will include several assets to increase the probability of success of your projects with Azure OpenAI.

Table 6-1. Potential risks for generative AI projects

Category	Risk	What could go wrong
Contextual	Regulation and compliance	The use case or potential project has to be aligned with upcoming regulations. Even if some of them are "work in progress," examples like social scoring, manipulation, and others are already clear examples of forbidden applications.
		For generative AI deployments, the required transparency obligations (*https://oreil.ly/sq8N1*) are key and need to be considered from the design phase of the project (e.g., by generating traces and changelogs directly from the MLOps and LLMOps systems).
	Proper usage	Both Microsoft (*https://oreil.ly/7ojQP*) and OpenAI (*https://oreil.ly/eQpg-*) have clear policies on how to use and not use the models. Failing to comply with this (in addition to using the models for use cases that are already forbidden by international AI and general regulations) may lead to limitations to service access.
	Internal concerns	Due to the new and complex nature of generative AI, multiple departments within a company will need to be involved in discussions, and they may not all be on the same page. While technical and business departments can have a clear idea of how and why to use Azure OpenAI, other departments such as legal or compliance may temporarily block implementations to first understand questions related to the nature of the service, data privacy, residency, etc.
		Leveraging resources such as the transparency note (*https://oreil.ly/B843c*), Microsoft's EU Data Boundary (*https://oreil.ly/Bor0w*), the compliance offering portal (*https://oreil.ly/IKBjQ*), and any legal and Data Protection Addendum (DPA)-related information (*https://oreil.ly/Fqfi9*) will help to unblock this sort of situation.
Business	Incorrect use case discovery and prioritization	One key challenge is to find and prioritize the most feasible and impactful use cases. Sometimes prioritization is based on ideas from the executive team, or from technical departments.
		Proper ideation and a clear design thinking process can help to analyze all relevant aspects from a list of potential use cases.
	Lack of quantitative usage scenarios	Another challenge for generative AI adopters is to imagine how much their new cloud native solution will be used by end users.
		Preliminary scenarios are required to properly size the envisioned solution at both the technical and budget levels. This can be achieved by estimating a total number of users by the average daily/monthly usage of the platform.
	Unexpected cost	Estimating costs is relatively simple because of the linearity of the pricing of generative AI tools, including Azure OpenAI Service.
		But to accurately estimate costs, it is necessary to not only have clear usage scenarios, but also to understand the pricing structure and to be able to create estimates based on the chosen models, by using the official Azure calculator (*https://oreil.ly/2SQ4C*) and other tools like OpenAI's tokenizer (*https://oreil.ly/DDQHG*).
		Also, general FinOps best practices such as resource tagging, pricing alerts, and the use of Azure Cost Management help monitor costs for your generative AI projects.

Category	Risk	What could go wrong
	Unclear business case	If the potential use cases are not properly prioritized, and there are not clear scenarios and cost estimation, it is difficult to draft any business case and ROI expectation.
		Any generative AI business must include an estimation of potential revenue, savings, or differentiation for the adopting company. For example, "human hours saved in a call center," "number of tickets being solved automatically," "item upselling in a recommendation bot," etc.
	Innovation dilemma	Even if most of the company is willing to adopt generative AI, some initiatives may be paused due to the innovation dilemma. This means questions such as "Is it too early to implement something like that?" or "Why this and not other innovations that require a budget too?" may be raised, and having a solid base to justify a new Azure OpenAI project will be key for success. Factors like the fast-evolving ecosystem and increasing competition are potential considerations for generative AI adoption.
Technical	High complexity	Despite the relatively accessible level of technicality for implementations with Azure OpenAI, it is common to see adopting companies, integrators, and individuals that are not confident about their level of knowledge, especially for complex implementations.
		The evolution of visual interfaces such as Azure OpenAI Studio as a way to test and deploy web apps and bot agents equipped with generative AI, as well as for model deployment and other visual capabilities such as prompt flow, will help reduce the entry barrier for less technical or nonexpert adopters.
	Low performance	Depending on initial expectations, generative AI applications' performance can be perceived as imperfect (which is obviously true) because of their tendency to produce sporadic errors. If expectations are not realistic, the testing phase can lead to disappointment, blocking the way to production.
		It is important to have an initial alignment and clearly defined expectations of what "good enough" performance would mean, as well as a proper plan to evaluate the solution with subject matter experts (SME) and/or end users.
	Lack of resources	Implementations can be stopped before or during the project due to lack of resources such as budget, data for customized models, and available people with the right skills.
		A good way to guarantee feasibility is to properly scope the envisioned implementation and plan accordingly based on project priority and technical complexity.
	Security concerns	As with any other data or AI systems, generative AI can suffer attacks at several levels: perimeter, data sources (those used for grounding), and prompts (through prompt injection techniques).
		Adopting best architecture and DevSecOps practices and planning red team activities to simulate scenarios can help increase the overall robustness and security of the systems.

There will certainly be other relevant topics that you'll need to consider, so any pre-mortem activity has to be prepared and discussed with all relevant stakeholders. One of the best ways to understand and reduce risk is to go very granular in terms of the envisioned generative AI solution details and the intended implementation. For that purpose, defining a detailed roadmap and related resources and activities will help a lot.

Defining Implementation Approach, Resources, and Project Roadmap

One of the most challenging activities for complex AI projects is to plan activities in a granular way, and to elaborate detailed roadmaps that specify major categories of work, duration, and required technical and human resources.

This section includes a nonexhaustive methodology that will enable you as an Azure OpenAI adopter to plan your new projects, step by step. To illustrate the examples beyond the theory in the following sections, we will refer to Azure DevOps (*https://oreil.ly/dGQEr*) (the native Azure service for project planning and more) and some of its features.

Defining Project Workstreams

Before planning project activities, it is key to define the implementation's work scope. For that purpose, creating categories of work (or workstreams) will help create buckets to add different activities and user stories. Following is a recommended list of workstreams (independent of each other; the bullet points don't represent a sequential approach) for generative AI projects with Azure OpenAI Service:

Cloud enablement
> All the design, deployment, and optimization activities related to Azure cloud landing zones, tenants, resource and resource groups, etc. It also includes security and monitoring configuration.

Dataset preparation
> All data preparation, engineering, and storage activities that enable customization of Azure OpenAI–enabled systems. This is not the typical data engineering and pipelining process from nongenerative AI, in which we need to work towards a consolidated data input that will be used to train a model. Instead, the dataset will include a diverse set of "pieces" such as documents, JSON/JSONL files, and generated embeddings. Topics such as data quality measurement and improvement are still very relevant and key for successful implementations.

Prompt engineering
> Everything related to the design, testing, automation, and optimization of system and user prompts. This is a specific kind of workstream due to the exploration and experimentation required to perform these activities (and therefore the complexity to plan and estimate them, from a project planning point of view).

Design and user testing

The end-to-end activities related to the design of the UIs (including previous user interviews), as well as the testing of the generative AI solution in terms of UI/UX and model performance and evaluation.

Deployment activities

A transversal workstream that includes all preliminary and production-level deployments, including initial pilots, temporary web apps for internal test, etc. This workstream will include key milestones and dates for specific steps within the full generative AI software lifecycle (i.e., proof of concept, minimum viable product), based on Evaluation Driven AI-System Development principles.

These workstreams can be represented as area paths (*https://oreil.ly/82ROJ*) via Azure DevOps, as these paths help organize any project into groups of work items. They will also serve as work categories for visual roadmaps, as we will see later in the chapter. Now that we have the workstreams, let's go into the details to define and quantify project resources.

Identifying Required Resources

The next step is to understand and plan the different resources we will need for an Azure OpenAI implementation. This will go from purely technical aspects to "man-hour" costs related to the development of the solution, as well as its maintenance. We can define the following resource categories:

Human resources

The different profiles and related skills will obviously depend on the type and scope of the implementation. However, there are some key roles you need to consider for any generative AI and Azure OpenAI Service–related implementation:

Business executives

To sponsor your generative AI projects, support business needs, and provide the required resources.

Architects/specialists

Technical profiles with highly specialized knowledge of Azure OpenAI and other generative AI services. They can evaluate functional and technical requirements, and define suitable architectures by leveraging chat, embeddings, text-to-image, and other models, as well as analyzing different fine-tuning and grounding options depending on the nature and format of the data sources.

Developers

Software developer profiles with previous back- or frontend experience, especially for API-enabled integration projects. Some of the main capabilities are related to Azure OpenAI APIs, and orchestration blocks such as Lang-Chain and Semantic Kernel.

Prompt engineers

Talent with hybrid technical and business experience, with a mix of skills that includes prompt design, test, iteration, and optimization, as well as the creation of templates for production-level reuse of prompts. Profiles with previous experience may include advanced testing abilities, and knowledge of security and prompt injection techniques (e.g., quality assurance or QA engineers).

Security professionals

As part of the AI red team (*https://oreil.ly/5Kf3c*) activities, or granular development activities to secure APIs, data sources, etc.

Cloud engineers/admins

Classic cloud professionals with the skills to administrate, deploy, configure, and consume cloud resources from Microsoft Azure. They may have an initial knowledge of the Azure portal, studio, and playground interfaces related to Azure OpenAI Service.

Responsible AI and compliance experts

Specific roles with ethics and legal knowledge, related to the data privacy and AI regulatory topics mentioned in Chapter 5. They are usually available on a part-time basis, and they may have specific knowledge of tools such as ChatGPT, Bing, Azure OpenAI Service, general cloud, product DPAs, etc.

Other tactical and technical roles

Project- and product-related roles, such as product managers (PMs) and product owners (POs), project managers, scrum masters, etc. They may have low to no generative AI experience, but we can expect these roles to continue upskilling and getting practical knowledge after a few projects. Also, classic roles such as the data trilogy (science, engineering, analysis) may be part of the team, and even take some of the core generative AI responsibilities, as an evolution from (or addition to) their current roles.

If you are hesitating between classic data and AI roles (e.g., data scientist) and the new LLM-oriented roles such as prompt engineer, Figure 6-1 shows some high-level guidance on roles and skills evolution.

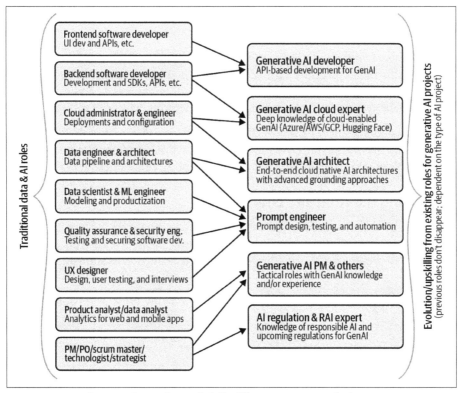

Figure 6-1. Evolution of AI roles and skills (illustrative examples)

Other technical resources

All product and services required to implement Azure OpenAI–enabled and other generative AI projects with Microsoft Azure:

Cloud subscription

In this case, all the required Azure services work based on consumption. This means there is no fixed price or license required, just the price for each of the Azure services being deployed for your specific generative AI implementations.

Other software licenses

Not a requirement for most cases, but some implementations could include specific licenses, for example if you use PVAs as an orchestration block and bot interface, or if you leverage other non-Azure generative AI services to create end-to-end architectures.

External costs

This could be related to external technical and consulting services, often leveraged by adopter companies to accelerate their generative AI projects.

This effort needs to be quantified during the ROI exercise we will review in this chapter.

Other post-implementation costs
This includes future cost scenarios related to maintenance activities, model improvement, or evolution of the grounding scope (i.e., adding new files and data to the existing knowledge base, generating new embeddings).

All these factors imply a total cost that we will use to plan and evaluate the sustainability of the business case related to the generative AI implementation. This is a key step to make sure it is really worth it for the adopting companies.

Estimating Duration and Effort

A second level of detail from the "human resources" defined in the previous section would be to quantify their participation and level of involvement in the project. A good way to present it is to list all roles with the specific details shown in Figure 6-2.

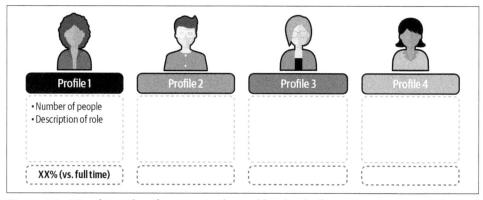

Figure 6-2. Visual template for project roles and levels of effort

In this figure, we see the distribution of roles, with the number of people per role, their scope of activity, and the level of effort compared to a regular full-time involvement. This simple visual can be your best ally when trying to present the required roles and their level of effort (number of hours per week). However, you will need to calculate them depending on the project and your company's context. An illustrative estimation:

- A prompt engineer is a highly specialized role that could be required to work on a single project part time. Depending on the scope and level of required effort, we could imagine a range of 25% to 50% of their time for one project, which would mean working on several generative AI projects at the same time (concretely, between two and four).

- On-demand roles such as compliance and RAI experts could have a maximum number of hours assigned to projects, for reactive ad hoc dedication. It depends on the project, but the average could be 5% to 10% of their time, which would represent 4 to 8 hours per week on average. Obviously, their involvement will vary depending on the project stage.

- Other roles like architects, engineers, admins, etc. will have specific knowledge required at different stages of the project. Some of them will even have two or more functional roles (e.g., an architect can initially define architecture and requirements, then play the engineering role to implement the solution). The same applies for generative AI developers, who may work on code-related activities, but also may deploy Azure OpenAI models and integrate them to the tools via APIs. All of them can go between 20% and 100% dedication, depending on the project scope.

Regardless of the type and number of roles, it is important to initially plan the resource requirements, to know how many people will work, how many hours per week, and during which phases of the end-to-end project. This means the important thing is to have a plan, not to look for the perfect one. The ability to plan and estimate in an accurate way will obviously depend on increasing project experience in relation to generative AI with Azure OpenAI, so it is normal to make incorrect assumptions during the first few projects. Even with that, we will have the key building blocks to prepare an initial roadmap for a generative AI project. Let's check the details in the next section.

Creating a "Living" Roadmap

Let's analyze what we should have up to now: a clear understanding of the potential use cases and implementation approaches, an initial definition of the architecture, a preliminary idea of the required resources at both the human and tooling levels, and an estimate of the availability of the different team members.

These are all key elements to create a project's "living" roadmap. Let's start from the basics. A roadmap is a visual way to communicate a plan for achieving a goal or outcome, in this case the project implementation. It includes the major steps or milestones needed to reach it, and it includes the workstreams we have previously discussed as a way to organize all required tasks.

The concept of a "living" asset refers to the ability to evolve it from its initial version. This is especially important for AI projects (including generative AI), as preliminary roadmaps tend to evolve during the implementation phase due to unknowns (e.g., how long we need to try and test different prompts) or unexpected events (e.g., limited access to cloud platforms, temporary leaves from team members). So you can consider the roadmap a canvas to plan and evolve your implementations in a visual, easy-to-read manner, an asset you can use with both technical and business/executive stakeholders to regularly discuss plans and progress. Figure 6-3 is an example of a visual roadmap for a generative AI project, with an illustrative case for an imaginary pharma company.

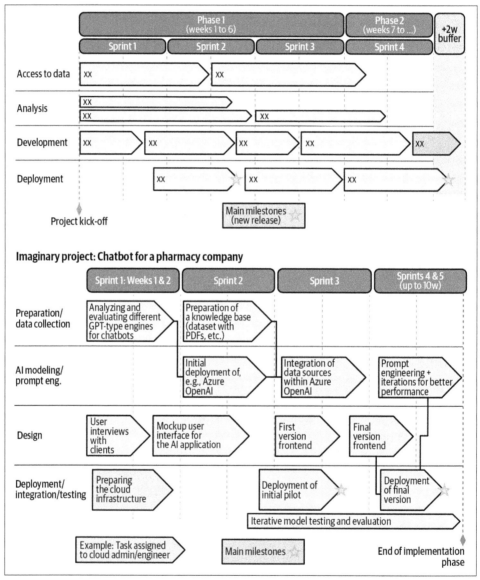

Figure 6-3. Visual roadmap template for AI and generative AI projects (top) and illustrative example (bottom)

In this kind of one-pager roadmap, the important thing is not to go into hyper-granular details, but to define the "what" and "by when" of the workstreams and activities. Using sprints to structure blocks of work for a two- to four-week period is the way to get more tangible details of the sequence and duration of the tasks.

From an Azure point of view, once you have defined a visual roadmap (in some regular format such as a PowerPoint slide), you can implement its details via the Boards feature (*https://oreil.ly/NKWy8*) in Azure DevOps. This functionality includes the ability to create Kanban (*https://oreil.ly/kEhyq*) and Scrum (*https://oreil.ly/0THjo*) boards, as well as delivery plans (*https://oreil.ly/v-hwK*), which represent the scheduled work items by sprint against a calendar view.

Now that you have a project plan and all its related details, let's see how to create Azure OpenAI usage scenarios to estimate the cost of the cloud-related services.

Creating Usage Scenarios

One of the most challenging activities for adopters and related partners (e.g., integrators, consulting firms) is to create realistic scenarios for potential usage of generative AI solutions. This is critical for sustainable business cases, but also to guarantee there is enough budget for the cloud-related costs (the cost structure of Azure OpenAI is well optimized for massive use, but it is still linear and depends directly on the number of interactions with the system). The challenging part is to imagine how many users will actually leverage the solution, and how.

For that purpose, the best option is to take a *multilevel scenario drafting approach*, in which we will calculate several factors for a chat-based application with a potential number of end users, step by step:

Number of expected (average) users
This is relatively difficult for any business-to-consumer (B2C) scenario in which we may have end users arriving dynamically, or even internal employees using internal generative AI applications. That said, the idea is to establish a maximum average number of users that we know will connect actively to the final solution.

Number of interactions per user, by day/week/month
Again, it is not easy to predict how many times a user will use the solution, but we need to define a maximum number. It can be based on the number of past interactions with existing solutions, or by allocating a maximum number of sessions by day, week, or month. This maximum number can serve as a session limit at the application level, to guarantee no one overuses the solution.

Max length of each interaction (in tokens)
This is relatively simple and it applies to both prompts and completions. We can limit at both the Azure OpenAI model (via "max length" settings but also by defining the length using the system message) and application level (by limiting the number of characters and words a user can write). If we handle the maximum

length for both questions and answers, we can obtain an average length for each interaction (e.g., 250 tokens for a 50-token question with a 200-token answer).

 The general rule is 1,000 tokens equal 750 words (for English text), but it really depends on the language and type of words. For an accurate estimation of what an X-token question or answer would look like, check OpenAI's tokenizer tool (*https://oreil.ly/DDQHG*).

If we get these three elements, we can technically imagine the maximum cost allocated to this usage scenario, by creating a very simple formula:

Number of expected users × number of interactions per user (for a specific period; for this, we'll say by month)

× max token length of each interaction

= total cost (aka total number of tokens by month)

In this case, if we have the number of interactions by month, the total amount of tokens will correspond to the total usage of tokens in one single month. If we take that amount, let's say 2,000 users × 30 interactions × 500 tokens max, we obtain a total of 30 million tokens.

As you know, the regular pricing for Azure OpenAI (*https://oreil.ly/7Gmq6*) service is based on "bags" of 1,000 tokens. This means that we pay a fixed amount (depending on the pricing of each model, which tends to change and get lower over time), in this case 30,000,000 tokens / 1,000 tokens per bag = 30,000 bags. If we assume a unit price of $0.002 (illustrative amount for a model "X"), this means 30,000 × 0.002 = 60 USD of monthly cost for Azure OpenAI usage, which means 720 USD per year. Obviously, this amount will be higher for bigger scenarios, and it does not include:

- Additional Azure OpenAI costs for embedding-based scenarios. This means if we leverage embeddings, in addition to the regular chat-type capabilities, we will use a different kind of model (e.g., Embeddings Large) with specific pricing by 1,000-token interaction.

- Other implementation pieces such as Web Apps, other AI services for document intelligence, cognitive search, vector storage, speech-to-text and text-to-speech, etc. These depend on the type of solution, and can be calculated as any other cloud service, by using the official Azure calculator (*https://oreil.ly/2SQ4C*).

- Any other related license or external software being used for the final architecture. A good example could be using PVA as deployment and orchestration options for your Azure OpenAI service. In this case, you will need to add its monthly cost (*https://oreil.ly/KpqfF*).

Provisioned Throughput Unit

At the time of writing, there is a relatively new purchasing option for Azure OpenAI Service, called *provisioned throughput units* (PTUs). PTUs are an alternative to the regular pay-as-you-go (PAYG) model that is based on the public, token-based pricing (*https://oreil.ly/7Gmq6*). PTUs offer dedicated AI resources for a specific GPT model, with latency, performance, and cost advantages, especially important for production-level scenarios. Keep in mind, PTUs are not just about the relying infrastructure, but also the platform and the resources optimized for that GPT model. Additionally, PTUs are the way to go for production-level deployments compared to PAYG, as they enable testing and experimentation.

From a company point of view, your PTU instances can serve all your Azure OpenAI use cases together if the number of PTUs is properly chosen. PTU pricing for Azure OpenAI Service is available via the official Azure calculator (*https://oreil.ly/2SQ4C*), with specific SKUs for hourly, monthly, and yearly purchasing options. Here are several pieces of information you can leverage:

What is a provisioned throughput? (https://oreil.ly/KCC6K)
The official documentation explaining the full extent of the PTU concept.

PTU onboarding process (https://oreil.ly/WZEku)
Constantly updated information with the logic behind PTUs, dimensioning scenarios, and measuring usage.

Getting started (https://oreil.ly/09g99)
Deployment instructions (bookmark this resource, and keep in mind that the process may evolve) and technical details.

Right-sizing PTU deployments (https://oreil.ly/O2YtJ)
The techniques to plan PTU scenarios.

Benchmarking PTUs (https://oreil.ly/R7NAn)
An official repo that includes a tool to benchmark specific PTU-enabled deployments with Azure OpenAI.

API Management (https://oreil.ly/2C3rb)
A useful resource that includes API management and load balancing techniques to combine both PTU and PAYG models.

Additionally, you can leverage a calculator from the Azure OpenAI Playground (*https://oreil.ly/e7jPN*) (you can access this functionality from the *Quota menu > Provisioned* section). As you can see in Figure 6-4, this calculator includes the number of tokens required for prompt and completion.

This Azure OpenAI calculator enables you to estimate the number of PTUs needed for your workload. The calculator assumes a static prompt and generation size as well as call rate and are provided as an estimation only. Variations on these values will cause changes to the overall throughput per PTU you receive. For more accurate evaluation, run a benchmark test after deploying with a representational workload and monitor the Provisioned-Managed utilization values in the metrics tab.

Select a model ⓘ   Model version ⓘ

| gpt-4 | ∨ | 0613 | ∨ |

Workload size

Improve accuracy of your estimate by adding multiple workloads to your PTU calculation. Each workload will be calculated and displayed as well as the aggregate total if both are running at the same time to your deployment. Read our sizing guidance in documentation to learn more about different estimation strategies.

▷ Calculate   Export results   ◁ Clear all workloads

Workload name	Peak calls per min* ⓘ	Tokens in prompt call* ⓘ	Tokens in model response* ⓘ	Output* ⓘ
RAG Chat	10	3500	300	Calculate to see PTU estimates
Basic Chat	10	500	100	Calculate to see PTU estimates
Summarization	10	5000	300	Calculate to see PTU estimates
Classification	10	3800	10	Calculate to see PTU estimates
Totals	0	0	0	PTUs: 0 (0)

Figure 6-4. Azure OpenAI Playground: PTU calculator

Remember, the principle behind this remains the same (calculating monthly cost for a given GPT model), but the logic behind it is different. If your company purchases PTU capacity, the goal will be to dimension your scenarios in terms of token consumption, aggregated for all your generative AI scenarios. You can combine models, and the main metrics you need to consider are:

RPM
　　The amount of *requests per minute* you can launch for a specific Azure OpenAI resource, which will be higher for PTU scenarios than regular PAYG options.

TPM
　　As with regular PAYG models, there is a specific quota (*https://oreil.ly/bEN4D*) based on the notion of *tokens per minute* (which usually follows an equivalence of 6 RPM per 1,000 TPM); this is increased when purchasing PTUs.

TTFT
　　The *time to first token metric* is the direct consequence of purchasing PTUs and dimensioning scenarios based on the expected usage of the service among projects. If you rightsize your PTU deployments, the models will answer faster and provide an API response in a timely manner, faster than any PAYG-based deployment.

In general terms, any "box" or building block from a visual architecture should be considered to calculate the total cost of the solution. Check the official pricing websites regularly to get updated information on the price per model. For company-wide scenarios, you can explore potential chargeback setups (*https://oreil.ly/fpA1N*) so you can bill the corresponding cost to specific business units or departments.

Once we have elaborated our usage scenario, in addition to all previous human and technical resources considerations, we are finally ready to elaborate our quantitative business case.

Calculating Cost and Potential ROI

Now we can put everything together and focus on both the aggregated cost and the total estimated value. These two elements will help us elaborate our business case with a clear ROI estimation:

Total cost
This includes all the building blocks we have previously mentioned (human resources, cloud cost, licenses, external expenses, etc.), everything that implies a direct or indirect cost for the organization, including the cost of the implementation team for upskilling and working on the project. The cost of the cloud must be calculated based on the specific usage scenario, keeping in mind the pay-as-you-go and PTU pricing modalities.

Estimated value
This will include any improvement that the adopting company may get from the generative AI project with Azure OpenAI:

Hard benefits
This will include any increase in revenue or generated savings. It is possible to quantify how much and by when with the financial impact usually starting after the initial implementation.

Soft benefits
Any additional advantage related to the creation of new lines of business, strategic differentiation for the company, creation of new intellectual property, generative AI project experience for the team, etc.

The ROI formula is simple, and it focuses mainly on tangible financial figures:

ROI = [(Quantified hard benefits – Total cost) / Total cost] × 100

It can include considerations such as the break-even, which indicates when the initial investment will be recovered. For example, you could say that the total project implementation cost is X, but it will help generate 2X in two years, so the ROI is 200%, and it is likely to happen between the first and second year.

You (and your company) need to consider these financial or company-level aspects while evaluating your potential list of generative AI use cases with Azure OpenAI. You can use Table 6-2 as an example and fill it with your actual generative AI projects.

Table 6-2. Generative AI use case discovery list

Use case	Description	Duration	Cost	ROI	Other benefits	Priority
UC1	Example: Chatbot for pharma company	7 weeks	X K$	Between 150% and 200% depending on the scenario	Improved employee satisfaction	Top
...						
UCn						

You can obviously add other relevant factors for your internal decision making, but this kind of analysis will facilitate internal discussions and prioritization of your next generative AI project. As with the other visuals from this chapter, these simple tables and slides remove complexity when dealing with all business and technical stakeholders.

Conclusion

This concludes our sixth chapter, which has focused on the key elements (e.g., project roadmaps, required resources, cost estimation) to build sustainable and realistic business cases for your generative AI projects with Azure OpenAI.

Remember, these business-related topics are as important as any other technical consideration, and the way to enable successful implementations and guarantee user adoption, for both internal and external use cases. If your generative AI system is great but numbers don't add up, then your company won't be able to adopt it and make the most of it. Try to include the recommendations from this chapter during your prioritization and design process.

We will now continue with the last chapter of the book, which includes several generative AI success stories from experts in the field. We are almost there—let's do it.

CHAPTER 7

Exploring the Big Picture

This chapter includes the last pieces of knowledge for your generative AI learning with Azure OpenAI and other Microsoft technologies. It includes some future visions, interviews with experts, and success stories. Remember, generative AI (and artificial intelligence in general) is a highly evolving domain, so use this book as your entry to a whole universe of knowledge and learning assets.

Let's start this last chapter by discussing what's next, from an Azure OpenAI perspective. For an avid learner and AI adopter like you, what are the other areas you should explore?

What's Next? The Evolution Toward Microsoft Copilot

Azure OpenAI Service is part of a wider ecosystem. All architectures, APIs, and integrations with other generative AI building blocks contribute to the notion of AI copilots, which we mentioned in the first chapter.

AI copilots are technology-enabled assistants, companions that help human agents become better, more efficient, workers. The principle behind them is to provide an interface (written or spoken) that helps people perform complex tasks, such as finding specific information or adding information to a third-party system (e.g., a CRM, a support ticketing system).

As you can see in Figure 7-1, the end-to-end Microsoft vision for AI copilots includes models from Azure OpenAI, but also their connection with other systems such as Microsoft 365, which already includes its own copilot (*https://oreil.ly/Jwuff*). This can be expanded with additional capabilities by leveraging the data from the Microsoft Graph API (*https://oreil.ly/3qy8E*), the development interface to access data from the 365 suite (including calendar and emails from Outlook, and meeting recordings and transcript from Teams, to name a few), and the Microsoft Dataverse (*https://oreil.ly/*

onOnS), previously known as Common Data Model, a data store for the Power Platform and Dynamics 365 (*https://oreil.ly/omP3a*) ecosystems.

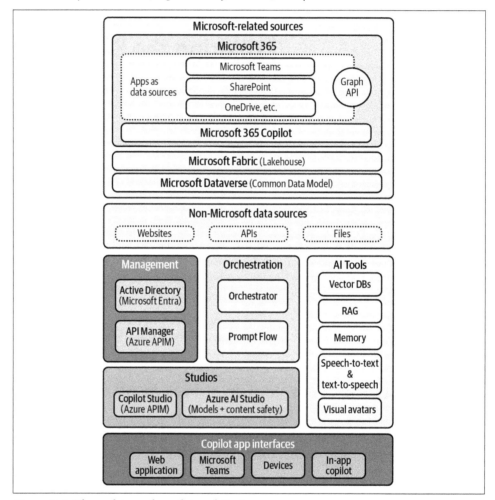

Figure 7-1. The end-to-end copilot architecture

The combination of all these building blocks enables new development patterns, augmenting generative AI models with other data sources and systems, and the notion of a copilot will certainly evolve over the next few years. You will see this kind of end-to-end architecture becoming an industry standard, so I recommend you understand how all these pieces connect and enable new productivity and generative AI scenarios.

That said, it would take two or three more books to explore all these pieces, but to leverage some official Microsoft resources, take a look at the Learning Pathways site (*https://oreil.ly/kljOi*) from the Microsoft UK team, and check the AI Learning Companion path (*https://oreil.ly/SntTJ*) as it contains a huge variety of videos, articles, and training programs. You can also explore an illustrative example (*https://oreil.ly/1_p3Q*) of the Microsoft Copilot technology stack, which includes Azure OpenAI and other Microsoft services—very useful if you have a technical background.

Let's now go to what I consider the hidden gem of this book: valuable and exclusive insights from interviews with some of the biggest experts out there, which will complement the content of this book with diverse perspectives on related topics such as design, data quality, the future of AI, etc.

Expert Insights for the Generative AI Era

It is pretty rare, and an extraordinary privilege, to get access to some of the most relevant experts on generative AI, people who have a hand in shaping generative AI and how organizations are adopting Azure OpenAI and other related building blocks.

This section includes a series of interviews with:

David Carmona (https://oreil.ly/FOSlv)
Vice president and CTO for Strategic Incubations at Microsoft and author of the *The AI Organization* (O'Reilly). This interview includes a discussion on AI adoption and advanced use cases, as well as his vision of the future of generative AI. We'll gain top insights from a visionary leader.

Brendan Burns (https://oreil.ly/e_vU5)
Corporate vice president at Microsoft, an authentic legend of the cloud native ecosystem thanks to his role as Kubernetes cofounder and the author of multiple O'Reilly books such as *Kubernetes: Up and Running*, *Kubernetes Best Practices*, *Managing Kubernetes*, and *Designing Distributed Systems*. This conversation discusses the convergence between the generative AI era cloud native architectures.

John Maeda (https://oreil.ly/4jxQ0)
Vice president of Engineering and head of Computational Design/AI Platform at Microsoft, and the main sponsor of the Semantic Kernel project. This is an amazing exploration of the role of design for AI solutions and the importance of LLM orchestration technologies.

Sarah Bird (https://oreil.ly/N_NK9)
Microsoft's chief product officer of Responsible AI. This interview includes a conversation with the leader in charge of RAI developments for the Azure AI platform, including Azure OpenAI. Sarah gives us a different perspective on such an important topic.

Tim Ward (https://oreil.ly/cersn)

CEO at CluedIn, is a great source for data management topics. This discussion dives into data quality as an enabler for generative AI developments, but also looks at how AI is changing the way companies perform master data management (MDM) and quality control.

Seth Juarez (https://oreil.ly/oIrgI)

Principal program manager for the AI Platform at Microsoft. Seth has been one of the more visible faces of the Azure OpenAI era, thanks to his role as host of the AI Show (*https://oreil.ly/h-Fvw*). Seth is one of the most well-known professionals for Azure OpenAI and Azure AI Studio topics, and a great storyteller who makes complex topics look a bit simpler.

Saurabh Tiwary (https://oreil.ly/qUK9P)

Corporate VP for Microsoft Copilot & Turing. This interview includes a great exchange about the vision for Microsoft Copilot as the end-to-end architecture that leverages Azure OpenAI Service.

Let's dig into these interviews!

David Carmona: AI Adoption and the Future of Generative AI

A.G.: So, I know your background, I know about your career at Microsoft, but who is David and what's your role at the Microsoft organization?

D.C.: Well, thank you for inviting me. It's a big pleasure. I think we share the pain of writing a book, so I am always in awe when somebody takes that big adventure. It's amazing that you did it, so congratulations for that. I think when I look at my role in Microsoft at the end of the day, it's all about creating new incubation businesses. I've been in Microsoft for almost 23 years now, and it's always been very focused on that function. I'm originally from Spain, I was working for Microsoft in Western Europe, then I moved 15 years ago to Corp in Seattle. I was part of the cloud incubation, which was amazing to be part of that.

Then after that, when the cloud became mainstream, and I didn't have to prove all the time the importance of the cloud, then I was offered to lead AI incubation. It was just when cloud was becoming mainstream at that time, which was eight, nine years ago as it was something that started in

Microsoft Research. I was working with Microsoft Research at that time, and it was all about creating a new business category for Microsoft. Just when that started to be mainstream too, I recently—two years ago, so just when I didn't have to prove again in every conversation the importance of AI—I moved to the next businesses. I'm working now on areas like the future of AI, which are the new frontiers of AI that we will see in the future. For example, applying AI to science, which is an amazing use case scenario. Then other areas like quantum computing, which I also have the pleasure to incubate, and some others like space, communications, future of communication, and so on.

A.G.: You're a good person to talk to about the vision of generative AI, artificial intelligence in general, and how we will be using them in the next few years. What's the potential and the cool things that you're seeing now? What's your vision for this generative AI era?

D.C.: For me, the big difference is the scenarios that you can address with this new AI that you couldn't address before, of course. The whole concept of reasoning on top of language, or any other modality, and not only data, that is something super powerful and we can speak about a lot. But for me, the big transformation, what is really the revolution of this new generation of AI is that it is broader, it is more generalized. In the past, to create an AI model, you required a specific dataset and a specific model. I still remember those early times of AI when we were creating these milestones for AI in Microsoft Research of image classification of human parity, speech recognition, etc. All of those require a very specific team, super specialized on that, with a very specific dataset and model.

The big change of that, the big impact of that is the possibility. Now that model has become something that is not only for data scientists to create, but for even end users to customize and use in their daily lives and jobs, which is the concept of Copilot. The rest is history after that. But for me, that is the core difference of this new AI.

A.G.: Exactly. Because we have been using AI. We had AI in different products, but most people weren't aware that they were using AI or being subject to AI. Now it's natural, and that's the concept of democratization, access to technology, because we use language, which is the purest way to communicate. I think it's very exciting.

D.C.: This is just the beginning. As you know, I'm super excited about what is going to come next. Not only on the technology itself, of course, the technology will evolve, but also I think as we understand the technology better, and we start using it in more use cases, we're going to see scenarios that we can not even think about today. The one that I mentioned at the beginning that I work on a lot lately is, of course, the applicability to scientific discovery, which is going to open areas that are just amazing, that we cannot even imagine yet.

A.G.: Yes. Bringing that scalability to situations where maybe in the traditional world we couldn't take care of that. There's this public case with the SERMAS, the health department of Madrid in Spain, with Julian Isla that you probably know. They're trying to leverage generative AI to spot the good information, to retrieve the good information for rare diseases. Usually, you have a business case behind everything, and with traditional AI, you will say, OK, there's not enough of a target public because it's a rare disease. With this, you can actually bring that to all the doctors in the world, and they can spot the situation in a faster and more efficient way. That's a perfect example of the kind of things that even if they don't sound super advanced because it's just retrieving information, I personally love it.

D.C.: Yeah. I'm in love with that use case. I'm also part of the nonprofit Foundation 29 (*https://oreil.ly/DCC5D*) that Julian Isla leads, with Carlos Mascias and others. For me, it is a great example, as you said, because it's focused, as you know, on diagnosing rare diseases. The problem that we have with a profession like doctors is that it relies a lot on the experience of the doctor. That works perfectly fine when you are diagnosing a common disease. But the exposure to rare diseases in primary care doctors is very low. It's very difficult for them to diagnose those diseases. Consider that the average time of diagnosis of a rare disease is seven years. Those are seven years that you are not applying the right treatment to that disease. With things like this where a model can help because it's always helping the doctor, so guiding the doctor, giving them clues on where the disease could come from, that is an amazing tool that I think is a great example of this new paradigm of humans and machines working together.

A.G.: Exactly, and improving the status quo. Something that is impossible to deny is that there's something that we can improve with technology. You have mentioned the models, you have mentioned the platform. This book is about Azure OpenAI, but how do you see Azure OpenAI as a piece of technology or as a platform, as a technology enabler for this era? How do you see this going? It's about the model, it's about the platform, the different layers, the thing around it. I have my opinion, but I want to hear yours.

D.C.: I think it's a deeper conversation, I could say. If you look at this only at one particular layer of the ecosystem, you are probably missing a lot of things. For me, AI is more than a technology, it's a new paradigm, it's a new economy actually. You look at the impact that AI is going to have even for core GDP growth and it's huge. We are addressing it with just a layer of the stack, it's not enough. You need to take a look at the entire ecosystem. In that entire ecosystem, you have many players. Of course, you have at the bottom of it, you have even the chips, even the pure hardware that you need to consider for this. On top of that, you have the big data centers that you need to address and to target one of these applications. Then on top of that, you have the foundational models, which are super visible, of course, they are a critical part of it. But on top of that, you also need the tooling, the platform to really get the most of these models. It's very easy and you know this more than anybody, it's very easy to start a proof of concept on a service and model. Very easy to start doing prompts and start getting more of that model. But to create a real use case, to create a full scenario, you need way more than that. You need to start talking about grounding, safety, things like services integration, such as plug-ins and many other areas that are satellite to the model but are equally important. Then on top of that, you still have more layers. You have responsibility, which is critical. You have the applications, you have the distribution.

In the case of Azure OpenAI, I think the key thing, of course it's a critical piece of that full stack. But in our case, the principle that we have from the very beginning since we started with AI, is that we believe in a speed of innovation that goes side by side with the platform. Even internally in Microsoft, the way that we look at innovation is providing that innovation as a platform to the rest of the company. Then at the same time, we bring that platform to Azure so our customers can use it. So Azure OpenAI is a perfect example of that because what we did was create the concept of model as a service, making it super easy to be accessible from customers, and making it like a first-class citizen of Azure. You access it just like any other service, which is again, bringing that to the broader platform for developers to create new applications with it.

A.G.: Yes. With all these layers that you have mentioned from the platform, that's why I was asking the question, because usually the discussion is around the model. We are creating a bigger model and this is, before it was like more parameters, now it's the one that is better on the benchmark. But I think the models are becoming a commodity, very expensive and difficult to create. But now the value, the real value is in the combination of these models with the rest of the platform. That's what I have liked the most from the evolution of Azure OpenAI and Azure AI Studio in general during this 2023-2024 period.

D.C.: Yeah. Completely agree.

A.G.: You have a general view of everything that's happening at Microsoft, like internally, externally, like platforms, models, cool projects, Microsoft research, papers, the new things that are coming. What's the part that gets you most excited? Is this about the large language models, the small language models—do you have any preference?

D.C.: From the research probably because, of course, in that full stack there are things happening on every layer. I'm excited with each of them because they are super important. In my heart, I'm a software developer. I'm especially passionate about anything that has to do with the platform because it's what really enables developers to create important cool stuff on top of it. I'm a super fan of, for example, Azure AI Studio and all the tooling that is there. Anything that has to do with the orchestration of the entire lifecycle of models, super big fan. In my initial role, I was very focused on how we can transform the development process with the cloud. The concept of DevOps, continuous integration, continuous deployment, and so on. We released what was at that time called Visual Studio Online (VSO) (*https://oreil.ly/IJeOu*), now it's Azure DevOps. I think that we always forget that part of the stack and it is hugely important. There's no way that you can be successful in an enterprise adopting AI if you just take a very specific tooling and model approach, so you need to look at the entire lifecycle, and orchestrate that lifecycle. That, I'm super passionate about.

But now, if you ask me about the wow stuff, the things that are coming from research that gets me excited, I have to say that, probably because of my current job, I'm a huge fan of all the work coming on applying AI to science. There are things in there that are just mind-blowing, that we're just scratching the surface of right now. One example that we recently announced was the application of some of these models to an actual scientific discovery. In this case, it was a battery discovery, the rest of the material to create a battery. It was discovered fully with these tools. They are the three things that these models can do, but in a sense, at the core of it the concept is as simple as saying, hey, just like AI can reason on top of text, just like AI can reason on top of images, video, and so on, AI can also reason on top of graphs. A very important graph that is all around us is molecules. They are just graphs of atoms. The possibility of AI to reason on top of those structures, on top of molecules, is just amazing. We see the same concept that we see with generative AI apply for images. Think of DALL·E when you write a prompt and the model will deliver an image like an output. We're starting to see that and Microsoft Research has already delivered some of those externally on models that can do that with molecules. Think of explaining the model, what are the properties that you are looking for in a particular model, and the model creating a lot of variance and a lot of possibilities for that molecule. That is mind-blowing, think of the possibilities of that.

But then, that is the generation part. Then the second part is the simulation. With AI, we can simulate the properties and the interactions of these molecules, which are, imagine the equivalent of that could be to go to a "wet lab" and do that in person. Now, if you are able to do it with AI, accelerating thousands of times, the time that was needed on traditional compute, what that allows you is to just expand your search space. Now, you can screen millions of molecules to find those properties. Then the last one is also helping us to synthesize those molecules, giving us the best and more efficient ways of synthesizing those molecules. The implications of that in any science—so from materials to health, to sustainability, to climate change, to many other domains—is just amazing. When you combine it with the concept of reasoning on top of knowledge, now you have on one side AI models that can simulate nature. On the other side, you have the concept of a copilot for the scientists, where the scientists can use it to reason with all the past scientific knowledge and all the current knowledge of that domain. It's just mind-blowing the possibilities of it.

A.G.: It's impressive, the impact at all levels, even the academic level. People that are learning can retrieve all the information, and they can accelerate their learning, and they can contribute more and more to the research. You see, that's why I invited you, because you have the vision of these kinds of things.

D.C.: It's funny because I think what we always talk about, the work that AI can do on behalf of humans, but with this concept of AI reasoning on top of the collective knowledge of the scientific community, what it can do is actually bring in that community even closer, because right now there's a big barrier for scientists to reason on top of the knowledge that was created by other scientists, because there's so much. It's almost impossible for a scientist to be on top of all the collective knowledge of the community. Now, with these tools, it will make it easier for scientists to build on top of the discoveries and the progress of others, which is amazing.

A.G.: To finish the discussion, I'll come back to your book, *The AI Organization.* Students are wondering OK, is this relevant? Descriptive AI, like traditional AI, do I need to learn this when I'm talking about generative AI? Now we have so many new experts talking about the topic. I said, yes, of course, the kind of consideration, the technical consideration, but also organizational considerations of adoption and the barriers and the tricks and the things that you need to do and the data component, the data strategy of the companies, this is very important. And I feel like your book includes a lot of good examples. I remember the one with Telefonica and Chema, Alonso, that I like especially because it's very illustrative and very creative. But what would be, if you had to sell the value of that book for the generative AI adopters at the company level, what would be the value of it?

D.C.: Yeah, I mean, the book was written just thinking of the learnings that I was seeing with big companies embracing AI, right? So, I've seen many of those in the early days, right? So, early days in AI are like eight years ago. So not a long time ago. And it's funny because usually the blockers that I was seeing for adopting AI at scale had nothing to do with technology. So that made me wonder, hey, there's a lot of books talking about the technology, but there's a gap in there on telling the broader story that leaders in organizations of any level should know to be successful with AI. So that was the approach to the book. I identify four big areas that you need to address to be successful in adopting AI at scale. So again, not proof of concept, not specific use cases, but really transforming your company with AI, right? And becoming that concept of AI organization. And it's, yeah, technology is one of them. So, of course, it's there and I talk a lot about technology, but I talk about the strategy. You need to have a full comprehensive strategy that is inclusive of the short term, but also the long term and connecting between those two, right? So I share the learnings in Microsoft as well. How we approach that, we call it the horizon framework and how we actually make sure that we balance those investments across the horizon. We have a connected strategy that is investing in the short term because it has value for the short term, but also in the long term and how to connect both, right? So that is good. I also talk about the importance of having an approach that is from the technology to the business, but then also from the business to the technology, right? That is critical. I see, and I was seeing at that time, a lot of conversations that started on the possibilities of the technologies, but not what the business needed, right? So you need a framework. And I also share the framework that we use in Microsoft to have a conversation that is business centric. And then connecting that to the technology to focus on identifying the use cases and the long-term bets in my company. So that's the strategy.

The second one is culture because that's another critical one. This AI transformation is not something that happens in a laboratory. It's not that you can create a center of excellence of AI and consider it like a black box and forget about this problem. This is something that will impact, as a leader, you need to know that this is something that will impact the entire organization. So every employee has to be part of it. And that's something that requires specific action and need. And I also share ways of doing that, some learnings from Microsoft. We have a lot of learnings on that one. And you realize how important it is if you compare failures with successes, you see that culture is usually a huge part of that. When you have the organization not fully bought in, where you have things that are isolated, that are not connected, it's very difficult to have an impact in the business by doing that. And then the last one is responsibility. So that is a critical one, as you know. And it's something that we tend to think that it's just creating principles for AI. It's far more than that, right? You need to turn those principles into reality. And now even more as at that time, there was no regulation, but now with regulation coming, it's not going to be like a good addition. It's going to be absolutely critical that every company does that. And it's not something that you can think of at the end of the process, it's something that you have to consider in every step of your development, from the ideation to the development to the deploying and monitoring.

A.G.: I totally agree. And look, these four pillars are exactly the same today. We have the same kind of cases, people get excited about technology, then forget the overall strategy of the company, creating a case that has nothing to do with the strategy of the company, or the return investment, or the potential value for the company. The culture, all the education parts, now it's becoming more obvious that people need to learn about genetic AI, and we see that trend beside the technology teams. And the responsible AI part, which is, I call it accountability. It's not AI at this point, because it's accountable. It's trustworthy, it's responsible, it's ethical, everything you want, but there's a regulation. So now we want to be compliant with regulations. So it's still the same. And that's why I think that it's still a very good classic for any generative AI adopter out there.

Brendan Burns: The Role of Cloud Native for Generative AI Developments

A.G.: I'm very happy to have you here. I know that a lot of people know you, but what's your current role and journey at Microsoft?

B.B.: Sure. I'm currently the corporate vice president for cloud native open source and the Azure Management platform. So that's a focus on, I guess the best summary is maybe all things DevOps and modern application development on Azure, with a special focus on containers and Linux.

A.G.: So everything related to cloud native and the Microsoft ecosystem, you're there.

B.B.: Yep. As well as the Azure Resource Manager, which is sort of the API gateway with policy, and all sort of infrastructure as code tooling.

A.G.: Very important for the kind of architecture we discuss in the book. And even if it's an obvious question, what's your experience in cloud native and Kubernetes?

B.B.: Sure, yeah. So I mean, obviously I started the Kubernetes project. It's closing in on a decade actually, which is kind of, I guess, why there's some gray hair, but, you know, I was responsible for the early days of that project, shaping, helping shape the community. And then I came to Azure and focused on really figuring out how Azure can be the best place to run open source and cloud native workloads. And as part of that also, I think helping a lot of enterprises, traditional Microsoft customers with their transition to cloud native applications. I think there's a sense that cloud native is like a new startup thing, but actually the truth is that I think most of the cloud native applications that are being built today are being built by large companies that need this kind of development agility and reliability for their applications.

A.G.: Yeah, which is connected to the current era of generative AI here at Microsoft. What's your personal point of view on this new wave?

B.B.: Well, I'm super excited about it. I think everybody's excited about it. I'm really excited about it at a personal level, because it's actually helped me. I think using things like GitHub Copilot actually really does speed up, especially when I'm learning something new. I was just learning Rust over maybe six months ago. And I found that when you're in a new language, it just made a huge difference in the speed with which

I could pick up the idioms. And you think, because sometimes, when you're learning a new language, you're programming it like the other language. So you end up writing Python, like you used to write Java, for example. I think having access to those idiomatic patterns helps you become fluent in the language a lot faster. Plus I found Rust also is a little bit, the error messages are not as good as they could be, I think. And so again, having that ability to be like, please fix this error message for me, right? It would just give me the code snippet that I needed. And that was pretty useful as well. So I think that's cool.

I think it's really exciting also how we can help our customers have similar reductions in complexity, whether it's for programming languages, or their infrastructure, or you know, any number of things. Becoming cloud native is a good example, actually, infrastructure as code (IaC) can be hard for people and enabling people to transition from, you know, ClickOps in the portal to infrastructure as code easily is really great. And things like mechanical export of an infrastructure as code template hasn't always been that great. And I think generative AI gives us the opportunity to go in a different direction and get better, more fluid templates than we do if we just, you know, sort of write code that tries to do it.

A.G.: Yeah, and I think it's exciting because it goes both ways, no? We can leverage generative AI for all cloud native purposes. And we can leverage the good practices of cloud native to implement generative AI on existing and new applications.

B.B.: Absolutely. Yeah, I mean, it's interesting to think, right? I mean, it sounds sort of grandiose to claim that generative AI wouldn't exist without Kubernetes. But I think actually, it's kind of true, right? In the sense of not like Kubernetes is special, but in the sense of it enabled a lot of people who wanted to build large-scale systems to kind of forget about machine management. The first step to doing AI inferences is no longer figuring out how to get a bunch of machines to work together. Containers and Kubernetes took care of that for you. And so you can just say, OK, I've got this fleet of machines with GPUs and everything else. How do I get my application out there to do the training? And I think that that's the history of computer science in general, building higher levels of abstraction to enable the next platform to build on top.

A.G.: And that's one of the cases I love the most. If you check the success stories at *kubernetes.io* or CNCF (*https://oreil.ly/epXxD*), they talk about OpenAI with Cloud Native (*https://oreil.ly/b5EfH*) and how that was enabling all the kinds of things that we have seen, like wider scale, a lot of people can connect to ChatGPT. Of course, there is the AI infrastructure from Microsoft behind that. But that's a new enabler for all these areas of applications and the AI compilers.

B.B.: Yeah. And a reduction in complexity again, too. So not only can generative AI reduce complexity, but having that orchestrator reduces the complexity for the AI engineers who just don't need to worry about that problem. And then when you get it from Azure, you don't even have to worry about running it. It just takes care of it for you.

A.G.: Saving a lot of people like me.

B.B.: I think it's also always the goal, right? It's much easier to consume the idea than it is to implement the idea. You can say, OK I know how to use a sorting algorithm. You can probably write a sorting algorithm, but it's going to take you a lot more time to write it than it is to use it. It empowers a lot of people, which is great.

A.G.: Yeah. And accelerates the implementation, something that would take so long before now is becoming like a, I wouldn't say commodity, but certainly like something easier to implement.

B.B.: Yeah. And I think you'll see, I think you see that creative explosion then afterwards, where a lot of people who maybe wouldn't have the patience or the skillset to implement generative AI, but they can have really creative ideas about how to use it. And so when you make that capability available, you're going to just generate a ton of creativity about how to use it.

A.G.: Certainly. From the cloud native perspective at Microsoft, how do you see all this explosion of the technology stack for Copilot (*https://oreil.ly/jGrqE*), Semantic Kernel, all the different cool pieces that we mention in this book? What's your personal opinion on that?

B.B.: Well, I mean, you still have to run your application somewhere, right? You know, you don't get to, generative AI doesn't enable you to not have a webpage there or not having a Restful API somewhere. And so not only do tools like Azure Machine Learning build on top of Azure Kubernetes Service (AKS), but we're actually also seeing a lot of people building, you know, the frontend application or the APIs that they need to have, even plug-ins for OpenAI on top of AKS. It's still a really great place to host code and integrate there. And of course, we have GPU support in AKS, so there are people who are doing their own inference or building their own models. And some of our largest clusters actually are built to do that kind of AI for a variety of different groups. And again, I think it's about simplicity, right? Because if you want to focus on AI, you don't want to focus on what it takes to run a 5,000-node Kubernetes cluster. It's not the easiest thing to do. And if you can just click a bunch of buttons or do an infrastructure as code template and have 5,000 GPU nodes, that's pretty good. And then know that my team is on call for those. Saves you a lot of time.

A.G.: Yes. And that's what we're seeing with Azure AI Studio now, and with all these applications and the ability to deploy any kind of model, because the book is about Azure OpenAI and a proprietary model. How do you see the role of open source as an enabler for generative AI?

B.B.: Yeah. I think, over time, I suspect that there's going to be more and more models that happen, that people tune, that people build for different situations. I mean, you're already seeing that kind of model sharing and model retraining happening. I think that's really great. I think you look at something, you know, Semantic Kernel is out in open source sharing our best practices. LangChain is out there in open source. I think it's all rooted in open source. I think also one of the things that is going to happen over time, I think will be higher level frameworks, too. I think people are still trying to figure out exactly what it takes to build a complete copilot. I think there's a lot of what I would call sort of vertical copilots, you know, copilots that are good at one thing. But I think there's value in sort of saying, well, actually, there are some really broad areas out there and you may actually want something that knows how to choose between copilots. I think of it sort of like search, maybe, right, when you do a web search, maps, video? Like there's a variety of different kinds of content you could be searching for. And I think the same thing is going to be true with Copilot. There's going to be multiple levels in terms of choosing what you want to generate. I mean, in some sense, it's like your friends, I guess. Like you go to one friend for tech advice, you go to one friend for sports or whatever. And you're going to find the same thing.

A.G.: On one side, there are all the building blocks that are being created and the orchestrators that you have mentioned, different approaches like retrieval (RAG), like the kind of knowledge bases that we can use, that can be databases, etc. And I feel like that's evolving a lot, of course.

B.B.: For sure. And I think there's a little bit of one of the questions I've had that, you know, I don't necessarily have the right answer for, which is, when do you do retraining versus when do you do retrieval-augmented generation? Because they kind of both do the same thing at some level, you can influence what your results are either by retraining or retraining on your corpus or by doing retrieval-augmented generation. I think questions like that people are going to need to struggle with for a while.

A.G.: Yes. There's no single answer for that. In one of the chapters from this book, I mention (very carefully as it is such a new topic) that we need to try and test depending on the dataset, depending on the kind of retraining, the kind of fine-tuning you want to have or the general behavior of the LLM compared to the kind of tasks that you're assigning.

B.B.: Or even the app. You're probably not going to be able to retrain it for every single customer. You may have to do it because you're like, well, I have such a diverse set of users. I want to provide personalized content for each user, but I can't retrain every user, so I'm going to use retrieval-augmented generation. But on the other hand, you can be like, I am my company and it's worth it to retrain because I know my company and I'm only going to have results for my company. I think it's interesting stuff.

A.G.: Right, and maybe it's a combination with segmentation or a recommender system, something that will pre-filter the kind of users you have in front of you. And then based on the ability that user may have to access the information, the knowledge base based on the active directory or whatever, you can customize that answer then.

B.B.: I mean, role-based access control (RBAC) is a fascinating part. We have this challenge even in the Azure Resource Graph, which is used for at-scale querying. It's an index of all your Azure resources. Applying access control to that is a very interesting problem. Because obviously you can't build an index for each user, right? There's one index of all the resources. And so then you have to basically be like, OK, I did the query. I found some data. Now, which of the data that I got back did this user actually have access to or put it into the query itself and actually say, as I do my search query, only show me things that also this person has access to. And yeah, obviously, it's important to get right.

A.G.: Totally. With all this complexity, what would be your recommendation in terms of upskilling, for people to follow in this area, like any kind of thing that will help learners and readers to keep track of everything that's going on?

B.B.: The two things I would say is, I would definitely recommend playing around with it. I think the Bing chat is a great way to get in and give it a try, because it's really important, I think, to get a sense for what it's good at and what it's not good at. Because I think when you see or read the articles or you hear, or even when you see examples, they've been kind of cherry-picked. They're never going to show you bad examples. And I think it's really valuable to get in there and realize that it's not perfect. Even beyond the hallucinations, which I think people are getting a handle on how to deal with, I think with some questions it just isn't very good. And I think that experiential is the way to go. Give yourself a task, try and figure out what the system is good at.

In particular, I would say I think it's really good at summarization in general. I found that it's quite good at taking information and distilling it down. It can be good at things like error messages for compilers. It can be really bad also sometimes. I think you have to get your own sense of what you think it is good at and what you think it's bad at. Because it will give you a sense of which ideas you could use it for. Because you may think, I could use generative AI to do this and you're like, well, in practice, that's not going to work out very well. So that's part one, and then I think part two is that I'm a big believer in getting your hands dirty with a toy project that's meaningful to you. I do a lot of hacking with random stuff in my house to turn on lights or whatever. Don't just go through the toy examples because you don't have a personal connection. And I think that personal connection helps you build. Of course, you can't build the whole app at the start. You need something small and constrained to make sure you continue to make progress. I think that's usually the way I go when I'm learning new tech. I really want to get a sense of how it works and how I put a whole piece of it together. That skeleton. And then, you know, then you can move on to saying, OK, I now have the knowledge to go build the real app that I was thinking about building.

A.G.: I think those two points are very precise on what acquiring the experience is like. Of course with Azure OpenAI, but also the different technologies out there or the flavors of Azure OpenAI on different products, and what the limitations and the advantages are. Because there are very good advantages, but also limitations. For example, I was checking something related to finding information related to a specific person. Maybe that's not always the best use case scenario because it's linguistics, you have Adrián González from Microsoft and another Adrián González, the baseball player. So, yeah, I totally agree on that.

And remind me, you have several O'Reilly books as well, right? You're in the club of authors with several books. Can you tell us a bit about them and what they are about?

B.B.: Well, I've written a couple of different books on Kubernetes. *Kubernetes: Up and Running*, which I wrote with Kelsey Hightower and Joe Beda. And then more recently, the third edition was written with Lachlan Evanson, who's another person at Microsoft. And then actually right now I'm working on the second edition of *Designing Distributed Systems*. And it's actually going to go into a little bit, probably not in as much depth as your book, but go into a little bit of how to build AI systems in the context of distributed systems.

And then actually the most exciting chapter that I'm adding there for the second edition is what I'm going to call the greatest hits chapter, which is all of the problems that people had, which discusses all of the mistakes that people make that keep coming up over and over again. Because we go to live sites and you sit through outages and postmortems and all this kind of stuff. And after you do it for a few years you see that there are patterns that repeat. And I've been taking some notes and I've written down a bunch of the ones that repeat over and over again. For example, one of the ones that comes up a lot is our monitoring didn't think that the absence of errors should be an error. If there were a lot of errors you'd notice. But if it goes absolutely quiet and there's nothing, it could mean you're totally OK, but it could also mean that you're not processing anything. And several times we've seen systems where they have a monitoring gap, where for some reason they stopped processing anything. With this idea that no news was treated as good news, they didn't alert anybody until a customer was like, hey, wait a minute, where are my deliveries? You could be monitoring delivery lanes, anything like that in terms of an online retailer, right? An online retailer could monitor how long it takes a package to get from point A to point B from my delivery center to the customer. And they could alert if that goes over 12 hours or whatever. But if you stop delivering all packages, that alert does not fire. Because there's no deliveries, it didn't take any time. It's subtleties like that and it doesn't occur to you in the first place because you're so used to the steady state.

A.G.: I think that applies to what we'll see in future editions of this book. Like the kind of learnings from the industry, the kind of things we don't know because we don't know it yet. It will be based on experience. We are just starting this wave for generative AI, but certainly the same case here.

B.B.: Yeah. Oh, yeah. I imagine it's going to change rapidly, actually, as more and more people get in there. The first couple of years when people got in, the same thing happened with cloud native open source, right? Even with UI frameworks. I think mostly people use React now, but like there was a solid two or three years where I felt like people were changing every three months. It seemed like every time I talked to somebody, they'd switch their JavaScript framework. I'm sure the same thing will happen with AI, right? Because I think it takes a little bit for people to figure out what abstractions actually work. What are the abstractions that make sense? What are the common problems that we can turn into libraries? I think there's a lot of free-form prompt engineering happening right now. I think there's going to be a lot more science that comes into that. And I don't know if science is the right word, but a lot more like rigor that comes into that kind of stuff over time as people figure out kind of what works and what doesn't work. The templates, operations, the best practices, the countermeasures. I think at some point you'll probably just be able to hit a checkbox and get a bunch of the fixes and all that kind of stuff, hallucination prevention and stuff like that.

A.G.: Hey, just a last question, because you mentioned the postmortem, but there's something we mentioned in the book, which is the premortem. Did you use the notion of a premortem to see what could go wrong?

B.B.: Yeah, it's sort of like what we call red teaming as well, where you're trying to break that, you know, you're purposely trying to break stuff. And yeah, I think that's really important. I think you check both bad stuff, obviously, like there's been stuff in the press and otherwise about, you know, ways you can trick these models, but also honestly, just to see if it does a good job. I think it's more prosaic. You know, nobody writes a headline about something that they're like, this query was not answered very well. But obviously, if you're building a product, that's really important to understand: does it actually work? And I think actually measuring, that's the other thing I think is going to be really interesting. And a lot of growth is happening. It's like measuring the quality of a model. I don't think we've done a ton of rigorous scientific measurement. I mean, there are scoreboards and things like that to measure against benchmarks but it's not clear that's 100 percent connected to the reality of a user experience once you build it into a product. And I think just as we've done a lot of work, you know, in the Azure portal and things like that on figuring out, where we are confusing the user? You know, where do we have a UI that's not great? I think we're going to do the same thing with these chat systems, right, where it's probably going to be, how many times did people click on the prompts we suggested or how many times did they hit the clear button or, you know, there's a lot of ways you can figure out, are we giving them the answers that they want?

A.G.: Totally, because right now with the benchmarks and the evals type of projects on LangChain and Azure AI Studio, we are focusing on the core model parts. But then you are mentioning all the quantitative and qualitative measures that we usually do in product analytics, for example. That's something I mention in the book. You'll see it in some of the chapters because obviously that part will evolve a lot, but getting the sense of the metrics, how good or bad you are doing from a user perspective, is crucial. I think that would also be very useful for companies.

B.B.: For sure. Yeah, absolutely. I think that it's in its infancy right now. It's going to be really interesting to see how we figure that out. So I also am pretty excited. Microsoft is also really big into accessibility and computing for all. And I think that it's also going to be a game changer in terms of usability, because we see people with challenges and we do a lot of work in our UX for accessibility, but I think a chat or a voice-based UX that is actually empowered by generative language could be significantly better than what we provide with a mouse-based or sound-based UI.

A.G.: I'm loving this case with the Portuguese government creating an avatar (*https:// oreil.ly/jMgb6*) for people who cannot write and then you have another for people who can write but cannot talk. I think that's where we are leading to. We're saying that this generative AI is equivalent to what the visual interface was to command lines. And I believe that's kind of true.

B.B.: Yeah, I think it's going to be really exciting to see how it transforms things. And it's fun to be a part of it. I guess that's why we're always here. It's fun to be involved in the transformation as well.

John Maeda: About AI Design and Orchestration

A.G.: I know you very well just because I'm some sort of groupie of what you are doing with your learning resources, but let's learn a little bit about who John is and what your role at Microsoft is as well as your previous background.

J.M.: I'm lucky to get to work in the middle of the AI Superstorm and there is a project called Semantic Kernel that I am helping to advance. It's a way to enable more enterprises to take advantage of this new kind of AI. Before that, I was in the physical security industry. I was a chief technology officer of a mid-cap security company called Everbridge. We took care of the world, countries, cities, and corporations. Before that I worked in places like venture capitals. I was at MIT for a while and did research and I also worked in a late-stage startup to really understand where the world is heading.

A.G.: Amazing. Such an interesting back-ground. One of the things I really like about you is that you are converging the design world and the AI world, which is very intuitive for some people. Like, of course, if we're interacting with artificial intelligence, we want to have an interface and a design with a human-centric process. But what's your opinion on the importance of this kind of design process and design thinking for AI applications, including generative AI?

J.M.: Yeah, well, I give an annual report at South by Southwest about the intersection of design, technology, and business. This year was called Design Against AI (*https:// oreil.ly/pOZmj*), which has two meanings. One meaning is design protest against AI, and the other is design competes against AI. So one is more of a kind of like, you know, give up. Stop it. The other is to, say, maybe I'll take it on. I think creative people should be competing with AI instead. Trying to see how to advance their craft. Many people say it's about collaborating with AI instead of just competing. That said, I think that this kind of AI is not about the pictures or the text. It really is about the tools, functions, actions. That's why in Semantic Kernel we say plug-ins, planners, personas. I've heard nowadays people say large action model instead of just large lan-guage model where large action model assumes you're using functions, plug-ins, function calling. I think that verb aspect of AI is going to be the thing that unlocks much more value than we could ever imagine.

A.G.: Yeah, because it's the interaction with tools. And in general, people are worried about AI replacing some basic functions of society. But some people are skipping the part where generative AI can be the interface to interact with very complex functions like designing 3D or analyzing SQL databases. So that draws the sign as an interface. Models and tools like Semantic Kernel.

J.M.: Well, I think plug-ins are so powerful. Whether you call them functions or tools or whatever you want to call them, when you integrate them with a large language model, of course, you get the kind of planning capability. And that's what we saw with Semantic Kernel. When you use GPT-4, you give it plug-ins that can plan. And once it can plan, it's basically writing code that you could never have written. It writes code on the fly, basically. From a design perspective, a lot of time has been spent making the perfect user experience. That's something very hard to do. We'll build a journey to take you step by step through it. In reality, though, with function calling, you don't need a journey. You just say, I want to do this, and it's done. You didn't have to have a user interface. That's why you hear people calling it sort of like a zero UI era, where you don't have a journey, you teleport to the goal.

A.G.: I love that notion because from my perspective with the book, I think that function calling and the planning part was the most difficult part to explain, to be honest.

J.M.: It is. It's so hard. It's hard because if you're a developer right now, you're just too busy shipping regular code. You're tired at the end of the week. You know, it's a weekend, you want to take a break, and like, what, this new thing, what, embeddings? What, you've got to do language model understanding, testing, what, these are all new tools. You know, Python may not be your thing you do every day too. It's like, oh, I don't want to, I played with Python, whatever. And so that's why we're trying to make it easier for enterprise devs who live in .NET or Java or boring languages. So I tell people, Semantic Kernel is for boring AI people.

A.G.: Boring AI people. That's such good marketing.

J.M.: Well, it's because enterprise likes "boring." I mean, we also have a Python branch, but I find that the Python stuff is so advanced that actually integrating into an enterprise, it's not so easy because it's a different developer. An app dev is more about shipping "real code." So we need an easier way to do that. That's why Semantic Kernel exists.

A.G.: That's very smart positioning. And how can you define Semantic Kernel? You have explained the plug-ins, the personas, but if you think of Semantic Kernel as a thing, today and in the future, if we're able to get a sneak peek here, what's your vision? How is it helping companies?

J.M.: Well, you know, I think the biggest way it helps companies is it helps you be boring because the latest thing is the latest thing, but the problem with the latest thing is it just got new today. And so you're just so distracted. Like, what do I do? Oh my gosh, it changes every day. So Semantic Kernel is good insurance for building on a middleware layer. When the lower parts change, it's easy to adapt it at the middleware level. So it's like insurance for the high speed of AI change. And it's grounded in the plug-in because the plug-ins are where function calling becomes valuable. We have so many ways to do plug-ins with native code or native plus semantic code, you know, pick your own language. And the planners are designed to not just leverage the plug-ins to call them automatically, but to generate a script basically that you can read yourself, not a Python program, but a handlebars-formatted plan. We found many enterprises are happy that AI generated the plan and they want to freeze the plan because they know it works. They don't need it to invent something new. So frozen plans. And we're all talking about agents now. So it also incorporates agents.

A.G.: Agents, we're talking about the difference with someone I cannot disclose right now, the difference between agents and copilots.

J.M.: I don't know if I could get into that conversation. It's very meta, I believe.

A.G.: It's very meta. I think it's a matter of the audience. The people talking about agents are probably a more developer-oriented audience.

J.M.: Yes. Good point. Well, if you remember the shift to object oriented programming, I remember that being a radical idea. It's like, how do you do that? I'm so used to programming in this linear, compartmentalized way. Object? What's an object? The number one thing you learn in object oriented programming is don't make everything into an object. I think agent oriented programming also, sometimes agents are useful. Sometimes they're not. It's just a new pattern, I believe.

A.G.: Yes, totally. I like that example because I was born during the object oriented era. And I could see how the previous era was like, this doesn't make sense. You're doing this in a linear way when you need to create relations between objects.

J.M.: And you remember, you suddenly make everything into an object and then you can't understand it anymore. You create some kind of compromise. I think agents are a new way of improving the output of models through iteration, through feedback loops. It's a more clever way to do prompting. It's more compartmentalized. But sometimes if you need a linear workflow, that might be what your application requires. In that case, you don't need agents. In that case.

A.G.: Interesting. And from an Azure OpenAI perspective and any kind of generative AI in Azure, how do you see that connection with Semantic Kernel? And how do you see in general the role of orchestration? Like in Copilot, we're talking about Prometheus and other orchestration engines. How do you make sense of this? There are so many things in this area.

J.M.: Well, you know, there's people who want to call the model directly, call the APIs. I'm sure you've seen things like Ollama (*https://oreil.ly/Eyl-u*) or LM Studio (*https://oreil.ly/qQBmG*), they're all adapting to the OpenAI API specification. I kind of feel like OpenAI has become a kind of interfacing body. And because Azure OpenAI is super tight, a fast follow, I think anyone in that ecosystem gets to take advantage of that. And then you may want to orchestrate directly to talk to the API, or you want to talk in a layer. And a layer is like clothing. There's all kinds of brands of clothing, basically. And the particular brand of clothing that is Symantec Kernel is plug-ins first. And then the plug-ins are the foundation. And the neat thing is planners are also plug-ins, and also our agents, personas, are plug-ins too. We say we're plug-ins all the way down. So we're very boring.

A.G.: This is like a multilayer architecture in which they're communicating, and then you have different options to communicate with this service and another.

J.M.: Everything is just code. We're not trying to make a magical spell that you're not programming anymore. You're still programming. And everything is a computational unit. It's a plug-in. And you can make plans that are also plug-ins, or you can make agents that are plug-ins. And it's just like connecting those dots.

A.G.: Amazing. Let me ask this question. I've got several people asking the same question. And you can tell me if this is not a good question, but what's the difference, convergence, compatibility between Semantic Kernel and LangChain?

J.M.: Very common question. Yeah. LangChain and Semantic Kernel are both open source projects. Open source projects support each other. All I have is good things to say about LangChain and also Harrison (*https://oreil.ly/ttbiM*), that community. I also love LlamaIndex (*https://oreil.ly/QZtYV*), which I think of as like a sister or cousin project, which I adore. And the difference really is in the fact that LangChain is running the fastest with the latest and greatest AI ideas. Semantic Kernel, that's not the role. The role of Semantic Kernel is to enable enterprises to leverage this large language model or large action model revolution. And they're gonna tend to move slower and need more sense of safety and security. So Semantic Kernel is architected with very few package dependencies, if at all. It's designed to be loved by the CISO (Chief Information Security Officer). And it's designed to be loved by procurement because it's free, but it's also part of the Microsoft world.

A.G.: Yeah. Which makes total sense. I think both of them are necessary.

J.M.: Yeah, yeah, yeah. I mean, like I say that if you want to drive a Tesla Model S Plaid, then LangChain's fun. If you wanna drive a Toyota Camry XLE Hybrid, then you've got Semantic Kernel. And the neat thing is with a Python branch, everything is becoming 1.0. .NET became 1.0 first. We're aligning Python and Java releases. If you're a Python team, usually a data science–oriented team, and you use Semantic Kernel, all of your YAML files and everything easily shift to the App Dev. So that's the advantage.

A.G.: And what's the role of orchestration? I know that it's a bit of a stretch, but what's the role of orchestration to bring the proper information and the proper format and good timing in a timely manner for compliance? I'm located in Madrid, in Spain, Europe, AI Act, similar things in Canada, in the future in the United States. I feel like there's a lot of potential for that layer in the middle to distribute information that is required at log level.

J.M.: Well, I mean, that's a nice thing about Semantic Kernel having been built 1.0 first with .NET C#, because it has all the logging everywhere. It's got all the Azure kind of security, safeness built into how it's architected. You often hear people who love how Semantic Kernel has been architected, because it's been Microsoft architected. If you haven't seen, or if any of your readers or viewers haven't seen how we wrap plug-ins, you're gonna be pleasantly surprised because it's so little code to enable function calling of complex plug-ins. And you're thinking, wait, this is all the code I need? And you're like, yep, we can get going. People love that. And that was architected by Stephen Toub (*https://oreil.ly/i7kqx*), one of the .NET architect legends. I remember when he said it's gotta be this way. And we're like, OK. And he said wow, that's really good. It's really good. But anyone who sees it, they're kind of, where's the code? It's all there because it's using the abstractions available already of an enterprise-class language.

A.G.: Learning is the goal of this interview and I know that you are a humble person because you are not talking that much about your activities and your background, but you're creating learning resources, which I personally love. That's why I'm writing this book. That's why we're creating all this stuff. And I have two examples, LinkedIn Learning and DeepLearning.AI. What are they about, for people to continue learning?

J.M.: Oh, thanks. Let's see, I have a LinkedIn Learning course (*https://oreil.ly/TXE5e*). Now I have multiple (*https://oreil.ly/G6grC*), including one for AI engineering for leadership (*https://oreil.ly/z-nXp*). Because AI engineering is about leading change. And most developers love to be introverts, but they sometimes become managers and they have to lead people. And this AI stuff is kind of scary for people. It's also very technical to understand. I have a whole new course themed on the kitchen. Also, Microsoft Dev Channel has a new show we've made, called Mr. Maeda's Cozy AI Kitchen (*https://oreil.ly/N9oCg*). Yes, we cook AI every two weeks in my kitchen. And we have guests and they try the AI.

And the DeepLearning.AI course (*https://oreil.ly/nxusL*) was an opportunity to talk with Andrew Ng (*https://oreil.ly/CDLm-*), who I think is one of the great minds of our time. And he gave this talk at the Wall Street Journal CIO Summit, where someone asked him if this is going to change how people's jobs are, and all the fear around it. And he said the best thing I've ever heard anyone say: you should think of AI as automating tasks, not jobs. Any given job has many tasks. And if there are a lot of tasks that you don't like to do as a human, that aren't of high value as a human, then automating them with AI makes a lot of sense and can improve your job. Whether it's a gnarly testing function you're writing where you're thinking, "Oh, that's going to be such a pain with all the cases," and boom! It's there. Or something like a shell script that is always different in every language with a little subtlety. You just say I need a shell script. Just a half an hour ago, I did that. I need a shell script. And then find out, oh, that was easy. And you debug it yourself too. So, it's taking tasks that I don't like to do and having it be done for me.

A.G.: I can really see that. Like, right after this discussion, I'm creating the transcription and I'm creating the action points and the summary of the most important information. No one likes to do that and that's maybe 10% of my job because we are having so many meetings. I just want to go back to your design background. Looking at this adoption pattern where companies and people are using generative AI, LLMs, and they are learning how to evaluate them, how to use them, how to orchestrate, from a design point of view, do you see anything happening in the near future that will be radically different from a design UX, UI point of view?

J.M.: Yeah. Well, I definitely think that this zero UI revolution is happening where you don't need a lot of user interface, user experience, psychology when the machine can discover your intent and execute the task. There's this thing called Jobs to Be Done by Clayton Christensen (*https://oreil.ly/Aq12m*). It's almost as if we create user experiences to get a job done, but if the machine knows what job you want to get done and you tell it what to do and it does it, did you really need any experience in the first place?

A.G.: That's amazing, that is funny. Just today I was getting that question from a student about how to define the jobs to be done for artificial intelligence. I was like, I don't know, I don't know.

J.M.: Yeah, because with tool calling and function calling, you give it, like in Semantic Kernel, just last week I had this weird moment where I gave it five plug-ins I wrote, and then I didn't have to construct the logic of how to make them all work. It was actually too hard for me to write the logic, and the planner just constructed the flow the way that I couldn't write.

A.G.: Wow, that's incredible. And just to finish, since you mentioned the kitchen, if you had to choose, did you have one recipe that you say, this is something that someone needs to learn for the next stage of adoption?

J.M.: Oh, good question. Yeah, I tell everyone that in the kitchen that you have to realize there's two kinds of AI models. One AI model does completion, the other does similarity. And this is called the embeddings model. This is called the completion or chat completion model. It's a combination of these two together that are making this revolution amazing. If you only have one, it's no good. If you have chat completion or completion, it's going to be ungrounded. It'll say things that make no sense. If you have similarity models, which are basically search, you can find something, but you can't synthesize. The two together make an incredible pair. It's like one is butter and one is flour. Like together you can make great cookies. And this is the core recipe for everything with large language model AIs. You can create function calling models, you can create sophisticated chat, you can create supply chain automation, all from these two models. But one model alone is not good enough, you need the two together.

A.G.: You're right. And I think this in the human comparison would be something like IQ and EQ together. Like the ability to remember information, traditional intelligence, but that ability to explain in a proper way that is adapting to the audience. Yes, I love it.

Sarah Bird: Responsible AI for LLMs and Generative AI

A.G.: Do you want to start by explaining your role in the organization and what you are doing at Microsoft?

S.B.: Yeah. I'm Microsoft's chief product officer of responsible AI. What that means is my team is responsible for figuring out how we take a new AI technology and ensure that it's developed responsibly. In the case of a lot of the AI we build at Microsoft, we're figuring that out ourselves. If we're partnering with other organizations such as OpenAI, then we work with them to ensure that the right things are happening as they develop the AI. But then it's not just about the model, it's really about how we ship a complete application safely. We take that new AI technology and look at what the entire approach we need to follow is to use this technology effectively.

For example, for GPT-4, an exciting new piece of technology, the first place we shipped this was in Microsoft Copilot, originally called Bing Chat. Our team went in and basically led the responsible AI (RAI) development of that. We developed new mitigations, we developed new testing tools, we developed new techniques for red teaming. All that we learned, we built into the Azure AI platform and that enables it to power all of the AI at Microsoft as well as enable our customers who are building their own AI applications to use the same best practices. That's the mission of the team, figuring out how we really put AI into practice, and then ensuring that we're using those best practices across Microsoft and empowering others to do that as well.

A.G.: That's a lovely mission. And it's not a new one. There's a journey at Microsoft with responsible AI even before the GPT models.

S.B.: Yeah, it's something that we've actually been doing a long time. I was fortunate to be part of founding the first research group in responsible AI in Microsoft, and this is the FATE group (*https://oreil.ly/hmo69*), back in 2015. This is something we've been doing for almost 10 years. But we've come a long way during that time. It went from just some ideas in research to, the next thing that we founded was the Office of Responsible AI, which was really starting to set what is the policy or the standard we want to follow. But even creating a policy without much experience in implementation is really hard. A lot of the journey since then has been figuring out how we really do this, and iterating between policy, engineering, and research to really mature our practices, tools, and technology. But even with generative AI, for a lot of people, the first moment they were aware of it was ChatGPT. But actually, well before ChatGPT came out, Microsoft shipped GitHub Copilot, which was really the first generative AI application that we produced at scale. A lot of the things that we used in Bing Chat and other applications were actually originally developed for GitHub Copilot, because that was the first real-time generative AI application. Azure AI Content Safety (*https://oreil.ly/uB6d-*), the safety system that we use in our gen AI applications today, was actually first developed for GitHub Copilot.

A.G.: It's funny because a lot of people forget, including ourselves, when we are talking about different Copilots, that GitHub Copilot is actually the patient zero, the first one and the original one.

S.B.: It was eye-opening for us working on it because the GPT technology was exciting, but it felt like it could still be, it was still a toy. Then when the GitHub team really showed the early prototypes of GitHub Copilot, we were like, wow, this is real, this is really exciting. But at that time, we weren't sure, is it just this one application? How narrow is the technology? How many more GitHub Copilots will there be? Then when the next wave of it came out, going from GPT-3 to GPT-4, GPT-4 was when we were like…oh, this is not narrow anymore. There will be many more Copilots that are possible. That jump in the technology, I think, really unlocked many more applications, but GitHub Copilot really showed the way first.

A.G.: Yes, and I think from an RAI perspective, the idea or the adoption pattern of having a regular completion, something that is a singular interaction with the machine, and then moving to something that is chat-related, with memory, with all the benefits and all the considerations. I think that that's probably the evolution of that learning, the engineering and policy duet that you're talking about.

S.B.: Yes, certainly. There are nuances in the GitHub Copilot application. I actually really loved the design of it because it is a paradigm people are already familiar with, with the autosuggest. We're already comfortable with the idea of…hey, the suggestion might not be perfect, but if I like it, I can keep it and I can still go and edit it. We all know that it makes us go faster in natural language. But then knowing that actually was going to be effective for code, that wasn't obvious. But we did have to look at both with that natural language risk, hateful content, violent content, things like that, and also code risks, like the ability to produce security vulnerabilities or known weaknesses in the code. We had to address both of those dimensions. Because the application is only useful if it goes faster than people actually can type, there were really extreme latency requirements.

Now, the transition to Bing and Copilot since then in the chat applications, as you said, adds this multiturn dimension. Now, if you're trying to look at an interaction and say "Hey, did the AI system do the right thing?" you actually have to score a multiturn natural language conversation, and that's much more challenging. There's a much bigger diversity of topics and types of interaction that the system is going to look at. We started with a strong foundation with GitHub Copilot, but certainly with the power of GPT-4 and the power of the search engine, and the breadth of things that we wanted to cover there, we really had to look much broader. So that's when you start having conversations about things like hallucination, because accuracy really matters, or missing disinformation because the search engine is so connected with information integrity. And so the aperture really broadened with that application.

A.G.: It must be very interesting, that moment that we realized we actually need new metrics, because you have mentioned the performance, and we had the ROC curve, the F1 and F2 scores for classification topics and stuff. And then we arrived there and we said, OK, we have a new kind of application that is based on something called generative AI. We need to test the performance of this. We have the metrics from traditional linguistics like BLUE and ROUGE. How was that? At the AI level, like what do we do now?

S.B.: You know, the thing is we always knew we needed metrics to actually address these risks, right? It's very hard to understand if mitigation is effective or if a risk is present without actual metrics. And one of the big challenges in RAI for a long time is that these metrics were really difficult to get. For example, let's go back to saying, "How do I rate a multiturn conversation?" So if you're looking at doing that for "hate" (as an AI content safety metric), our guidelines internally are more than 20 pages long to kind of score that conversation, and they're built for expert linguists. And so that meant that we can measure for response by risk, but only very infrequently as sort of the outer loop. OK, an application is basically ready to ship. We can run one set of tests that are very manual, and have the human reviewer score them. And if the results look good, great, we can ship it. But with that, you're not able to really innovate in the inner loop and really try different things, and find which one works the best.

Actually, one of the most memorable things for me about developing Bing Chat quite early, as we were using GPT-4, was realizing that it actually had the potential to help us automate these metrics. We were actually able to use GPT-4, with a lot of prompt engineering, and get it to score similar to the level of those expert humans. And so that meant we went from…hey, we're gonna be able to check this very rarely, maybe once a month, maybe at the very end, to every single night when we make a change to the system, we can run the safety test overnight, look at the scores, and iterate. And so that unlocked just a whole new wave of responsible AI innovation. The technology is obviously a significant breakthrough for AI, but it's also a significant breakthrough for responsible AI and safety and security because it's this amazing new technology that just understands language and context so much more. We've really put that to use in our own development of AI.

A.G.: And you have mentioned the key words like safety, security, even compliance, regulations, and responsible AI. Everything is converging at this point. Everything is going towards something that in the beginning was the ethical way to do things, like the willingness to do something that is good, towards something that is responsible, that is accountable. And I think that that's a wonderful thing from a technology perspective, that organic evolution.

S.B.: Yeah, I think with generative AI, one of the things that's been exciting, but also challenging, frankly, is that with a lot of the responsible AI work we did before, just the AI developer could manage it. And everyone kind of got the benefit, but they didn't need to really understand the details as long as you work with a great AI provider like Microsoft. You were set. With generative AI, we really end up needing both for safety and security to use a defense in depth approach where the model developer needs to do things, the safety system developer needs to do things, the application developer needs to look at the meta-prompt and the grounding information, the final application developer needs to look at how the human interacts. What does that UX look like?

There's so much more that needs to be done to use this technology effectively. And it's not surprising, it's a much more general-purpose, more powerful technology. This went from something that was really just housed in a small number of responsible AI experts to something that now every organization, every security professional, every AI developer needs to think about. It's been really fun to see the interesting growth and support for the work, but also the explosion of demand means there's so much more that we have to do. And that's really exciting, but also can be challenging.

A.G.: It is very exciting. And I think it's very aligned with the kind of artifacts and material that the Responsible AI Initiative at Microsoft (*https://oreil.ly/tCL6L*) is putting out there, available for organizations at both the technical and organizational level. I'm thinking about the impact assessment (*https://oreil.ly/bJAeg*), the HAX toolkit (*https://oreil.ly/AtDRJ*) for the interfaces. What's your favorite? If you had to choose different pieces of material that are useful for organizations in terms of responsible AI, what would be your selection?

S.B.: Oh, it's so hard. I love all the responsible AI things. But I think what you've called out is really important because it is a mix of practices, policies, and technologies. And you really have to look at the whole spectrum and customers and organizations are asking us for that. So, for example, one of the things I really like is that we've put out our Responsible AI Standard (*https://oreil.ly/j5tBY*), which is really the guide for how we do this overall out there. So organizations can look at it. They can adopt something similar if that works for them. We also put it out there so we can get feedback. People can tell us what they think we're missing, what they're finding works, what they're finding doesn't work. And so that's really kind of where everything starts with us. But then if you want to go and put that into practice, you need to first start with a process like an impact assessment where you're really mapping the risk. You then need to be able to measure risk effectively. And so actually we just released new safety evaluations for generative AI (*https://oreil.ly/GcCSo*), which are the tests that we run ourselves to really measure these risks. And that's actually the breakthrough I was telling you about earlier.

And then you also need to be able to mitigate the risk. Azure AI Content Safety is a great way we mitigate the risk. That's the safety system layer. The HAX toolkit really helps with the application, the UX layer. We've also put out prompt engineering guides and meta-prompt templates to help with the prompt layer. You really have to look holistically across all of these to adopt that. Another one that we get asked about a lot from customers is how to red team, how to do that kind of final expert validation. We put out red teaming guidelines (*https://oreil.ly/oDBO_*), but we know red teams are limited resources. So we've just released PyRIT (*https://oreil.ly/azSbW*), which is a tool that helps accelerate the productivity of red teamers by helping them get more ideas for the next thing to try, basically using AI to assist them the same way we're using AI to assist many other roles now with what we've developed.

We're finding that people really need all of these pieces. A lot of the work we're doing is trying to make sure that they understand that complete spectrum of practices and policies and tools that they're going to need to achieve this. And we want to make it easy for everybody to just pick these up and go running with them, but also customize them as they need. We know different domains are different, organizations are different, and so we don't want it to be just the Microsoft way. We just want to make it really easy for people to start with the responsible AI state of the art and then adapt it to them.

A.G.: Yeah, and this is useful. In my case, I'm using it with partners, with integrators, with consulting firms, with clients also who are asking for inspiration or some good practices on how they can approach responsible AI. Traditionally, it was about defining the AI principles, like we want to be accountable, transparent, etc. But now we're going farther on how to approach this at an organizational and technical level.

S.B.: Yeah, and I think we have people ask both, how do I do a practice like red teaming or evaluation that we mentioned? Or they ask, how do I address a particular potential risk, such as hallucination or prompt injection attacks? We see people looking for guidance in both of those dimensions. And the answer for something like hallucination is…here are the steps: here is where you identify that risk, here's how you measure that risk, how you red team it, here's layers of mitigation for that. They're actually a horizontal and vertical pattern, but we hear people asking for guidance in both of those ways.

A.G.: Yes, indeed. And I think you have mentioned the experiences with GitHub, or Microsoft Bing/Copilot, that I think have been extremely illustrative for everyone trying to create their own copilot or whatever platform, even for competitors. I remember people saying…"Hey, Jordi Ribas (CVP Microsoft) and the team are releasing learnings every week, and this is so useful now for everyone." So that's very exciting, that movement from model to platform, and all the learnings that go with it.

S.B.: Yeah, and we're still learning every day now, as technology becomes more accessible to more people, all of the exciting new use cases that people can think of. But I think those early days were very special. The rate of learning was just insanely high. And we had the first ones where we had brought experts from around the company to work on this. Quite a few folks from Microsoft Research volunteered to work on that full time. We had these great minds all working together, iterating every day. And I think for a lot of people, that experience also kind of changed their work after that in their research directions, because they went in and really saw what the real challenges we have right now are, but also the real amazing potential of the technology. That hands-on experience where you were learning so much and we were all learning together, I think was really shaped in the way we've done AI at Microsoft and many different people's outlook on that. So that certainly I think was a really special innovative time for us.

A.G.: That must be amazing. I can imagine those days and those discussions, the daily work. It was very exciting also from the consumer point of view, just to see the news and all the new functionalities, not only the models, but everything that goes with that. What's your vision for the next…it's too difficult not to say two or three years, but just for the next year, your vision of how this will evolve, the kind of things that we may see, the kind of challenges that we may have, what do you think will happen?

S.B.: Yeah, I think there's a couple of patterns that we're seeing. Certainly one of them is multimodal, right? A lot of the applications are still kind of mostly text, but there's so much more potential when you can understand together different modalities, images, audio, video, etc. We're starting to see very exciting examples of that technology. I think over the next year, a lot more multimodal will come in, and that certainly brings new types of risks from a responsible AI point of view. I think there's a lot of excitement about the next wave of technology and AI agents, having the technology that can perform more actions. That of course greatly increases the space of things you need to think about in terms of responsible AI, but also the level of quality and inaccuracy that you need, because if you're taking an action, a mistake can have a much bigger impact.

Those are kind of two big ones that are on my mind, but maybe in the kind of bigger picture sense, Kevin Scott (Microsoft CTO) says regularly that right now this technology is on an exponential curve, but we only get to see the next points on the curve every year or two, when the next wave of technology comes out. I think a lot of us are asking ourselves, "Is the next one really gonna be exponentially better than GPT-4?" And if it is, what does that really mean? Like our minds have a hard time thinking in exponentials, we really kind of project out linearly. There's also this chance that we're gonna be just seeing another extreme breakthrough, sometime soon. And so, I think, one of the exciting open questions is just how much better will the next wave of technology be?

A.G.: Yeah, I think it's exponential, the kind of performance that we'll see, and the kind of considerations that you're mentioning. Like I said, there are multiple dimensions that we need to consider on that journey of new applications being created. A good example is what we saw with OpenAI releasing Sora (*https://oreil.ly/ppSjf*) and just putting it out there, and showing the benefits but also sharing it with different parts of the community to analyze the potential considerations, because we can do a lot of things with this technology. But it's exciting.

S.B.: Yeah, I think it's as a technologist, it's your hope, but certainly not expectation, that you're gonna be around when the technology goes through a critical transformation, really crosses the threshold from being something that's an exciting research idea to something that is really ready for practice. And so, I remind my team every day, we need to be enjoying every moment of this, because obviously I think the impact of the technology will only grow and that will be really exciting as well, but nothing is quite like the beginning in terms of the change that that brings, and the rate of learning and everything. And so, we're just enjoying the ride, but also very, very aware that we're in a position of leadership where we need to steer the direction of the future of this technology, and we need to help the world be able to use it in effective ways, but also ensure that it is not used in ways that I think society really doesn't want. And so, I think we're also very aware of the weight of the responsibility of being here in this position at the beginning and really making sure that we make decisions we think are going to be right for the future.

Tim Ward: The Impact of Data Quality on LLM Implementations

A.G.: Of course, you're the CEO of CluedIn, but what's your role in the company? What's CluedIn doing in terms of data management, data quality, and so on?

T.W.: Yeah, sure. I'm actually joining you from a hotel room in Seattle. I am literally about 200 meters away from the Microsoft headquarters in Redmond, so I've been working with that group all week. This has a little bit to do with my role. I run the CluedIn team, I'm the CEO of CluedIn, but I come from a very product-driven software engineering background. I've been architecting products and building enterprise-grade products for some time. What we do at CluedIn is bring some pretty critical and necessary elements to Microsoft customers, and that is in the form of data quality and master data management (MDM).

Data quality is probably one of those aspects we're all aware of, we know we need to fix. MDM is somewhat one of those mysterious topics that I think people might even say is synonymous with data quality. What's MDM versus data quality? At CluedIn, we really see there's quite a lot of similarities between what data quality fixes and MDM. What we've really done is find those different elements or categories, and here is the kicker: CluedIn is a tool that's really targeted at nontechnical users. That's because we think that data quality doesn't seem like one of those stubborn things that we're always tripping over, and we know we need to do it. What we believe and what we've seen with our customers is we were never able to bring the business in and make them responsible for this. Often, the tooling was a little bit too complex, and so what I'm happy to say is that we bring those capabilities to anyone that's in that Microsoft ecosystem. They've got Fabric, they've got maybe Purview, they've got Azure Data Factory. But at some point, they need to go, how do I bring the business in and have them play a role in this supply chain of data as well.

A.G.: Well, that's amazing because I'm pretty sure you heard with this initial generative AI wave like…oh, we don't need data anymore, so we don't need to care about the quality. Then what happened, people were saying they would like to customize development and use their own data, but wait, we haven't taken care of the data quality for a while, so what to do?

T.W.: Exactly. Now, there's somewhat a race condition here in that to yield value and insights with data, and specifically AI, we probably need AI to help us with the data quality piece. There's this quite self-fulfilling recursive nature to the yin and the yang between solving data quality and actually yielding value AI. Spot on with, I think, your analogy there.

A.G.: Yes. Before we go into the details of data quality, because I think it deserves some discussion here, but how was 2023 for CluedIn from a generative AI perspective? I know that you have been working on a lot of things, including your own product. How did you experience this?

T.W.: Many facets. Number one thing, being a company just "slightly" smaller than Microsoft, just slightly, that I guess we adopted AI ourselves, just internally as a business very early on, and it started with GitHub Copilot. It then progressed. Fortunately, due to our great relationship and partnership with Microsoft, we were given early access to Azure OpenAI in a private preview. That was something we instantly realized, wow, that's how we're going to build this in our own products. This also gave us a bit of time to learn about the guardrails that were necessary.

You and I both know, Adrián, GenAI forms some pretty spectacular demonstrations, but being in the data management space and data governance and data quality, often the discussion goes to how do I make sure that our generative AI initiatives are actually going to survive the tumultuous nature of the enterprise? Is it secure? Is it governed? Do I have an audit trail of what happened? Is someone responsible for the data that's being used? What about all the data sovereignty questions about where is data? Pretty early, we were having those discussions internally, but also with our early customer adopters that were saying, as soon as you guys start to implement AI in your platform, please let me know because there just seems like such an opportunity to apply AI to the actual data management practices itself, not just use it as an end consumption piece of software.

A.G.: Which makes total sense from a Copilot point of view of interacting, of adding something to the user interface, we are saying, MDM or data quality in general, they are traditionally some sort of technical task, but we want to bring this to a business because they know their data, they know the information, so we can put this layer to infuse generative AI, and that's what you guys did, and did it very early.

T.W.: Yeah. I would argue that's been the biggest gap that we haven't been able to bring the business into, because we often give them this software and we say, hey I bought this great MDM platform for you, just put all your data quality rules in there. Then someone comes in and says, OK, it says put a regular expression. Sorry, what's a regular expression? I've been a software engineer for 19 years, and I still don't know how to build regular expressions, but we're asking people to somehow do this and that's how they'll play a role. And I think that's why often these initiatives get thrown back to IT naturally because this seems like it's for them. Then IT says, "No, I've got my tools, I've got Fabric, and I've got Azure Data Factory, that allows me to play my role, but it asks me to be very technical." You could argue, Adrián, haven't we been trying to bring the business in for 30 years? What has changed? Well, apart from the fact technology has just changed in general, getting access to different software is easier and easier all the time, and the cloud of course brought part of that.

The other piece is we've been handed in this nice little wrapped up bow an easy way to interact with LLMs; that is that chasm, it's that bridge between, you can tell me what you intend and I'll translate it underneath into what the underlying system needs. Because the thing is, for detecting patterns in data, especially in a deterministic way, regular expressions are somewhat just the way we do that. You need some underlying function to be able to do that, especially in a cost-efficient economic way. We can't at this point, which is one of the things I'm looking forward to, we can't just throw a large language model at every problem. Actually, we shouldn't. I personally wouldn't sleep as well if I realized my whole supply chain was just running off a model that sometimes gets things right and sometimes gets things wrong. It's that bridge, how do I use the general knowledge to bridge that technical thing that these tools will still ask you to do, but now it's not so much in this very like, oh, I need to be technical to do it.

A.G.: These are the cases where when we're interacting with the tools, or we are processing information, or we are trying to fulfill some JSON file by using generative AI, the engine itself becomes more deterministic. It's like we are not giving that much creativity because we are trying to find that connection with the system. In your case, you have software, you have a backend layer with all the data, you are connected to the data. I think that that's the perfect example of evolution on the interfaces. When Bill Gates said this is like the evolution from the command line to Windows, and then from Windows to this kind of generative AI interface. How do you see the relationship? I know that this is not an answer for now, it could be an answer for later, and for later, and for later on the roadmap of the different products. But how do you see the current relationship between a company like CluedIn, or even the MDM and data quality solution, and the Azure OpenAI engine?

T.W.: So I think the relationship is somewhat symbiotic, and a good example is the plug-in architecture for Azure OpenAI. The fact that you can plug in something like Uber, KAYAK, or TripAdvisor, and the LLM knows. I know when you want general chat and general knowledge, but then I also can do the smart thing of saying, actually, when do you just want to talk to KAYAK or TripAdvisor, and book a trip? A very similar thing happens on the data management side, via CluedIn's copilot that we have in our platforms, very similar to what you have in Microsoft 365 or Power BI, or up-and-coming Fabric. If you had a big dataset with a million records, right now, without actually training your own model on that data, there's really no easy way via context windows to just, not in an economically viable way anyway, to say what's the value in column 4 in row 464,000? But the symbiosis is, how do I translate that language into an underlying language that can then do that query in a very efficient way? That could be translating it locally into SQL. In our case, it's translating it locally into something like an elastic search query that says, I'll build the query, so the LLM is not actually looking at a million records, it's transposing into the local environment.

Listen, I think at some point you will have these unlimited token sizes where you can either just say, I want the whole one million rows in the context, or potentially it's going to be…load that data into a model, and your copilot is running off your custom model. And Azure AI Studio is a great tool that makes it so easy already to build your own copilot of Llama and Mistral and things like this, and also throw your own data from quite heterogeneous file types as well. Everything from PDF to images, to CSV, to Excel, to text, to video, and even C# and SQL files, it can swallow that stuff up. At some point, you are going to get to a point where you might not even need to do that local translation in all situations. You could literally talk to your entire data estate with a native feel in chat.

A.G.: Yes, there is another discussion with Dr. John Maeda, he was mentioning the notion of plug-ins, everything is interacting, and we are even building the code based on needs. It's like function calling, but imagine automatic function calling, on which the model can realize, I need to check on my storage or Cosmos DB, I need to check on whatever source of information I have. Even more, if I was imagining (and I know this interview is about asking you questions), but just imagining the future, and this is not even related to roadmaps or whatever, but imagine in the future you have your data state, then you are handling general data governance with a solution like Purview, then you are going to the details of data quality and MDM to prepare all the data, and then there's a smooth two-clicks way to push to a data store.

T.W.: I then have to comment on this, Adrián, because very early on when OpenAI came out, almost within a matter of days, this concept of LangChain came out as well, in that I want to chain multiple things together, and of course this was one thing we said is we have to have this included, because what we want via the plug-in architecture is to say, go get me all of our employee files that we have, bring them in, map them into the same concept, and trade the semantics of column names for me. If you've got F name, first name, first, of course it easily swallows that up, but in many cases you might bring on an SAP system, and it's column names, not that obvious, they are German acronyms in a lot of cases. And for it to be able to chew that up and say, "I know what you mean," but then to chain things, and then after that, check every column and apply appropriate data quality checks, and that's the one thing I love, the fact that you can just be very dynamic. That you're not being prescriptive and saying, "No please enforce this standard of phone numbers," that will work, but also the fact you can be very dynamic and fluid in the way you interact.

I am in the data government space, but to be honest, I don't know ISO codes off the top of my head, I don't know how fun that person would be at a party if they actually did know that, and you're wanting the large language model—the truth is it knows that stuff, it knows the ISO codes, it knows what they do and that chaining of things, I think this is what takes the use of GenAI from something that saves you 5, 10 seconds, to something that genuinely saves hours of research or trial and error. And that's where I think the key thing is in bringing it into products, we have this kind of standard or set of ethics we have on the use of AI in our product, and we take a couple of these from inspiration from Microsoft as well, one of them being your data is your data, we're never going to use cross-customer data to train this general model.

But one of the ones we've added ourselves is, no AI for AI's sake, and what that means is, if we build something on our platform, and actually you could probably do the same thing in the old way, probably faster or relatively the same, why bother using AI? You know a good example would be, it's technically impressive in a chat to say "Find me all the employees that are over 64," but actually by the time you've just used our rule builder, you've probably taken the same amount of time to do it by hand than using AI, and at that point it's like, what's the value there? And I would argue, it's not so much. There are cases where it is smart, for example if I said, "Go get me all of our customers in the Nordic region," and I don't have to say, "where the country is Denmark or Iceland" or this or this. Now that's great you've saved 15 seconds, but really the things we should be focusing on is, how did I save you complexity? How did I increase simplicity? And what were the things that saved me one or two hours, three days, that's what we're really trying to focus on here at CluedIn.

A.G.: Yes, I love that vision of how the end-to-end architecture chains different functions that handle the data and AI activities of any company. But I am seeing cases in which people are using generative AI to re-create chatbots all the time, for example, because I want it to be deterministic, I want to use it like a knowledge base, and then I have 10 questions, 10 answers, and I say that's not necessarily something we maybe want to do with generative AI. Do you have interesting stories or insights on how data quality is already impacting, either in a negative or positive way, generative AI implementations with Azure OpenAI, or any other technology? Like clients saying that because we have been working on data quality, and we have this data state properly done, we have seen the difference.

T.W.: One of the things that's so interesting about the form factor of chatting to your data is that it surfaces bad data quality quicker than probably any other form factor like search, or anything like this. It becomes abundantly clear, and I think also it's because people have high expectations of LLMs, so even when it does something slightly silly, in my head I go like, "I appreciate this so much, this is so amazing," like with my children, I will forgive my ChatGPT more often than I don't, and I think one of the cases is when you start throwing your own data into a LLM, what happens is the chat interface starts to surface your data quality issues really clearly.

A good example would be a case where, pulling in HR data on employees as part of a HR onboarding process, to make new employees feel a little bit like they don't have to go and find out, "Who do I talk to about this and that?" Now of course they have a HR system where it's tagged with information like, this person is a software engineer, and they've got these responsibilities, but also with the large amount of employees, it was improbable that that would be the best way to do it, so the form factor of being able to use your own natural language was great. What happened is when you typed in something like, "Can you give me the contact details for the person that knows the most about Azure OpenAI?" or something like this, it would come back very confidently and say, "Not a problem, I've got this and this and this phone number." And you know, there's a couple of challenges with that, number one is, you're more confused now, the second thing is, without proper attribution, you're not 100% aware if the AI is making this up.

One of the great elements about Azure AI Studio, and if you're using that particular place to host your copilots and anything you've done with your custom models, you get attribution at a file input level, for free. The challenge is that the data lineage doesn't start there, it started a long time ago in a different place, but you get it at one of the places where it landed, so you could put it into your AI model, but actually the lineage of what happened to that file, where was the source system, what happened along the way, who changed what, why did they change this…this is some of the lineage that things like Microsoft Purview brings in at an asset level, and CluedIn is bringing us at a record level. Purview can say, these four assets on employee data were fed into your model, great. Then CluedIn says, see that Martin there, and that Martin there, there's no way for me to stitch this data together, but I actually put those together into the same record, and so once you're using the Copilot on this cleaner data, the answers are much more precise, and much more trustworthy because you can see…here is the phone number for Martin, oh, and that's where I got it from, that's what made me decide on it, so it becomes so abundantly clear, when you start to use the copilot, you're like technology is great and super interesting, did it just make this up? And you'll know from these AI models, they're not self-aware. They cannot let you know if they made something up. Isn't that a weird difference between the large language models and us? Like I am self-aware if I've made something up, but the LLM is not.

A.G.: And it depends. I really like that, because imagine you are a data scientist, and you are performing an exploratory data analysis. If you don't have the context on the business, you're not able to understand if something that you see on the data, or even your own analysis, will be actually true, and I was thinking about that notion of EDA or exploratory data analysis, like the next barrier, because you have probably seen it in your projects. The best EDAs are those that include people who are from a mathematical and technical background, but also those that are from the business side, and usually they (business folks) don't perform EDAs because they don't have the technical means to explore the data, and to ask questions to the data.

But this notion that you're bringing, exploring the data and understanding that something is wrong, leads to the discussion where people are talking about "model hallucination." I don't like that expression, hallucination, because it's not like a human, but they were talking about the model, and I feel like this chaining of capabilities shows that it's not only about the model, it's also about the data. Because you can have the best model, GPT-5 or whatever, and even if it's very precise, we combine it with our information, which is feasible for a lot of scenarios, and we need to take care of that data so the LLM retrieves the good information. What's your vision for these topics on generative AI in regards to CluedIn for this and the years to come? How do you see this evolution of a platform at a functional level?

T.W.: You know, the part where I realized that LLMs were something super powerful was the first time it clicked that I can translate my input to a targeted output, where I can say, here's what I want, and can you actually return your answer, like this JSON structure? And it was at that moment that I went back to our team, and I said, all right, let's look through all of the functionality that includes, and I want us to go through and really understand, could I use AI in every different part of the platform? And you could look at some of the things, like that when people make a change we cause an audit trail, and you can think, no, that's like a log, why would AI have anything to do with that? And you realize, well, some of these records over time, they change a lot, and instead of having to go through a huge changelog, can I summarize the history of the change? And you could literally put this in all different places and have a net positive.

For me, the vision is, where are the biggest wins? Where are the wins that are 2 hours instead of 20 seconds? We need to focus on the things that actually are time-saving, and hit some type of business metric, make more money, lower operational costs, lower risk, complexity, etc. so we can just get things done without stressing all the time. So, I would argue to some degree, this space of AI is moving so fast, that for ChatGPT or even the DaVinci model, we haven't milked all the value out of that. There's just so much you could start to do, and, of course, the beautiful part is we get to wake up every day, and think…that same prompt, it's just more reliable with an answer now, and I didn't really have to do anything besides change to a model that also supports that functionality, like function calls, or completions, or something like that. For me, the vision of CluedIn's use of GenAI is very much self-aware that you need AI to solve the data quality problem in a more complete way. You will still use traditional techniques that are kind of deterministic, I can sleep at night because it'll do the same thing, every time, you still need those.

And then, I think, what our job here at CluedIn is, I need to bring that to the data management process, so we can finally bring the business in, and make them responsible for data quality, because up to this point, I think it's one of those elephants in the room we never talk about. Like why is data quality never cracked? Why is it never cracked? That's just hard, and yes, it is, but actually, the thing is, we've never brought the business in and said, "Right, see this list of clients, that data comes from across 15 different places," and so I love the fact that, even in their own 15 systems, it's perfect.

The problem, when we start to bring data together, is that there are things, despite all the governance that we could set up in the world, that take their own path, and someone needs to be responsible for that. And IT will still play a role in that, definitely in things like, "I can get the data to you reliably, I can get it with rollback, we can process it again really fast, we can scale," but at the end of the day, someone from the business comes in and says, "That's wrong and I know it because I work with this data every day." And being an engineer myself, I know how to work with data, but I don't know how to do those things, I have no idea how to just look at a record and go check if it meets all the right patterns. But I didn't know that those were actually the same company, and there's some real impact that happens if you don't crack that, it could be as simple as sending the invoice to the wrong email address, and then you wonder why aren't they paying us, and then you realize that's not the team that pays it. And you go, "Wow, I'm now 30 days overdue," and realistically, I need to send them another invoice and wait another 30 days,and cause maybe a cash flow issue. And you realize that's where it really hits the bottom line, and you need to be exposed to that reality to then appreciate the effort of cracking that data quality. AI just in a way exacerbates the need for it, because as soon as you use it, it will stand out really obviously because of the form factor.

A.G.: I love this part of the discussion. I was thinking about the roles and responsibilities of data governance in the company, even if you take a framework like DAMA or whatever, with the different roles, this is a new archetype, this is like the Ultron (Marvel reference) of the DAMA roles, like you have an Ultron (well, maybe not an Ultron, let's get a Jarvis), a Jarvis working for you, to do the things that, let's be honest, humans are not doing, because it's a manual process, and we don't have time to do that every time, every day, in a proper way.

Seth Juarez: From Generative AI Models to a Full LLM Platform

A.G.: So, what's your role at Microsoft? What are you doing in the organization?

S.J.: So, I work in the Azure AI platform as a program manager. My job is to work in incubations and narrative. Those are the two mandates that I have. Incubations, meaning we build stuff. For example, if we want to explain how something works, we will build prototypes, etc. Wherever those prototypes may differ from what our product is doing, we feed back into our product prioritization and what it is that we build, just to make sure that the narratives work out, which leads us to the second part. We also do technical narrative, which is to explain what is going on and how these things work. Again, anytime the ideal story doesn't match with product truth, we feed back into our product group, and sometimes they even put us in charge of certain features. We're like every person, the primary goal being incubations, building samples and stuff that help people understand how to do this, and then the technical narrative that follows from that.

A.G.: You are like Marvel's The Watcher, seeing everything that's happening at the product level, accelerators, repositories, prototypes, and new functionalities.

S.J.: That's right. But it's not just me. Obviously, there's a couple of us that work on this. For example, you may know Cassie (*https://oreil.ly/33PBM*). She's appeared on the AI Show (*https://oreil.ly/h-Fvw*) as well, but her and I work together on this stuff.

A.G.: Wonderful. Thank you for the introduction. You have seen the whole evolution of Azure OpenAI Service, and the convergence with the rest of Azure AI Studio. How do you see something that started as a model, and now is becoming a platform, and a very good one with a lot of functionality?

S.J.: That's a great question. It turns out that there's a lot of AI models and the Azure AI platform has been in the business of surfacing models, enabling you to customize these models and then enabling you to create your own models for a number of years, maybe half a decade already. The idea that a new model comes in, the reason why it was awesome for us is because we already had the infrastructure in place to make these models shine. While the new GPT series of models, and LLMs and AI models in general, may seem like a new thing when it comes to infrastructure and how these things are actually run, it's not new to us. We were able to ramp up quickly and deliver these models to folks at scale, which is really nice, obviously in partnership with OpenAI.

A.G.: That was one of the things I was surprised about during these recent months, to see this model as a service. Basically, being able to consume the APIs so quickly and so easily, that was almost magic for any developer out there.

S.J.: Yeah, and the cool thing is that the reason why it seemed magical is because we've been doing this, like I said, for a number of years with our Cognitive Services or AI services. We've been delivering, for example, text-to-speech, speech-to-text, translation, etc. as APIs. And those, if you think about them, are basically models as a service as well. They just happen to be more at the application layer, but it's actually the same thing. These models as a service are similar. The weights happen to be different, and the model structure is different, but the things that are needed to run them are actually quite similar.

A.G.: Yes, I like this convergence with the AI Studio and the model catalog. Just to see all the models available out there, and not only Azure OpenAI. How do you see this platform evolving, in which we have different models, a full catalog, so easy to deploy, with the APIs out there, we just consume them, we have Llama, Mistral, and then we have this ecosystem of prompt flow that I know is another part of the platform, all the evaluation, etc. What's going on? How do you see it?

S.J.: Yeah, that's a wonderful question. It turns out that we want to commoditize the ability for folks to find, consume, and refine models. That's basically what we want to do. So generative AI happens to be one of the most exciting in my opinion. For example, if you have an idea and you want to add AI to it, the basic thing is go to the model catalog, see if you can find something, look at some of our services, and see if you can incorporate it. My particular opinion on this, and this is something that I'm coming to realize, is that much like in the early 2000-2005s, if you didn't have a phone app, an iPhone app, people were like…are you a technical company?

My sense is that people will think the same thing when it comes to AI experiences inside of your applications, where people will think if you do not include these things that normalize human interaction with computers, they're going to feel like your app might be fundamentally broken. We're coming to a place where we will no longer have to adapt to computers, but computers will adapt to us using AI, making experiences more natural. So my sense is that we need to start thinking about how we can add those niceties and soften the edges around our software, and how can AI help with those experiences? My sense is that we're going to start to see these things included wholesale into almost everything we do, to the point where someone's going to come to you in 2025 and be like, wow, your app doesn't have AI? Maybe you should add it, because people will feel like it may be fundamentally broken.

A.G.: I love it. This is very related to the discussion we were having with Dr. John Maeda on Semantic Kernel, and the influence of design for artificial intelligence, and then this reflection about how AI just brings a new kind of interface, which is way beyond just the visual interface that we know today. And I know that this is just a personal opinion, something that you imagine, but what's your vision of what's going to happen in the next one or two years?

S.J.: Two things, and they're going to seem diametrically opposed, but they work together. The first is the expansion and proliferation of the use of these models inside of software. You're going to see these models being used to do all sorts of things, to make experiences more delightful, to make experiences more user and customer focused. You're going to see a big expansion of the use of these models, and we're already seeing that today. I mean, it's only been like a year and a couple of months since ChatGPT came out, and it's actually now everyone's expecting it to be part of the experience. So that's getting bigger in terms of the volume of people using these things.

But there are also things that are going to get smaller. There's going to be more specialized GenAI models that are going to become smaller and that are going to be used in a more targeted way to do specific things. Like the GenAI models we have now are quite general and big. However, you can make small language models (SLM), much smaller but more targeted. The smaller the model, the more targeted the task you need to make it do. You're going to see the proliferation of small language models included perhaps even on devices within the next two to three years. You're going to have those experiences move into a native local experience as well as a larger cloud experience together, and together those models are going to work to really get to laser focus into what the customer experience is for each task that it's solving, as well as a general way to actually solve other language problems. This is for language models, for example. Two diametrically opposed things, things are going to get bigger in terms of volume of people using, and things are going to get smaller in terms of the models that people use, and those two things are going to be used in combination, I think quite effectively.

A.G.: I believe so. For the second point that you mentioned, this kind of multilayer or multimodal architecture on which we could dispatch our first model, depending on the topic that it identifies. We can even fine-tune that first model and then use GPT-4 for one purpose and another model for another purpose. How do you see it?

S.J.: I think that's a great way of putting it. We're going to get into this multimodal, which means multiple models, as well as multimodal, which means multiple modalities like maybe speech, vision, and text, for example.

A.G.: What about combining models of different providers?

S.J.: Yeah, I think that's great. In Azure, on Azure AI Studio, we really don't care what models you bring, and we are trying to forge partnerships with multiple folks. We've announced a partnership with Meta last year (*https://oreil.ly/ehdf3*), and some of the Llama 2 models are already in there. We recently announced another partnership with Mistral (*https://oreil.ly/SU0PT*), and we have Mistral Large directly in our model catalog, and some of these models you can even fine-tune.

But the reality is that the Azure AI platform is built on top of something we call Azure Machine Learning Studio, a general-purpose machine learning, MLOps platform for you to build any model that you like. In theory, you could start from something like PyTorch or TensorFlow, build your own model or do any code, and you could train those models directly in Azure Machine Learning, and surface them in AI Studio. The reality is, we really don't care what AI models you bring, whether they're stuff that we've forged through partnerships or things that you literally make yourselves, all of those things should and will be available to you in your applications.

A.G.: Even that curation of models from Hugging Face, we have basically a variety of good models out there.

S.J.: Yeah, Hugging Face is an amazing partner. They've done a really good job of surfacing tons of functionalities, and we hope that with those functionalities, you will be able to deploy and use them reliably in your applications.

A.G.: Yes, and you mentioned machine learning operations (MLOps), now LLM operations, and we know that this is a new area. We've been discussing responsible AI. But if we go to the core aspect of measuring the performance of the models, how do you see this? Because this is evolving and getting more and more complex but also more intuitive. Because one year ago, it was not easy to know how to measure the performance of an LLM. I think that is getting clear now. Where are we going with that part?

S.J.: Great question. We'll start first with DevOps. DevOps is not an old concept, but it's one that's pretty well known. DevOps is a union of people, processes, and products to enable the continuous delivery of value. MLOps is the same thing. The union of people, processes, and products enable a continuous delivery of value, but with machine learning, LLMOps is the same thing but with LLMs. The idea of unifying this three-legged stool, people, process, and products, is super important. Because the thing about DevOps, LLMOps, and MLOps is that a product is not going to solve your process problem, and it's not going to solve a people problem. If people don't buy into the process, then no tool is going to satisfy that need.

I think that's the first thing to bring out is that there is no magic bullet or elixir or product that's going to solve a process thing, and the fact that people buy into the process. That's the first thing. The second thing is, once you do want to buy into a process, people want to buy into a process, the question is what do we do in LLMOps to make this process reliable and useful, when it comes to how we evaluate the prompts that we do, and how to evaluate or how to make sure that the thing is working in production. In Azure AI Studio, we have a number of ways to do that.

There's two kinds of evaluations that I think exist (but obviously, this is an evolving space, and so we're learning a ton here too). But the two kinds are unsupervised checks and then supervised checks. Supervised checks are probably the easiest. Imagine you have a call to an LLM and you want to make sure that it gets a certain answer out that's similar to what you have. Basically, you would need to have a dataset of inputs and the expected outputs. To me, that's a supervised test because you have the answer that you want. There's a number of metrics that you can do. Here's a simple one: for example, you can take the answer that's ground truth, project that into, for example, an Ada embedding or any other embedding, and take the answer that the LLM gives you, project that into an LLM embedding and then measure the angle. Maybe there's a particular tolerance that you have that gives a semantic closeness or meaning. That's one way of checking.

You can also use what we like to call GPT star metrics where you have the ground truth, and once you get the ground truth, you give that to a GPT star metric like similarity, and you ask the LLM as a language problem, how similar are these things on a scale of one to five? You give it some few-shot learning. That's an example of two supervised learning methodologies, one that's more empirical and one that's more stochastic because it's using the actual LLM to do it. The other one is also stochastic because it's using embeddings, but you have a way of just projecting these things and then measuring an actual metric.

Then there's these other ones that I like to call unsupervised that look at the structure of the actual thing that's going into the prompt and the context, and with the answer it measures what the structural integrity of the entire thing is. Let me give you one example: groundedness, which is a measure of how grounded the answer is in the context that was given to the LLM. For example, and this is the canonical example we use, we have a "Contoso" outdoor store and you ask a question about tents. Notice you have the question and then whatever the answer is, but the internal structure of the prompt flow or LangChain or whatever you're using fetches some information from a data source, which we know to be true. That to me is the context, and that generally gets embedded directly into the prompt in something we call retrieval-augmented generation (RAG). You get the question, you fetch some data, you put it into the prompt. With this particular call to the LLM, you have a question, you have the answer, and then you have the context that was fetched. With those three things, we're going to measure something called groundedness, which is how grounded the answer is that we fetched in the context, the answer that it generated from the context that we fetched. This is a normal interaction. You might ask me a question and I'll start answering with facts and good faith, and you might say, "No, that's not what I meant" and that's totally cool. We want the LLM to be grounded in that way.

There's a measurement on a scale of one to five of how grounded the answer is in the context we fetched and the question that was given, which is super nice. It turns out that this measurement is another GPT star metric where we give the question/context/answer, and then we say, "On a scale of one to five, how grounded is the answer in the context?" and then we do some few-shot learning in the actual prompt. This is something that you can also control. For example, you can change the entire groundedness prompt to directly match your few-shot learning priorities. Let's just say you're an outdoor company, you put those things in there and it's able to do that. Those are the two kinds of evaluations that I see coming out. A supervised one where you have ground truth and you measure ground truth against the answers, and then unsupervised evaluations where you're measuring the internal consistency of the truth versus the answers that you provide.

There are other ones like fluency, coherence, relevance, and those are all GPT star unsupervised metrics, and you can even invent your own. There's some clever ones that folks have invented like the apology metric, which is how many times it apologizes, and do we want to minimize that. But you've entered basically a world where you can evaluate these things in a way that is tailored to your business needs, your voice, and maybe even your ground truth, if that makes sense.

A.G.: That's why the platform evolves so much along with the evaluation flows that we have on the platform, and what we can do with these metrics. By the way, you have explained this in a better way than the book. This is why I wanted to interview you, because I know that you are so good at explaining these terms! This is amazing.

S.J.: Yeah. It's like I said, I remember talking to some nontechnical folks, business folks, and they were concerned about using these LLMs because they're like, well, how do we ensure that they're doing the right thing? I showed them and they're like, oh, so I can use English or the language of my choice, because they are trained in multiple languages, to actually evaluate these models. And I said, absolutely, and that's not all. For those unsupervised tests, notice that you do not need ground truth. As you deploy in Azure AI Studio, you have something called a model data collector, which enables you to capture the input/context/answer and store it in your storage (we don't see any of this stuff, we take this very seriously). Then even in production, you're able to create jobs that look at this data and measure those same metrics, and even alerts you when those things go out of whack.

Now we're getting into the actual LLMOps, which enables the continuous delivery of value. That's the thing. If the value goes down, you need to be alerted and to fix it, and then have that go back into the process. With these unsupervised evaluations and metrics, you're able to actually run them on a subset of your production data if you so choose, which makes this even better for folks who are concerned about these things staying on track in inference time or production.

A.G.: That's amazing. I just want to see the roadmap of what's coming next in this aspect, because there is so much discussion on LLMOps, but it's such an initial discussion for obvious reasons. This is a pretty new area. If you had to recommend one resource besides the AI Show, and the documentation, and all the official resources from Microsoft, do you have something in mind that you would recommend to learners and people who are listening to the discussion, that you consider good for their upskilling journey?

S.J.: Yes. I will say this, and this is going to be counterintuitive again because I like being counterintuitive. You are your own ultimate resource. My sense is that there is no amount of reading, or looking, or thinking about this stuff that really beats getting in there and trying something. That's what I would suggest you do. Try something, make a prompt, have the answer come out and see what happens. In my mental model, maybe this will help: you should not think of these "LLM things" as repositories of knowledge. They're not databases that have information. They are basically language calculators or language synthesizers. Think of your prompt as the language arithmetic that you're putting into the LLM and think of the response as the answer.

For example, this paragraph plus this paragraph minus this paragraph, what does that look like? I use LLMs like this all the time, even this morning. I wrote down a jumble of thoughts that I wanted to make so that it was smoothed out and GPT-4 was super nice and said, yeah, you should write it like this. It wasn't perfect, but it enabled me to start with garbage, get something more refined, and now I could become an editor. Editing is much easier than creating. Think of LLMs as language calculators and start using them to solve tasks. Once you do that as your own resource, you're going to get super far. These things are not hard to get started with, you just see the endpoint and you need to just put in a prompt and have something come out.

A.G.: Yeah, there are plenty of examples of notebooks where people can play with the API and test and see how it reacts. This notion of a calculator, I love it. It's aligned with the notion of a copilot for a person that will be interacting with the system by using the linguistic ability of the models. It's amazing.

Saurabh Tiwary: The New Microsoft Copilot Era

A.G.: For those who don't know, could you please explain who you are and what your role at Microsoft is with which unit?

S.T.: I lead a team called Turing, and the team has been training LLMs and applying them. It's an applied team, so it uses these models in a variety of products from the Edge browser to Bing question answering, or if you are getting emails in Outlook, you will see those text predictions as you type, you will see the sentences complete, so a lot of features like that. More recently, my team has been driving the Copilot experience across many of the Copilots that Microsoft has announced. Most of the heavily used ones like the Windows Copilot, Edge Copilot, Bing, in a similar way, even on the enterprise side. The backend of all of those Copilots is the same with an extensibility model, and so my team is building that.

A.G.: It's amazing. Legend has it that you created the Turing team, along with that first set of GPUs with which you were preparing the first models. That was some time ago.

S.T.: Yeah, it was quite some time back, like maybe eight or nine years back, at least on the product side. Obviously, Microsoft Research has been pushing the state of the art for a very long period of time. But on the product side, I kind of bought the first GPUs, then built the first clusters, and ran the software layer on top of it, so that you can do some large-scale (which is not large-scale by any standards now), but some large-scale training on that small cluster, then evolve that to a bunch of GPU running in Azure, and now there we are, where even the inference GPUs are massive.

A.G.: You mentioned Microsoft Bing Chat, and Microsoft Copilot now. How was that journey? Because I think that after GitHub Copilot, this has been the best exponent of experimentation and learnings; it has even been shared by Jordi Ribas and the team on the blog, and it was amazing just to see what you were doing. How was that?

S.T.: This is a phenomenal experience. Obviously, the team has been pushing very hard in terms of adding features, improving the experiences, etc. Let me maybe share a little bit of the backstory behind this. As I was mentioning, we were training our own LLMs in the past, and we had this conviction that conversational AI will be the next step in the journey. Even before ChatGPT or GPT-4 came out, we had our own conversational experience like a chat experience, which we were running in a stealth mode in India and MSIB countries (Malaysia, Singapore, Indonesia, and Philippines). We were working on it for a few years, I would say a couple of years before ChatGPT came out. We were iterating safety mechanisms, like not touching controversial topics, how do you address jailbreaks, etc. A lot of these things we were already experimenting with at a much smaller scale, and the surface area and the interaction mechanism was also a little bit different.

But, even within that experiment, we were finding that there was a lot of user engagement, in the sense that I remember one of the longer conversations was running for 13 or 14 hours. The user was talking to the bot for 13 to 14 hours straight with, I don't know, maybe 1,800 messages back and forth going between the user and the bot, etc. That actually, that initial experiment gave us some baseline footing, so that when we got access to GPT-4, we had our paths somewhat mapped out. Hence, within a fairly short period of time, I think we got access to GPT-4 somewhere around August or September of 2022, and then we released it within four or five months on February 7, 2023. We released what was called the Bing Chat experience, which is right now the Microsoft Copilot experience.

It has been a fantastic journey, lots of late nights. Actually, the team worked through Thanksgiving and holidays and stuff like that, but it was a very exciting journey and seeing it populate across all the different surfaces that Microsoft has, whether it be Word, PowerPoint, M365, Edge, Bing as well as across our app family, the mobile app family, it has been just amazing. The partnerships have been great. The company has been working like one to propagate this belief or mission about Copilot across all these surfaces. If you take a step back, being able to do something like this is just phenomenal.

A.G.: It's true. From the field, I see it like this belief that there is a notion of Copilot that is everywhere, aligned with all the products. Even this end-to-end architecture of what a Copilot is, that is certainly new, but it's something exciting. I feel like one of the most incredible things was to see the day-to-day, night-to-night, week-to-week progress of Bing Chat, Microsoft Copilot, all the learnings that you were sharing with the industry, even with the competitors on the blog, I was like, "This is gold!" All the improvements, I could really feel the improvements on the product. That pace of innovation is something that I think is difficult to replicate.

S.T.: I will say kudos to the team members who have been working super hard, and across Microsoft, working towards this common goal, and providing a delightful as well as a useful experience. It's not just conversations. At the end of the day, we have our mission statement of making every person and organization in the world more productive. Along that particular goal, we don't just want just a chit-chat experience. We also want people to accomplish things, do things. Within that mission, how do we connect all of the Copilots, add features like these plug-ins and GPTs that we have added? Actually, some of the things which might be coming up soon are even going towards task completion, etc. We are trying to evolve the product in a very significant way.

A.G.: Yes, and the notion of the end-to-end Copilot. People ask, what's Copilot exactly? Then there's this and the other Copilot, all the Copilots on the products. But this notion of end-to-end Copilot that goes way beyond the model…it's not just the model, it is the orchestration, it is the combination with Copilot for 365, etc. All this architecture, how do you design something that is so massive and so interesting from a combination of capabilities point of view?

S.T.: Yeah. The design principle of Copilot is that it is in the true sense a Copilot, as there is in aircraft. That if you are interacting with any piece of software from Microsoft, whether it be Teams or Outlook or wherever you are, the Copilot will be there next to you to help you. Obviously, it won't be a static experience depending upon which interface you are in, so if you are at the operating system level, at Windows level, you may want to do system-level commands, like for example, turn on focus mode or change my Bluetooth settings or open an app. If you are in Outlook, you may want to summarize your email while having general-purpose conversations as well.

The way we have architected it is so that irrespective of whatever surface you are using the Copilot in, you get a slightly different experience, which is conditioned on what surface area you are in. That's where we are pushing this default idea of a Copilot, that it will be there for you to help you do your work or do your task or whatever you're planning to do, with a much better experience than if you were to do it alone.

A.G.: Yes, and one of the original tasks, I mean, the main one is search. How did you and the team reinvent this notion of internet search by combining LLMs with traditional search? How was that, getting to that idea? I feel like it's mind-blowing.

S.T.: Yes, I have been working in search for quite some time. One of the things that we were thinking was that, if you look at us as a user, either it's me or you or anyone else. Why do we want to search? Search is actually a simplification of what the technology can offer to us and users or us as humanity have gotten used to using it in a particular way, which is that, for example, you will see in search, if you look into search logs, you will see a lot of queries which are very like two words, three words each. You will see something like "best elementary school," for example. Now, it's very abstract. The reason why people search, the uber problem that the person may want to solve with a search like "best elementary school'" is something like…I have a kid who has been going to this prep school and is looking for something that is nearby and good quality, or maybe the user is planning to buy a house, and they're wondering whether they should buy the house in this particular neighborhood or somewhere else and so on. There might be a lot of deeper intent, which the user does not express in search engines, because they have learned from past experience.

People who have been in this business for a long time may remember Ask Jeeves (*https://oreil.ly/yuhNk*), which existed around 20 to 25 years back. With Ask Jeeves, you were told to just express yourself in long sentences and it will find the information. At that time the technology was not great, and most of the time when you ask questions like, "I'm trying to buy a house, can you share what will be the good elementary school in this particular area?" and so on, it wouldn't find the information, which is why search engines trained humans to type in very specific keywords. Even when you type those keywords, if you look into a user session or how we engage, what happens is we try to click on a search result, we read some content, then we click on something else, then we modify the queries, and for this example, we may find that there are public school and private school options. We might decide we should look into those depending upon whether they're affordable or not, and then you iterate and so on. Given that the large language models have become a lot more powerful, we can try to compress this complex effort, which as humans we have broken down into these very specific sets. Let's issue this first query, look at results, then modify it, then ask the other thing, and then the other thing. At the end of the day, you may open a map and then say, where is that region and where is the house, and what's the distance, and so on.

Instead of that, with LLMs and with this Copilot experience, you can type what you really want. You can say, "I'm new to this area, I'm looking into buying a house, I have two young kids, where should I find good schools in this region?" etc. You can express all of that. Then the model is actually, as a Copilot, breaking that, because they know they have access to the search engine, the model itself. It will now break your complex scenario into smaller subcomponents, issue search queries, look at results, follow up again, etc., and then provide that comprehensive view. Instead of you doing all of these tasks, the model is helping you do that. That was our initial thing, because we have seen our users struggle in a session, trying lots of different things, iterating, making changes, etc. Anyways, that's the story behind this improved search experience with the Copilot.

A.G.: I guess you had started with the models, and then there was the orchestration part, now we talk about LlamaIndex, LangChain, Semantic Kernel, but Prometheus (*https://oreil.ly/Vkgtt*) was there. That concept of orchestrating knowledge and combining pieces, skills, etc.

S.T.: Yes, one of the other things for people who have been playing, or trying to build bots using LLMs, with one of these options like LangChain and stuff like that, one of the challenges that initially doesn't show up, but it happens when you start doing more complex things, is that when you have a database, or an interface through which you can pull in information, it's very easy to write a prompt, and you can add things over there. In Microsoft's case, there are many, many different complex things which the system can access. For example, even for Bing, there is a search index which is there, and that is one interface. But we also have our Ads engine, we have introduced image creation as a capability, we have GPT4-V for image understanding. There are many, we have actually introduced this notion of plug-ins if you want real-time flight information from KAYAK, being able to access that.

Once you start adding many of these pieces, what happens is if you start using the raw prompt-based method, the prompt will become just ginormous, and even the model quality will suffer because it now has to follow instructions, a very long instruction set, and just like humans where if you give too many instructions, you will be confused at the end of the page about what was written at the top. You see similar behaviors over here as well, that the model quality may not follow everything to the right intent of what is written. Hence, we had to build a more sophisticated orchestration engine which can do state-based prompting, it can do dynamic prompting so that the prompt which is sent to the model is a lot smaller. There's a lot of sophistication which has gone inside it so that we can provide a really compelling experience for our users.

A.G.: Totally. There's the model, the orchestration, and the third leg of this chair, I think, is the user interface. How did you experiment with that experience, how to adapt, because there is a learning process for users from traditional keyword search to something where we will be interacting and then understanding the results? How was that, all that experimentation?

S.T.: Yeah, right now, there are some standard interfaces which a lot of companies who are entering this area have settled on. But since we were almost first to market, we had to design and iterate on this a lot. From day zero when we released the product to where it is now, it has gone through a ton of iterative improvements. One of the first things that we did was we introduced the conversational interface on top of our search engine. So the question was, well, most of the users don't even know this product exists. So how would they engage? Because maybe you and I are more connected to technology, and maybe we have read the latest news, but how does a common user engage with this kind of technology? How do they even know this is there? One of the very subtle things that we did was on Bing.com, you would have icons to go to Copilot, like you can click and go on. But if you do a mouse scroll, you can switch seamlessly between conversations and search results. So that provides a very natural way in which I type this query and most of the time, the user will be typing the query for the search results. They get the search results, but let me just do a mouse scroll, just a couple of clicks. You land into the conversational interface and you can have that conversation.

There were other very subtle things that we did, for example, for question answering or weather, sports, etc. We had these follow-up queries, which we show on the Bing search page itself. When you click on that, you land into the chat interface. This is how we were trying to educate, instead of having a tutorial or a notification bar that now you can do this, we were having these subtle ways in which, now if you click on this, you see you go into a conversation interface, the Copilot will respond to your follow-on question and then the user knows that, OK, there is something else, something smarter, richer, which is behind the scenes, and then they can engage further with that.

A.G.: Yeah, totally product-led. So people will just get into a product and they will learn in an organic way how to handle this new functionality, very smart. So, because this book is about Azure OpenAI, then this transition, this evolution towards the Microsoft Copilot notion, this new era of AI that we are living today…what's your vision of what's next and the evolution in the industry or even the upcoming research topics that you think may be interesting to take a look at?

S.T.: Yeah, I mean, that's a very important and challenging question. A lot of people have argued that the last year has been transformational and a lot of stuff has been happening. But given the trend lines that we are seeing, I think, and it is hard to believe, but I think the rate of change will actually accelerate and not slow down, that's our belief. I know we have released Copilot across many surfaces, but the way we see the Copilot today, I believe it is going to evolve from these conversational text-based interfaces to a much richer experience very, very quickly. Yes, typing is something and there are certain places, so for example, messaging apps, etc., have educated us that you can type and you can get back and forth conversations, etc. We are following that mode. But models are becoming more powerful, think about true multimodality, just like we have as humans.

For example, when I'm talking to you, I'm seeing this Microsoft Teams window, I'm seeing your face, I also see your name written next to it. As a human, I'm not going into a text mode or an image mode like, I'm just looking at the face and now I'm going to read the text, etc. Everything is very seamless for me when I'm looking at your screen. In a similar way, even for the Copilot, we will start seeing things where the engagement will be very natural. People could speak and the model could produce an image. They could actually put in an image with some text and it may respond back, etc. Very similar, it's not going through pipelines of like, this model has got called and then text to speech, and so on. So that is one axis which will be fairly powerful that the models may start operating at the pixel level. So instead of a text model or image model, it just looks at pixels and some of those pixels end up being text and some of them end up being images and that's OK.

Another thing that I feel is where the world is heading is towards this behavior of agents. Meaning, right now, I was giving the search example earlier that you had a very complex task, and as a user we were interacting with the search engine by breaking down that problem into very small pieces, issuing those queries, looking at results, and we were the orchestrator in our mind, doing this complex thing even though we never explicitly said that we are the orchestrator. I think the same is true even with our Copilot today, they are limited to a certain extent because they are a lot about information gathering. We are trying to do some of the task completions with the KAYAK reference that I was adding.

Ultimately, what you want to do is, one of the popular examples in our Copilot is, "Can you plan an itinerary for me?" If I'm going on vacation, do whatever, pick your favorite place. London, for example. It will search, pick up various places, etc. It can create an itinerary, and it can also recommend hotels and so on. But ultimately, what you want to do is, you want to just plan the vacation. Because right now, for example, my wife hands that task to me, and it's super painful. I need to go read all the reviews, make sure that the hotels are good, nearby to the places we want to go, etc. I have to do a lot of these things, then go to the website, search for the hotel, do the booking, and so on.

I would say it is not a simple process. It takes quite a bit of cognitive load as well as time and energy. But if you think about it, a lot of these capabilities are there on the web. They are designed for humans because we can open a browser, we can click on results, we can book stuff, and so on. I think where these models are heading is towards having this agentic behavior or an agent-like behavior where you just tell them, obviously with some user interface, etc. Obviously, you can't run it in a fully autonomous way. "I want to go to London for X number of days. Can you plan that trip?" But plan here means really planning that trip and not just a text interface. Where it goes and it starts doing booking, looking for flights, and all of that. Checking weather, that's another thing, whether the weather is good or not. If it is not, if it is going to rain on a particular day, maybe you want to plan some different activities on those days, etc. Being able to do that where the Copilot on users' behalf can start doing those types of things like open web pages, clicking on things, and these are all arbitrary interfaces. I feel like that's where the world is heading towards.

A.G.: Yes, I think so. It's not even orchestration. It's a multilayer architecture in which you are going and performing all these actions, and instead of being the agent ourselves and booking all the vacations, the hotel, and the trip, etc., we have a system that is relying on the existing interfaces that we have today, the frontends and the backends.

S.T.: Think of it as your own personal assistant. If you had a personal assistant who really knew you well, obviously, it's just like if you were to hire a new personal assistant for yourself. Initially, it will be like, OK, just do simple things, etc. But at some point when the trust grows, and you know that person can do these things and they understand my interests and boundaries and so on, they can start acting on your behalf much, much more. I think that's where I feel like these models will go. On day zero, obviously, they won't do anything because people will be freaked out like, why did you make this particular choice or that particular choice? But as things evolve, I think we are going toward that future.

A.G.: I think so, it's very promising what we'll see in the next one, two, three years. That's why I don't ask for your vision for the next five years because I know that it's impossible to do so. Look, this is super interesting, wonderful insights. I'm just so happy that you are sharing all this information here. Did you have a last recommendation for our readers to continue exploring?

S.T.: I think this field is moving so fast that, personally for me because I have been in this area for the last 9 to 10 years, I think a lot of the social sites generally are useful, Twitter, if you follow the right set of people and so on. Right now, actually, things have evolved a lot. There are newsletters that are there, which actually provide the latest, and are actually using LLMs to simplify and summarize a lot of the conversation so that you can have a synthesized set of information and obviously you can drill down a little bit more if something is of interest. I think those are probably the more interesting routes.

I can give one other example. Generally, conferences were used for knowledge dissemination. Right now, if you look into the deep learning space, conferences are mostly for networking. The papers were already put on arXiv (*https://oreil.ly/O9tW3*) probably three months to six months back. If they were useful, they would have already been discussed till death by the time the conference happens. Even the research community has shaped itself. Then I will say the same is true for us as well. I would say just keep being on the cutting edge and the latest edge. I think things are evolving very quickly in this world.

A.G.: So quick. Even this Azure OpenAI book has evolved a lot, I don't know how many iterations every week, just to keep updating and adding all the information.

S.T.: Maybe even after publishing, you may have to iterate on, I don't know, like a book pointed to an appendix or something.

A.G.: Yeah, appendix, second, third edition…almost every month.

Conclusion

The experts interviewed in this chapter offer exclusive insights related to the current state of generative AI and LLMs (e.g., why data quality matters for RAG patterns, new LLMOps trends for model performance tracking, advanced use cases, the underlying cloud native infrastructure) but also insights into its future. There are two recurrent topics here: multimodality for models to analyze different kinds of information, and the evolution of AI agents, as a sort of combined automation of steps leading to complete complex tasks—all of this without forgetting the responsible and safe implementation of generative AI systems.

Overall, this last chapter was my way to bring together all the topics from Chapters 1 to 6, and to discuss them in a highly applied manner with an amazing set of professionals. From technology building blocks and architectures to organizational considerations. From Azure OpenAI Service to the rest of the related "pieces" that enable your cloud native generative AI developments.

And here we are, at the end of this book's journey. More than 200 pages full of explanations, examples, and technical topics related to generative AI and Azure OpenAI. But this is, of course, just the beginning. Companies are adopting Azure OpenAI, and the Microsoft product teams are working to continue evolving the platform, by adding not only new AI models, but also product features related to the operationalization of enterprise-level deployments. This is an amazing race, and the generative era has just started. This book is a small contribution for AI adopters around the world to get the most from Azure OpenAI Service. Let's keep innovating.

Other Learning Resources

There are tons of resources out there, but the goal of this appendix is to provide you with a curated list of books, repos, documentation, and reports to further your GenAI knowledge.

Relevant O'Reilly Books for Your Upskilling Journey

This selection of books includes readings that will help you at the company level, but also support your general Microsoft Azure upskilling, particularly with AI and generative AI technicalities. All of them complement what you have learned here, and you can also follow the authors' profiles to keep learning from these renowned professionals. Let's explore them:

The AI Organization, by David Carmona (https://oreil.ly/FOSlv)
> Personally, one of my favorites. This book includes real experiences from AI adopter companies, with expert interviews and lessons learned from an AI strategy point of view. Also, David Carmona is an absolute reference (and Microsoft colleague) for advanced AI topics.

> *Description*: This practical guide explains how business and technical leaders can embrace this new breed of organization. Based on real customer experience, Microsoft's David Carmona covers the journey necessary to become an AI organization—from applying AI in your business today to the deep transformation that can empower your organization to redefine the industry.

> *Why this book?* The learnings for AI adoption include culture, technology, responsibility, and business topics that are very relevant for any company leveraging AI and generative AI technologies. In my honest opinion, this book is a modern classic, and an easy-to-read resource for all kinds of profiles, including technical and business folks.

The AI Ladder, by Rob Thomas (https://oreil.ly/Ipe6t) and Paul Zikopoulos (https://oreil.ly/1gCVc)

Another O'Reilly classic for AI adoption topics, with other real-life examples from adopter companies.

Description: Authors Rob Thomas and Paul Zikopoulos from IBM introduce C-suite executives and business professionals to the AI Ladder, a unified, prescriptive approach to help them understand and accelerate the AI journey. Complete with real-world examples and real-life experiences, this book explores AI drivers, value, and opportunity, as well as the adoption challenges organizations face.

Why this book? Much like *The AI Organization*, this book includes real-life scenarios for AI adoption. But what I like the most is the step-by-step data preparation, highly necessary for anyone wanting to train their own AI models, or to implement RAG or fine-tuning patterns for generative AI.

Designing Machine Learning Systems, by Chip Huyen (https://oreil.ly/AFnId)

One of the most relevant authors for AI topics out there. Great balance of technical details and easy-to-understand explanations.

Description: In this book, you'll learn a holistic approach to designing ML systems that are reliable, scalable, maintainable, and adaptive to changing environments and business requirements.

Why this book? Chip created a terrific resource, an absolute reference for anyone who wants to understand the end-to-end operations for machine learning systems—and the reviews concur. Applicable to generative AI and LLMOps, I highly recommend this book if you want some technical knowledge and a holistic vision.

Machine Learning for High-Risk Applications, by Patrick Hall (https://oreil.ly/b-WAX), James Curtis (https://oreil.ly/Jexy2), and Parul Pandey (https://oreil.ly/CXpVc)

A great introduction to responsible AI topics, from a highly applied point of view.

Description: This book describes approaches to responsible AI, a holistic framework for improving AI/ML technology, business processes, and cultural competencies that builds on best practices in risk management, cybersecurity, data privacy, and applied social science.

Why this book? We covered responsible AI topics in Chapter 5 and during the interview with Sarah Bird. But RAI is a very important topic, and it deserves a proper deep dive for those wanting to explore not only the potential but also the considerations of GenAI technologies.

Machine Learning Design Patterns, by Valliappa Lakshmanan (https://oreil.ly/UC8s5), Sara Robinson (https://oreil.ly/FoRMy), and Michael Munn (https://oreil.ly/0I6en).

An introduction to ML models, related MLOps, scalability considerations, etc.

Description: In this book, you will find detailed explanations of 30 patterns for data and problem representation, operationalization, repeatability, reproducibility, flexibility, explainability, and fairness. Each pattern includes a description of the problem, a variety of potential solutions, and recommendations for choosing the best technique for your situation.

Why this book? An extensive, pre-generative AI guide with a highly technical focus on model training patterns. A good complement or alternative to *Designing Machine Learning Systems*. Highly recommended as an additional learning asset for professionals with a technical background.

Deciphering Data Architectures, by James Serra (https://oreil.ly/3CDHj)

A key resource to learn about the architectural patterns, from the classics to the lakehouse architecture, that can feed your generative AI implementations.

Description: Data fabric, data lakehouse, and data mesh have recently appeared as viable alternatives to the modern data warehouse. These new architectures have solid benefits, but they're also surrounded by a lot of hyperbole and confusion. This practical book provides a guided tour of each architecture to help data professionals understand their pros and cons.

Why this book? James Serra, one of the most knowledgeable Microsoft architects, is enough reason for anyone to read and recommend this book. This is an updated guide that shows everything required for a modern company's data platform, including lakehouse patterns that will feed your generative AI developments.

Data Management at Scale, by Piethein Strengholt (https://oreil.ly/EJRyo)

A perfect complement to the previous book, with a special focus on federated data systems.

Description: As data management continues to evolve rapidly, managing all of your data in a central place, such as a data warehouse, is no longer scalable. Today's world is about quickly turning data into value. This requires a paradigm shift in the way we federate responsibilities, manage data, and make it available to others. With this practical book, you'll learn how to design a next-gen data architecture that takes into account the scale you need for your organization.

Why this book? Much like James Serra, Piethein is a top voice in this space, and a huge source of knowledge for data management topics. This is an incredible continuation of the discussion with Tim Ward from CluedIn, and a highly necessary one for any enterprise-grade implementation. Another must.

Learning Microsoft Azure, by Jonah Carrio Andersson (https://oreil.ly/gZGyw)

An amazing introduction to the Microsoft Azure cloud, from one of the community MVPs. Highly recommended if you want to expand your Azure knowledge beyond this book.

Description: If your organization plans to modernize services and move to the cloud from legacy software or a private cloud on premises, this book is for you. Software developers, solution architects, cloud engineers, and anybody interested in cloud technologies will learn fundamental concepts for cloud computing, migration, transformation, and development using Microsoft Azure.

Why this book? For me, the perfect way to learn "all things Azure," in case you are missing the fundamentals for core infrastructure, networking, administration, security, and other topics. Jonah is also one of the technical reviewers of this book.

Azure Cookbook, by Reza Salehi (https://oreil.ly/W3lgM)

A technical guide with step-by-step explanations, and a perfect complement to the previous Azure book. A great way to expand your Azure knowledge beyond Azure OpenAI capabilities.

Description: How do you deal with the problems you face when using Azure? This practical guide provides over 75 recipes to help you to work with common Azure issues in everyday scenarios. That includes key tasks like setting up permissions for a storage account, working with Cosmos DB APIs, managing Azure role-based access control, governing your Azure subscriptions using Azure Policy, and much more.

Why this book? For me, this is the second step for any Azure learner after Jonah's book. Reza created an extensive cookbook that is useful for any professional wanting to leverage Azure resources. The deployment and administration steps are applicable to Azure OpenAI and other AI resources.

Azure AI Services at Scale for Cloud, Mobile, and Edge, by Simon Bisson (https://oreil.ly/xQwY2), Mary Branscombe (https://oreil.ly/JjlGg), Chris Hoder (https://oreil.ly/cR_Xk), and Anand Raman (https://oreil.ly/szRmD)

This resource is a perfect preamble to my Azure OpenAI book. It includes general information for the Azure AI platform. This is a great complement for you to combine LLMs with other vision, language, and speech models.

Description: This book shows you how cloud AI services fit in alongside familiar software development approaches, walks you through key Microsoft AI services, and provides real-world examples of AI-oriented architectures that integrate different Azure AI services. All you need to get started is a working knowledge of basic cloud concepts.

Why this book? This book complements what you have read here, going beyond Azure OpenAI Service, and focusing on all Azure AI services.

Cloud Native Infrastructure with Azure, by Nishant Singh (https://oreil.ly/MjRMB) and Michael Kehoe (https://oreil.ly/QEOtQ)

A must for you to integrate the cloud native aspects of Microsoft Azure, and very necessary for cloud native generative AI solutions with Azure OpenAI.

Description: With this practical book, the authors show you how to build a true cloud native infrastructure using Microsoft Azure or another cloud computing solution by following guidelines from the CNCF. DevOps and site reliability engineers will learn how adapting applications to cloud native early in the design phase helps you fully utilize the elasticity and distributed nature of the cloud.

Why this book? If you liked Chapter 2, this book should absolutely be next on your list. It explores cloud native fundamentals, architectures, and development lifecycles with Azure. Even more, if you like cloud native topics and you want to get some official certification, you can visit my *Kubernetes and Cloud Native Associate (KCNA) Study Guide (https://oreil.ly/-z6Tt)* as well.

Application Delivery and Load Balancing in Microsoft Azure, by Derek DeJonghe (https://oreil.ly/megO6) and Arlan Nugara (https://oreil.ly/iNdh5)

An Azure-first book for technical topics related to load balancing, an increasingly relevant area for any generative AI application with Azure OpenAI.

Description: With more and more companies moving on-premises applications to the cloud, software and cloud solution architects alike are busy investigating ways to improve load balancing, performance, security, and high availability for workloads. This practical book describes Microsoft Azure's load balancing options and explains how NGINX can contribute to a comprehensive solution.

Why this book? This is a technical guide, focused on very specific topics that will impact your generative AI developments with Azure OpenAI. Networking and load balancing are very relevant when designing your AI landing zone, including combining different models with dedicated capacity (PTU) and regular pay-as-you-go options.

Building Intelligent Cloud Applications, by John Biggs (https://oreil.ly/S3bup) and Vicente Herrera García (https://oreil.ly/OadSv)

A great introduction to the concept of serverless architectures in Azure. Another complementary topic that you may want to explore after Azure OpenAI.

Description: Serverless computing is radically changing the way we build and deploy applications. With cloud providers running servers and managing machine resources, companies now can focus solely on the application's business logic and functionality. This hands-on book shows experienced programmers how to build and deploy scalable machine learning and deep learning models using serverless architectures with Microsoft Azure.

Why this book? As you saw in Chapter 2, the different cloud-as-a-service levels are very important for your generative AI development. This book is another technical deep dive for you to understand the logic behind serverless, model-as-a-service APIs. This is important for Azure OpenAI Service, but also for other generative AI models in Azure AI Studio.

Generative Deep Learning, by David Foster (https://oreil.ly/1twy1)
A deep dive for generative AI topics, from a technical point of view. A great continuation to this book if you are willing to learn more about generative AI fundamentals.

Description: The book starts with the basics of deep learning and progresses to cutting-edge architectures. Through tips and tricks, you'll understand how to make your models learn more efficiently and become more creative. This book also explores the future of generative AI and how individuals and companies can proactively begin to leverage this remarkable new technology to create a competitive advantage.

Why this book? This book is the go-to option if you want to understand the technical, scientific details behind generative AI models. Very technical, and obviously not required for regular practitioners, this book will help you to become an authentic AI expert.

Prompt Engineering for Generative AI, by James Phoenix (https://oreil.ly/5m3x-) and Mike Taylor (https://oreil.ly/Z3lmO)
Another deep dive, in this case for prompt engineering topics. A great source for an evolving topic, and highly relevant for your generative AI applications.

Description: With this book, you'll gain a solid foundation in generative AI, including how to apply these models in practice. When first integrating LLMs and diffusion models into their workflows, most developers struggle to coax reliable enough results from them to use in automated systems.

Why this book? This prompt engineering guide is a perfect continuation of the best practices from Chapter 5. Great reading if you want to continue developing your technical and functional understanding of prompt-based systems.

These are just a few examples of relevant O'Reilly books, but there are of course other resources that will be useful for your generative AI upskilling journey. It will really depend on what you want to learn next. Let's now explore a list of technical resources.

Other Resources and Repositories

Here you will find a mix of resources, learning assets, reports, and repositories:

Report: Well-Architected Framework (WAF) (https://oreil.ly/jHwtt)
> This report and its content are the ABC of any Azure-related implementation. Your generative AI development needs to rely on a proper Azure architecture that is well designed and implemented. The WAF is the reference guide for any technology adopter, including integration and consulting partners.

Report: FinOps Guide (https://oreil.ly/LG42a)
> Much like the WAF, the FinOps Guide is the official resource to optimize your Azure cloud deployments, from a financial operations management and optimization perspective. This is less known than WAF, but equally important for the financial sustainability of your developments with Azure OpenAI Service.

Report: Microsoft Solutions Playbook—Working with LLMs (https://oreil.ly/rFN5n)
> An LLM 101 that includes topics we have already covered in this book, but that can be useful if you need to share generative AI content internally in your company. Not all of your colleagues will want to read a generative AI book, but they should explore the fundamentals of it. This resource is a good starting point.

Training: Microsoft Learn—Short course for Azure OpenAI Service (https://oreil.ly/XsmRk)
> Microsoft Learning Paths are a great option for interactive training. Much like the previous report, this course includes relevant pieces of content that can help you and your colleagues learn more about implementations with Azure OpenAI. Additionally, you can explore the Learning Pathways (*https://oreil.ly/kljOi*) collection from my Microsoft UK colleagues.

Training: Introducing Semantic Kernel (https://oreil.ly/TXE5e)
> If you like the AI orchestration world, and the discussion with Dr. John Maeda got your attention, then go and explore this Semantic Kernel training. A perfect deep dive to continue learning about this technology building block.

Training/article: Introduction to Prompt Engineering (https://oreil.ly/T7PuQ) and Prompt Engineering Techniques (https://oreil.ly/u6Xdy)
> From the official Microsoft documentation. Once again, entry-level knowledge that can accelerate your organization's prompting learning. Additionally, there is good non-Microsoft content out there—for example, the already famous Prompt Engineering Guide (*https://oreil.ly/JBB67*) (a very good online resource full of content and tips). You can expect some additional prompting resources in the future, as this is a rapidly evolving area.

Certifications: Azure AI Fundamentals (https://oreil.ly/iERfL) and Azure Data Funda-mentals (https://oreil.ly/G4I4B)

The entry-level certifications for any Azure data and AI learner. Even if you have read this book, taking both exams may be a good career investment. You will learn more about data systems, and the AI Studio. Highly recommended.

Videos: The AI Show (https://oreil.ly/LXyME)

An incredible series of didactic videos, hosted by Seth Juarez and other Microsoft folks. An extensive collection with explanations, Q&A sessions, applied examples, and new functionalities.

Repositories

A list of evolving repositories with Azure OpenAI–related and generative AI examples. It is always a good idea to watch them and leverage the updated content:

- Azure Accelerators (*https://oreil.ly/u7ylD*)
- Azure OpenAI Samples (*https://oreil.ly/eTD52*)
- Vector Samples - Azure AI Search (*https://oreil.ly/DToU2*)
- 30 Days of Azure AI (*https://oreil.ly/Nl0mt*)
- Partner Resources - Azure OpenAI (*https://oreil.ly/8UDF_*)
- Awesome Prompt Engineering (*https://oreil.ly/ZmTev*)
- Vector Search and Databases (*https://oreil.ly/OKmx8*)

These are living resources that you can bookmark and keep in mind when you look for new project ideas, code samples, or if you just want to catch up with recent news and developments. The journey never stops, so keep learning!

Index

H

hallucination, AI model, 119, 194
HAX Toolkit, 139, 185
Hugging Face, 13, 199
Hughes, Chris, 14
human resources, business cases, 145-149
Huyen, Chip, 121
hybrid search-based grounding, 63, 96, 97

I

IaC (infrastructure as code), 168
IBM, generative AI role of, 15
image detection, classification, and generation, 5, 11, 25
Image Generation API, 74, 84
implementation of generative AI, 59-100
  Azure AI Document Intelligence, 112
  Azure AI Speech services, 85, 113
  Azure API Management, 114
  Azure ChatGPT instance, 88-90
  building blocks, 65-88
    deployment interfaces, 78-81
    development interfaces, 65, 82-87
    interoperability features, 87
    visual interfaces, 65-78
  business cases, 141-156
  comparison of approaches, 97-98
  development frameworks and SDKs, 102-107
  fine-tuning GPT models, 62, 86, 91-97, 124
  knowledge scope of Azure OpenAI-enabled apps, 60-63
  Microsoft Fabric's lakehouse, 112
  minimal customization with one- or few-shot learning, 90
  performance evaluation methods, 98-100
  Power Platform suite, 107
  production deployments (see deployment of generative AI)
  vector database, 108-111
in-product recommendations use case, 6
index-based retrieval, RAG, 63
infrastructure as code (IaC), 168
integrations
  AI Builder, 107
  Bot Framework SDK, 106
  CI/CD, 33, 40
  Databricks Vector Search, 110
  Semantic Kernel, 103-105

interfaces, generative AI, 65-87
  AICI, 116
  deployment interfaces, 78-81
  development interfaces, 65, 82-87
  UI (see user interface)
  visual interfaces, 65-78
interoperability features, generative AI, 87
Isla, Julian, 162

J

jailbreak detection (Prompt Shields), 135
JARVIS/HuggingGPT, 114
JavaScript Object Notation (JSON), 68, 87
Juarez, Seth, 160, 196-202

K

knowledge scope of Azure OpenAI-enabled apps, 60-63, 92
Kubernetes, 37-38, 167, 168
Kubernetes: Up and Running (Burns), 172

L

lakehouse platform, 24, 112
LangChain, 102-103, 170, 178, 191
language capabilities of generative AI, 11
language-related AI models, 51
large language models (LLMs)
  agents for, 102, 208-209
  baseline, 60
  data quality, managing, 188-195
  development and integration tools, 101-116
  grounding techniques, 62-63, 97, 201
  LangChain, 102-103
  metrics versus ML, 124
  search integration, 205-206
  securing, 128-133
  tokens as unit of measure, 28
  value of practicing interaction with, 202
Learning Microsoft Azure (Andersson), 34, 56
Levenshtein distance metric, generative AI performance, 99
LIDA library, 115
LinkedIn Learning, 179
live internet results, in grounding, 63
"living" roadmap, creating, 149-151
Llama 3 LLM, 14
LlamaIndex, 105, 178

Neo4J, 111
.NET developers, Azure OpenAI library for, 87
neural networks, 3
Ng, Andrew, 179
NIST (National Institute of Standards and
    Technology), 137
NLP (see natural language processing)
NVIDIA, 15

O

OCI (Open Container Initiative), 37
OCR (optical character recognition), 112
Olive, 116
Ollama, 177
one- or few-shot learning, 90, 97
ONNX Runtime, 114
Open Container Initiative (OCI), 37
open source software (OSS)
    expansion in generative AI space, 170
    security risks of, 133
    support between different programs, 178
OpenAI, 12, 19-29, 94, 152
OpenAI LP, 12
operations research (OR), 4
optical character recognition (OCR), 112
Orca/Orca-2, 116
orchestration, role in AI, 37-38, 167, 179, 206
OSS (see open source software)
output handling, insecure, 132
overreliance on LLMs without supervision, 133
OWASP Foundation, 132

P

PaaS (platform-as-a-service), Azure OpenAI as,
    19
parameter customization, 84
Partnership on AI, 138
performance evaluation methods, 98-100, 103,
    124, 200-202
performance optimization, with microservices,
    36
Personally identifiable information (PII), 134
pgvector, 110
Phi-2, 116
Pinecone vector database, 111
pipelines, serverless workflows for, 39
platform-as-a-service (PaaS), Azure OpenAI as,
    19
plug-ins, 176

AI applications, 101
architecture, 190
insecure design vulnerability, 133
programming value of, 178
PostgreSQL, 110
Power BI, 24
Power Platform, 107, 158
Power Platform Copilot, 24
Power Virtual Agents (PVAs), 81, 107
predictive maintenance use case, 7
premortem managerial technique, 141-143, 173
privacy and compliance management, 5,
    133-135
private endpoints, 130
private networks, 135
Profisee, 131
programming use case (see coding use case)
project workstreams, defining for business case,
    144
prompt, 118
prompt engineering, 10, 117-121
    Azure ML and prompt flow, 125-128
    context prompt, 84
    LangChain, 102
    meta-prompts, 67, 129
    Microsoft guidance for, 185
    workstream for, 144
prompt flow, 125-128
prompt injection, 132
Prompt Shield, 128
Promptbase, 115
PromptBench (Python), 115
PromptsLab, Awesome-Prompt-Engineering
    repo, 120
protected material detection, 135
provisioned throughput unit (PTU), 153-154
PVAs (Power Virtual Agents), 81, 107
Python, 87, 176, 178
Python Risk Identification Tool for generative
    AI (PyRIT), 116, 185

Q

querying vector databases, 108
question-answer dynamic, 10
    (see also prompt engineering)
quotas panel, Azure OpenAI Studio, 78

About the Author

Adrián González Sánchez is a senior cloud, data, and AI specialist at Microsoft, as well as the industrial AI lead for the Spanish Observatory of Ethical AI (OdiseIA). He has previously worked as a senior consultant and product owner in AI and data science with CGI Canada and IVADO Labs, head of AI customer success for Peritus.ai, and other data-driven companies in Europe and Latin America.

He is a trainer for the École des Dirigeants at HEC Montréal, the Continuing Education Department at Concordia University, and online training courses for O'Reilly Media and the Linux Foundation. He also collaborates with 2U/GetSmarter as a tutor and facilitator for MIT Sloan's AI and blockchain executive courses, and Harvard VPAL's fintech course.

His areas of expertise are AI strategy and project management, responsible AI systems implementation, big data and cloud computing, data and AI governance, ethical and regulatory impact of technological innovation, telecommunications, and the Internet of Things.

Colophon

The animal on the cover of *Azure OpenAI Service for Cloud Native Applications* is the great blue turaco (*Corythaeola cristata*), a member of the bird family of "banana eaters" (*Musophagidae*). The great blue turaco is the largest of the turaco birds, at around 28 to 30 inches in length.

As their family name suggests, great blue turacos subsist primarily on a diet of fruits and other plant matter. They and their *Musophagidae* kin are one of very few bird families that are endemic to Africa. Turacos, in particular, are native to sub-Saharan Africa, where they can be found living in the trees of the forest, woodland, and savanna landscapes. They are poor flyers but excellent climbers.

The great blue turaco has been categorized by the IUCN as being of least concern, from a conservation standpoint. Many of the animals on O'Reilly covers are endangered; all of them are important to the world.

The cover illustration is by Karen Montgomery, based on an antique line engraving from Lydekker's *Royal Natural History*. The series design is by Edie Freedman, Ellie Volckhausen, and Karen Montgomery. The cover fonts are Gilroy Semibold and Guardian Sans. The text font is Adobe Minion Pro; the heading font is Adobe Myriad Condensed; and the code font is Dalton Maag's Ubuntu Mono.

O'REILLY®

Learn from experts.
Become one yourself.

Books | Live online courses
Instant answers | Virtual events
Videos | Interactive learning

Get started at oreilly.com.

Milton Keynes UK
Ingram Content Group UK Ltd.
UKHW052250050724
445066UK00003B/8